The Challenge of Famine

Recent Experience, Lessons Learned

editor
John Osgood Field

Kumarian Press

The Challenge of Famine: Recent Experience, Lessons Learned
Published 1993 in the United States of America by Kumarian Press, Inc.
630 Oakwood Avenue, Suite 119, West Hartford, Connecticut 06110-1529 USA

Cover design by Laura Augustine. Cover photos (clockwise from upper left
corner): UNICEF/Stephenie Hollyman (Ethiopia); UNICEF/Stephenie Hollyman (Ethiopia); UNICEF/John Isaac (Ethiopia); UNICEF/John Isaac (Ethiopia)

Production supervised by Jenna Dixon, Bookbuilder
Copyedited by Dorothy Brandt
Typeset by ProProduction
Proofread by Sydney Landon Plum
Index prepared by Barbara DeGennaro

Printed in the United States of America on recycled acid-free paper by
McNaughton & Gunn. Text printed with soy-based ink.

Library of Congress Cataloging-in-Publication Data

The Challenge of famine : Recent experience, lessons learned / editor,
    John Osgood Field — 1st ed.
        p.   cm. — (Kumarian Press library of management for
development)
    Includes bibliographical references and index.
    ISBN 1-56549-019-3 (cloth : alk. paper). — ISBN 1-56549-018-5 (pbk. :
alk. paper)
    1. Food relief. 2. Food relief—Africa. 3. Famines. 4. Famines—Africa.
I. Field, John Osgood, 1940–   II. Series.
HV696.F6C44   1993
363.8'83'096—dc20   93-975

---

97   96   95   94   93   5   4   3   2   1
First printing, 1993

Contents

Figures and Tables

Figures

Tables

Foreword

Famine is the ultimate public health catastrophe. It is unfortunately a recurrent human phenomenon, even in modern times. Since the end of World War II, there has not been one year in which there was not a famine. The causes of famine—drought, floods, earthquakes, biological invasions, wars—along with the combination of poverty and civil disorder are responsible for the millions of deaths that threaten several areas of Africa today.

Famine is such a massive phenomenon that it leads to a breakdown of all of our societal protection systems. People convinced that there is food somewhere, particularly where there is a large hospital, start migrating. In the process, children are lost, and adolescents form marauding gangs that are progressively more difficult to rehabilitate even when the situation is normalized. When people drink water out of ditches by the road, epidemics start and spread. Faith in government institutions is eroded as local authorities think it is to their advantage to minimize the extent of the disaster, while the opposition thinks it is to their advantage to exaggerate it. Rumors lead to further migrations, and information on what the situation really is—whether mortality is increasing, peaking, or decreasing, where the supplies are, or even who is in charge—becomes more and more difficult to obtain. The problems of relief and rehabilitation are enormous. How to keep populations where they are, whether to give preferential treatment to the police lest it becomes a party to the pillaging of convoys, at what point it is harmful and at what point it is useful to install price controls, how to define needs and to coordinate the action of relief agencies—all these represent complex practical problems.

Throughout the past, even in the recent past, each famine has largely been dealt with as though it were a unique phenomenon and each response has had to be reinvented at the reoccurrence of each famine. Yet, there are centuries of experience and at least 100 years of very substantive observations on what has worked and what has not worked in famine relief. For example, the Indian Civil Service, for close to a century, encouraged local administrators to keep a "famine book," which contained descriptions of past famine and relief efforts, successful or not, as well as inventories of food stocks, maps, and lists of the available means of transportation. Since World War II, the archives of UNICEF and other relief agencies have become useful sources of information.

Professor Field is rendering an enormous service by putting together a number of case studies that offer insight and innovation on more recent famines. The book will be a valuable addition to the knowledge of people working in the fields of nutrition, political science, and the economics of poor countries. Most of all, if read in advance by a sufficient number of administrators and politicians throughout the world, it will save lives.

Jean Mayer
Chancellor
Tufts University

Editor's Note: A nutritionist and educator who made world hunger his personal cause, Dr. Jean Mayer was very much the inspiration for this book. He passed away on January 1, 1993, as work on this book was nearing completion.

Acknowledgments

This book is derived from the Workshop on Famine and Famine Policy held at Tufts University from 1986 to 1989. The workshop was generously supported by the Lloyd A. Fry Foundation of Chicago I am grateful to the Fry Foundation for its support and to the workshop's many participants, especially those who assumed the burden of converting oral presentations into manuscripts for publication.

I also wish to recognize the capable—and unflappable—support of the following colleagues in the School of Nutrition at Tufts: Judy Bradford, Nancy Radford, Ketsia Louis-Charles, and especially Marlene Smith and David Hastings. We pulled this off together. Thanks.

About the Contributors

Hussein M. Adam is an associate professor of political science at the College of the Holy Cross, Worcester, Massachusetts.

Mary B. Anderson is president of the Collaborative for Development Action, Cambridge, Massachusetts.

Leonard Berry is vice president and provost of Florida Atlantic University, Boca Raton, Florida.

Joel R. Charny is overseas director at Oxfam America, Boston, Massachusetts.

Peter Cutler is a health economist and consultant on famine located in St. Albans, Hertfordshire, United Kingdom.

Thomas E. Downing is a research associate with the Environmental Change Unit, University of Oxford, Oxford, United Kingdom.

John Osgood Field is a professor in the School of Nutrition, Tufts University, Medford, Massachusetts.

Jack Shepherd is academic director of the War/Peace Studies and Conflict Resolution Program and an adjunct professor of Environmental Studies at Dartmouth College, Hanover, New Hampshire.

J. Dirck Stryker is an associate professor of International Economic Relations at the Fletcher School of Law and Diplomacy, Tufts University, Medford, Massachusetts, and president of Associates for International Resources and Development, Somerville, Massachusetts.

William I. Torry is an associate professor of anthropology at West Virginia University, Morgantown, West Virginia.

Paul Ulrich is a doctoral candidate in the Food Research Institute, Stanford University, Stanford, California.

Peter J. Woodrow is interim executive secretary of the New England Regional Office of the American Friends Service Committee, Cambridge, Massachusetts.

Introduction

John Osgood Field

There is no romanticism in hunger, there is no beauty in hunger, no creativity in hunger. There is no inspiration in hunger. Only shame. . . . Thus, if hunger inspires anything at all, it is, and must be, only the war against hunger.

Perhaps of all the woes that . . . plague the human condition, hunger alone can be curtailed and ultimately vanquished—not by destiny, not by the heavens, but by human beings. We cannot fight earthquakes, but we can fight hunger. Hence our responsibility for its victims. . . . There is "response" in responsibility. And this responsibility is what makes us human, or the lack of it, inhuman. . . .

And it is because we have known hunger that we now must eliminate hunger. It is because we have been subjected to shame that we must now oppose shame. It is because we have witnessed humanity at its worst that we now must appeal to humanity at its best.

—Elie Wiesel, "The Shame of Hunger,"
WHY Magazine (Summer 1990)

Famine is both tragedy and challenge. Short of nuclear war, it is the ultimate scourge of human populations. Short of physical torture, it is the cruelest way to die. Many millions of people have perished from famine since the dawn of recorded history; millions more remain at risk today. Yet, there is no reason why the future need repeat the past. Famine is preventable in an interconnected world of plenty. Humankind possesses the knowledge and the means to put an end to famine. The challenge is to do so, and an awesome as well as awe-inspiring challenge it is.

This book is part of a rapidly expanding literature on famine and shares with it the burden of trying to understand famine so as to improve management of famine episodes. Derived from the Workshop

1

on Famine and Famine Policy held at Tufts University from 1986 to 1989, it reviews experience during the famine-plagued 1980s and seeks to distill lessons from that experience.

A brief word concerning the Tufts workshop is in order. Held at a time when famine was a grim reality in much of Africa, as it still is, the workshop was an attempt to come to grips with famine—and its management—conceptually and in comparative perspective. Scholars and practitioners joined together to share their knowledge based on study and experience. This book enables those of us involved in the workshop to share what transpired with a broader audience. Those presentations that regrettably could not be included here have been or soon will be published elsewhere.

The eleven chapters of this book have been organized under four topical sections. Part I is a conceptual overview of famine as both event and process. Seeing famine as a process is important to detection and preemptive intervention, the principal concerns of Part IV. Seeing it as an event helps to define its emergence and also helps to distinguish famine from chronic malnutrition. This is an important distinction in policy terms. A major theme of the book is introduced in Part I as well, the value of viewing famine in relation to socioeconomic development and the need to integrate famine policy with ongoing development policy for the sake of both.

Part II analyzes national and international responses to famine during the 1980s, emphasizing Africa generally and Ethiopia in particular. Themes addressed include the astonishingly weak relationship between severity of drought and emergence of famine. Far more important are economic resilience, government policies, and the presence or absence of armed conflict. Actual success with managing drought and avoiding famine varied enormously in Africa during the past decade and related strongly to these conditions. The contrasts in Chapters 2 and 3 between Botswana (excellent management), Kenya (effective management), Niger (both effective and ineffective management), and Ethiopia, Sudan, Mali, and Mozambique (poor or no management) are striking.

Part II also dramatizes the intensely political nature of famine. Famines occur not only because of a process of destitution, but also—and critically—because they are allowed to occur. The primacy of politics in famine response (see Chapter 4) is a fact of life within famine-prone countries and internationally. Moreover, national governments, donor countries, UN agencies, and private voluntary organizations all face powerful constraints in responding to famine preemptively. These constraints are not immutable; and politics can facilitate as well as impede action, but the latter is more common. At both national and international levels, when action is not politically appealing, it tends not to happen. Ethiopia in the early 1980s is a case in point, with the government's priorities lying elsewhere and with the Reagan administration's determination to exploit famine for political advantage (see Chapter 5). Ethiopia is a compelling case both of how famine response is shaped by international political relationships and calculations and of how public opinion can force a change in policy once aroused.

Part III explores the often tenuous relationship between famine relief and development. Relief is often necessary because development has failed to reduce people's vulnerability to famine; but relief can also be an important step back to development, just as development is historically the best means of eliminating famine conditions and the need for relief. One of the challenges confronting those who manage famine is to bring relief and development together and then, through development, to make relief unnecessary.

All this is easier said than done, of course. Part III distills lessons from more than forty grassroots projects around the world that have successfully incorporated development into relief activities (see Chapter 6); but it also reveals—through Oxfam America's experience (see Chapter 7)—how difficult this is to do when people are in acute need, when political pressures cannot be deflected, and when a relief agency is expected to spend large sums of money rapidly. That Oxfam America encountered difficulty in reconciling relief and development is all the more sobering given Oxfam America's well-articulated policies concerning both. The good news is that relief and development can be brought together to the extent that both purposefully tap and enhance people's capacities and work toward lessening their vulnerabilities. Welcome evidence that these linkages are being forged in the West African Sahel rounds out Part III (see Chapter 8).

The Challenge of Famine concludes, in Part IV, with the theme of improving famine detection and response. As revealed in an experiment with participatory monitoring in Darfur, Sudan (assessed in Chapter 9), it is proving very difficult to establish famine early warning systems that are manageable, that are effectively linked to decisionmaking and response, that are capable of activating policies and specific interventions that have been designed in advance, and that are compelling enough to mobilize timely international assistance. It is not even clear that detection is the problem; many analysts believe that the real problem lies in the political and administrative response to impending famine once the signs of stress appear. Both perspectives are examined in Part IV, including presentation (in Chapter 10) of a relatively simple index showing the terms of trade between livestock and grain prices in Kordofan, Sudan, the results of which were dramatic in 1988–90 and helpful in justifying and then targeting relief.

Whatever the detection system and diagnostics employed, there is reason to believe that technical early warning is less important and less effective in spurring action than are political and administrative incentives to early intervention. This inference emerges from comparing how famine has been managed in India since 1880 with how it is typically handled in contemporary Africa. The comparison pits use of human judgment, local decisionmaking and response, and preparedness planning—all leading to early, preemptive action—against use of complex data sets and highly sophisticated technologies, decisionmaking remote from the scene of stress, and lack of preparedness—all disposing to delay and reliance on relief after the worst has already happened. Clearly we can and must do better. To do so we need improved understanding of the dynamics by which famines emerge, fewer and simpler yet powerful indicators of the process as it unfolds, and much sharper thinking concerning the objectives of intervention as well as the nature and timing of intervention. These themes appear often in this book; analytically they come to a head at the end of Part IV (see Chapter 11).

A double irony underlies *The Challenge of Famine* as it does famine management itself. On the one hand, even though famine is dramatically clear when in full force, it is shrouded in ambiguity before it reaches that advanced stage. Until famine happens, one cannot be sure that it will happen. The boundary, if there is one, between famine and nonfamine is extremely difficult to locate. Nor is there consensus on how to recognize famine before the camera proves its existence. Some in positions of authority rely on judgment; others require data. Some acknowledge famine when it is officially declared; others bemoan the tardiness of official recognition. Moreover, if famine is a judgment call, whose judgment counts? If data are essential, what data should be used and how are they to be analyzed? Ultimately, who is responsible for detection, decision, and response? Are they the same people or different people? Are they to be found locally, in national capitals, or internationally?

All too often the very uncertainty and confusion associated with famine dispose to fragmented responsibility for managing it. Uncertainty and confusion also dispose to a response that is late. Herein lies the second irony, because famine—unlike an earthquake or typhoon—is a slow-onset disaster. Famine is a process as well as an event. Moreover, it is typically a lengthy process and one that is as much human-induced as it is a cruelty of nature. One can chart the process and identify the key indicators as famine unfolds. Most important, one can intervene to arrest the process and either forestall a famine outcome or mitigate its consequences. And yet, again all too often, governments and international agencies, seeking certainty in inherent uncertainty and clarity in inherent ambiguity, delay decision and action. The usual response to famine is relief after the fact, not preemptive intervention. Indeed, few governments have developed the capacity to intervene early and effectively to prevent famine. The potential to do so certainly exists, and the logic for doing so is incontrovertible; but there is much work to be done before the art of managing famine is likely to improve on a significant scale.

This book is not a cookbook. It offers no recipes, but it does ask many of the right questions. In assessing recent experience and crystallizing the issues involved in famine management, it points to innovations in both thinking and policy that can improve future performance.

Part I

A Perspective on Famine

Introduction

Chapter 1, a conceptual introduction to famine, takes off from a double irony: While the process that leads to famine is shrouded in ambiguity, famine finally becomes dramatically evident; and while governments and donor agencies could intervene early and preemptively, they typically settle for relief after the fact.

An examination of the historical record reveals that famine is not tied to any particular ideology, economic order, or political system and makes clear that famine is a product of underdevelopment in a far more profound sense that the word *poverty* suggests. On a more positive historical note, both the frequency and the geographical scope of famine appear to be diminishing. Famine today is largely an African tragedy, associated more often with conflict than with either nature or poverty.

Since highlighting the distinctiveness of famine tends to divorce it from development policy and limit famine response to relief, Chapter 1 concludes with an argument for integrating famine policy with ongoing development policy.

1

Understanding Famine

John Osgood Field

Famine is a nasty turn of events that intrudes on our consciousness from time to time. We are shocked at pictures of starving people and reports of large numbers of acutely malnourished children, rampant disease, a rising death toll, and massive suffering in some far-off land. Many among us are moved to contribute to famine relief, reminded uncomfortably that famine still exists in a world "awash in grain" (Insel 1985). Those who think about it recognize that famine is related to poverty, that it is often triggered by climatic instability, and that it is both an instrument and tragic by-product of political conflict. But few among us know very much about famine beyond such fleeting insights. Even fewer are aware that our collective response to famine is woefully deficient.

Better management of famine entails more than honing the mechanisms of relief. It really means going beyond relief to the more ambitious agenda of preventing famine from occurring in the first place. Famine prevention, in turn, requires improved detection of the many factors disposing to a famine outcome combined with a more timely and effective response. Such a response can be achieved only when governments are committed to preemptive intervention and when they have preparedness plans to activate. Ultimately, famine management involves integrating famine policy into the mainstream of a country's broader development policies so that each reinforces the other in reducing vulnerabilities and building capacities in society, economy, and state.

Improving the management of famine may be a formidable task, but it is by no means an impossible one. Some countries—notably

11

India and Botswana—have managed famine with remarkable success, and it is possible to learn from their experience.[1] Equally relevant is a sharpened understanding of famine from its origins to its consequences, accompanied by strategic thinking concerning how best to anticipate, prepare, and respond, all of which are well within our intellectual and operational grasp.

This essay addresses the conceptual side of famine. The pages that follow seek to capture the essence of famine as revealed in a vibrant literature on the topic. Themes to be addressed include lessons distilled from famine's long history, why famine is both similar to yet different from chronic undernutrition, and reasons for thinking about famine as an issue in development rather than as something to turn to when development fails. These themes enhance an understanding of famine in terms of policy responses appropriate to it, and they set the stage for pursuing the principal objective of this volume, the attempt to learn from experience with famine in the 1980s so as to improve management of famine in the 1990s and beyond.

The Nature of the Beast

Famine may be seen as "the regional failure of food production or distribution systems, leading to sharply increased mortality due to starvation and associated disease" (Cox 1981, 5). While other definitions exist as well,[2] this one usefully emphasizes regional, not family failure; points to the importance of markets and, by implication, of shifting market demand for different foods in addition to their aggregate supply; identifies "excess deaths"—deaths that otherwise would not have occurred—as the core feature of famine; and attributes those deaths to morbidity as well as to seriously reduced consumption. Indeed, most famine-induced mortality tends to occur after the worst of the food crisis is over but while the crisis of infectious disease persists (Bongaarts and Cain 1982; Greenough 1976 and 1982; see also the studies cited by Drèze and Sen 1989, 44).[3]

What this definition does not adequately convey is that famine is the endpoint of a lengthy process in which people in increasing numbers lose their access to food. Most famines have long gestation periods, typically covering two or more crop seasons. Because the descent into famine is slow, early detection is possible. Because it is also typically shrouded in ambiguity, early detection is rarely definitive and seldom produces early response. Herein lies a dilemma that continues to plague famine early warning systems.[4]

Moreover, famine entails more than a severe shortage of food and grotesque distortions of normal food prices. Famine features a deepening recession in the entire rural economy, one affecting production and exchange, employment, and income of farm and nonfarm households alike (Sen 1981; Greenough 1982; Ravallion 1987; Desai 1988; Drèze 1990a). Landless laborers, artisans, and traders are among those most vulnerable to famine because of shrinking demand for their labor, goods, and services. Pastoralists and fishermen are also vulnerable because they rely on the exchange of meat and marine products to obtain the cheaper grain calories they require and because, in the dynamic leading to famine, the terms of trade turn sharply against what they sell relative to the grain they seek to buy. In the Bengal famine of 1943–44, for example, the price of cloth, fish, milk, haircuts, and bamboo umbrellas deteriorated 70–80 percent versus grain (Mellor and Gavian 1987). In Ethiopia animal calories normally cost about twice as much as grain calories, with herdsmen meeting half of their caloric requirements through consumption of grain; during the famine of 1972–74 the calorie exchange rate declined as much as 84–92 percent against animal products in some areas (Sen 1981, drawing on calculations by Seaman, Holt, and Rivers 1978 and Rivers, Holt, Seaman, and Bowden 1976). In Swaziland, cattle lost six to eight times their value relative to maize in the little-known famine of 1932, placing herders in acute distress (Packard 1984). As a rule of thumb, when grain supplies and animal stocks both decline, the exchange rate worsens for animals. This double jeopardy underlies Sen's observation that the Ethiopian pastoralist, "hit by drought, was decimated by the market mechanism" (Sen 1981, 112; see also Wolde Mariam 1984). By contrast, large producers of grain and grain merchants can usually ride out a famine far more successfully than others in the afflicted environment.

Similarly, the definition of famine offered above fails to capture the extent of social disintegration that usually accompanies the downward slide into famine conditions. Social reciprocities and supports crumble under increasing stress. Hoarding and related pathologies (smuggling, black market profiteering, crime) become commonplace. The distress sale of assets (jewelry, animals, land) accelerates. Families divide in search of work or succor; wives may even be cast adrift and children sold (Greenough 1982; Vaughan 1987). Out-migration increases as ever more people abandon their lands, homes, and communities in desperation. Abnormally high mortality may be the hallmark of famine, but societal breakdown is its essence.[5]

Finally, so far as these initial observations are concerned, it is important to note that famine occurs not only because a chain of events disposes to a famine outcome but also because nothing, or at least nothing effective, is done to break the process. It has been rare for the governments of famine-prone countries to possess the means with which to intervene to prevent famine. India over the last century and Botswana more recently are exceptions in this regard (McAlpin 1983; Drèze 1990a and 1990b; Holm and Morgan 1985; Hay 1988; Moremi 1988; Morgan 1988). Elsewhere the record has been quite dismal for the most part, while international assistance typically arrives after the worst has already happened. The usual way in which famine-prone areas become less famine prone is via economic development. In the long run, that remains the best solution even today (see Eicher 1987; Drèze and Sen 1989). However, we now know that intervention is possible and that it can work. Preparing for famine so as to prevent it, although not a new idea, is one that we should be thinking about and working to realize. The reasons are humanitarian, social, economic, and political.[6] We can both protect development and promote it by preparedness planning to "deny famine a future" (Glantz 1987).

The Lessons of History

Famine has a long history (Arnold 1988; see also Rotberg 1983 and Newman 1990). Reference to famine appears in the Book of Genesis, when Joseph interpreted another man's dream as meaning seven years of food scarcity to follow seven years of plenty and persuaded Pharaoh to store grain (an early example of preparedness/prevention). Famine is believed to have contributed to the decline of the Roman Empire and to have visited the Mohenjo Daro and Harappa civilizations in ancient Asia (Carlson 1982). The early kingdoms of Ghana, Mali, and Songhay in western Africa experienced localized famines (Franke and Chasin 1980), while in Ethiopia there have been at least thirty major famines over the past five centuries, including the Great Famine of 1888–92, triggered by a rinderpest epidemic that decimated cattle herds and cost more than a million human lives, almost 20 percent of the country's population at the time (Pankhurst 1966). India has had 127 famines since 298 B.C., thirty-two in the nineteenth century alone (Greenough 1976). China is said to have experienced one famine per year, on average, between 108 B.C. and 1911; in 1876–79 some nine to thirteen million people died in northern China in what might be the largest famine of the nineteenth century (Carlson 1982). The most celebrated famine of that period, the Potato Famine of 1846–48 in Ireland, resulted in only one million deaths out of a total population of eight million, although another million emigrated, leaving Ireland with only three-quarters of its original population (Woodham-Smith 1962). History's most severe famine occurred in Europe during the Great Bubonic Plague of 1345–48, which so disrupted the sowing and harvesting of crops that forty-three million people died of disease and starvation, including two-thirds of the

Italian population (Mellor and Gavian 1987). (Little wonder that during the Middle Ages famine was considered one of the four horsemen of the Apocalypse!) The twentieth century's greatest famine occurred not in India or Africa but in the People's Republic of China between 1959 and 1962 during the Great Leap Forward, in which thirty million people perished (Ashton et al. 1984; see also Coale 1981 and Aird 1982).

Several points are worth making based on the historical record. First, famine is not confined to any particular ideology, economic order, or political system; it cuts across the broad spectrum of thought and type. Russia, for example, experienced seventy-four famines between 971 A.D. and the revolution in 1917; subsequently the Soviet Union weathered three significant famines, in 1921–22 (five to nine million deaths), in 1932–33 (five to eleven million deaths), and in 1946–47 (two to five million deaths) (Dando 1981).[7] A possible exception to the apolitical character of famine is that it would appear to be much less likely to occur in a stable, functioning democratic system, presumably because rural interests are well represented and because opposition parties and a free press sound alarms that invite government action to forestall its emergence (Sen 1987; Mellor and Gavian 1987; Drèze and Sen 1989; Ram 1990; Watts 1991). A definite qualification is that famine is both associated with and accentuated by warfare (the Soviet Union after both world wars; Holland, Leningrad, and Bengal during World War II; Ethiopia and the Sudan in recent years) and by politically inspired social engineering (the collectivization of Soviet agriculture; the rapid expansion of communal farms during the Great Leap in China; and the near miss resulting from dislocations induced by the Khmer Rouge in Cambodia).[8]

Second, famine is inversely related to development. It thrives on generally low-yield agriculture whose performance is contingent on highly variable rainfall; on segmented, locally confined markets requiring self-provisioning of carryover stocks of grain; on restricted opportunities for employment, including alternatives to usual employment when it collapses; and on incomes that are seldom above subsistence and assets that are either too few to protect people in times of stress or are not fungible for food. Vulnerability to famine is greatly reduced as economies expand and diversify, raising incomes and options for employment; as transportation and communications integrate markets and permit the flow of goods and services, especially food, over very much larger areas—railroads, cargo ships, paved roads, trucks, mail service, the telegraph and telephone being important instruments for the prevention and alleviation of famine; as education expands, creating new capacities and career options; and as governments themselves develop, broadening the services they provide on a regular basis and enhancing their ability to intervene in times of crisis.[9]

Again, however, there are at least two qualifications to be made. One is that the commercialization of agriculture would appear to be associated, for a time at least, with increased vulnerability to famine as monocropping replaces multicrop and multiplot modes of production and as food prices become more volatile, alienation of land accelerates, and social supports decline in the face of expanding market-based transactions (Alamgir 1981; Leibenstein 1982; Packard 1984; Timberlake 1985; Devereux and Hay 1986). Second, not all development is equally beneficial. Development that widens disparities in society without strengthening the base does little to reduce vulnerability to famine. Export-oriented agriculture may actually increase vulnerability (Lofchie 1975; Lappé and Collins 1977; Franke and Chasin 1980; but note Pinstrup-Andersen 1983; Kennedy and Cogill 1987; and Downing, Gitu, and Kamau 1989).

Third, with rare exception famine is a rural phenomenon. This is paradoxical, perhaps, inasmuch as it is the areas that grow food that are most likely to experience the starvation, disease, and death associated with famine. The reasons lie in rural poverty, the market draw of urban wealth, and—more often than one might think—the procurement policies of government (Bates 1981; Greenough 1982; Wolde Mariam 1984 and 1987).

Fourth, also with rare exception, such as several noted above, famine takes as its toll only a small percentage of the total population, granted that it makes destitute large numbers of others. The Bengal famine of 1943–44 killed roughly three and a half million out of a rural population of fifty-five million (Greenough 1982; nationalist opinion in India claims as much as five million). The famine that struck Bangladesh in 1974 resulted in at most one and a half million deaths, or 2 percent of the population (Bongaarts and Cain 1982). Mortality associated with the Ethiopian famine of 1972–74 was only 200,000 in a population of twenty-seven million (Sen 1981), while that in the Sahel during the Great West African Famine of 1968–74, "among the greatest tragedies of the 20th Century" (Franke and Chasin 1980, 5), amounted to only about 100,000 (mostly pastoral nomads) out of twenty-five million population. Even China's massive famine of 1959–62, the one that produced thirty million excess deaths, amounted to less than 5 percent of China's total population of 647–654 million people at the time. The numbers may appear large, and they certainly are tragic; but proportionally they are surprisingly modest.

There is an interesting corollary to this point. The numbers who die in famine are typically such a small percentage of the total society that famine rarely plays the role defined for it by Thomas Malthus back in 1798, the role of "natural regulator" of overpopulation.[10] Famine is not nature's way of restoring the balance between population load and the carrying capacity of land. To illustrate, the Bengal famine of 1943–44 was no longer statistically discernible by the time of the censuses of 1961 in West Bengal and East Pakistan. Population was right back on trend line, even above it, as if the famine had not occurred. The reason is that the age groups most likely to perish in famine are the very young and the elderly. Adults in their reproductive years are the most likely to survive, and the many that do quickly make up their losses (Bongaarts and Cain 1982). As Table 1.1 demonstrates, the same thing happened in China in the aftermath of the Great Leap famine. The high mortality and reduced fertility of the famine triggered a boom in births immediately thereafter, to the point where 36.6 percent of the deficit was erased within three years and the previous trend line exceeded within twenty years, as in Bengal (Ashton et al. 1984). The famine deaths in Bangladesh in 1974, one and a half million (2 percent of the population), were outstripped by a population growth rate of 3 percent, meaning that these excess deaths were compensated for in less than one year. To the extent that overpopulation is a serious problem, famine is not a solution.[11]

Table 1.1 The Effects of the Great Leap Famine on China's Population Size Are No Longer Evident

Year	Population (millions)	Population Change (millions)			Trend Line Population (millions)
1953–54	582.6				
1954–55	594.7	+12.1	Trend line is approximately		
1955–56	608.3	+13.6	13 million added to the		
1956–57	620.3	+12.0	population each year.		
1957–58	633.7	+13.4			
1958–59	647.3	+13.6	*Difference from Trend Line*		
1959–60	653.5	+6.2	–6.8		
1960–61	651.0	–2.5	–15.5		
1961–62	646.6	–4.4	–17.4		
1962–63	653.7	+7.1	–5.9	–45.6	699.3
1963–64	677.4	+23.7	+10.7		712.3
1964–65	696.4	+19.0	+6.0	+16.7	725.3
			Deficit = 28.9		
Mid-1982	1,000.0		Excess = 40.7		959.3
Mid-1984	1,034.5		Excess = 49.2		985.3

Source: Calculated from Ashton et al. 1984.

Fifth, and finally, there would appear to be a historical trend reducing the frequency, severity, and geographical scope of famine.

Whereas famine once covered all geographical areas and touched most human populations at one time or another, today it is confined mostly to the semi-arid and conflict-riddled countries of Africa.[12] This is not to say that famine no longer exists elsewhere; it is to say that the likelihood of its occurring is very much lower elsewhere, except possibly Bangladesh.[13] Most societies have learned how to compensate for the weather and to protect those victimized by its adversities. When the rains fail in the Netherlands (one of the most densely populated countries in the world) or the U.S. South, nobody starves; when the rains fail in the Sahel (among the least densely populated regions in the world) and in Ethiopia, people starve in large numbers, just as they used to in much of Europe, Russia, and India. Outside of Africa, famine today denotes severe social dislocation, failed information systems, and either government brutality or paralysis—a threatening but unlikely combination. Even in Africa, famine is associated more with conflict than with nature. The extended drought of the early to mid-1980s affected thirty-one countries, but famine emerged in only five: Chad, Sudan, Ethiopia, Mozambique, and Angola, the most war-wracked countries on the continent (Glantz 1989).[14] On the other hand, Africa's distinctiveness at the present time is a function of all the major elements of famine: weak economies, weaker governments, social institutions in transition, crisis-prone environments, and a propensity to protracted political conflict. The rest of the world, Bangladesh included, is fortunate in comparison.[15]

Famine in Relation to Malnutrition

Famine can be seen as the dramatic endpoint of a continuum featuring different degrees of malnutrition, morbidity, and early childhood mortality. Alternatively, it can be seen as a unique phenomenon with a dynamic of its own and with consequences that are exceptional. The former perspective emphasizes the common origins of malnutrition and famine in the high vulnerability and low capacity of underdevelopment. It has the merit of encouraging famine to be interpreted in its developmental context, as malnutrition now is, the endemic conditions disposing to malnutrition-morbidity-mortality disposing in the extreme to famine as well. Even the vulnerable groups are much the same, granted that famine takes a broader toll across different age cohorts.

On the other hand, most analysts of famine prefer to emphasize its distinctiveness. In this view, famine is more than malnutrition writ large. The surge in mortality associated with famine is more epidemic than endemic (Cox 1981). The circumstances of famine are more exceptional than usual, even in places where famine is recurrent. Whereas malnutrition in many societies is common even in normal times, the entitlements of some people simply being insufficient to maintain nutritional adequacy, in famine the entitlements of many collapse entirely.[16] A society experiencing famine is in disequilibrium, a state of breakdown. Crop production is abnormally low; employment opportunities shrink among the rural labor force; trade is curtailed; food prices rise as incomes decline relatively and, for some, absolutely; the exchange rate between animal products and grain deteriorates markedly, the same being true of fish and other higher status, if less efficient, sources of calories; and consumption is curtailed as people lose access to food. As famine unfolds, antisocial behavior—hoarding, crime, and the like—increases, social arrangements erode, people sell or abandon their assets, and out-migration accelerates. In the midst of all this, malnutrition rates soar, infectious diseases spread, and people die in unusual numbers.

The advantage of separating famine from malnutrition should be apparent (see also Rivers 1988; Drèze and Sen 1989). Malnutrition, the silent holocaust, coexists tragically with steady-state conditions that are normal, familiar, and not easily subject to change. Famine is change in the wrong direction. It is, moreover, a jolt that overwhelms social institutions even as it victimizes individuals. If malnutrition is a constraint on development, as nutrition advocates have claimed (for example, Belli 1971; Berg 1973 and 1981), famine is the bottoming out of development. If the principal effect of malnutrition is functional impairment followed by mortality, the principal effects of famine are destitution and mortality followed by acute dependency on the part of survivors. Ironically, the deaths associated with famine may be less than the deaths associated with malnutrition, but they are more concentrated in space and time. Unlike malnutrition, famine wreaks social and economic havoc. Also unlike malnutrition, famine disposes to political instability (see note 6).

Famine in Relation to Development

The problem with treating famine as aberration and breakdown is that this perspective drives a conceptual wedge between famine and development. To be sure, famine undermines and erodes development, just as development is clearly the best and perhaps only long-term solution to famine, the economic immunization, as it were. In the short run, however, the exceptionality of famine tends to divorce it from development. In normal times governments and international agencies pursue development. When famine strikes, they are forced to switch gears and provide relief. The switch may be necessary, but it is also usually unwelcome. Institutional mandates are altered, agendas disrupted, resources diverted, and personnel redirected. Development is put on hold. The relief offered assumes the aura and often the frenzy of crisis liquidation. When the worst is past and as many lives as possible have been saved, governments and donors alike return to what they really care about: development. The aberration of famine elicits, at best, an exceptional response. Not only is famine relief not part of development, it is at the cost of development.

The irony becomes a dilemma. A keener understanding of famine, highlighting its distinctiveness vis-à-vis chronic malnutrition, disposes to removing it as a concern in development and to a very limited response in the form of relief. Appreciating this distinctiveness has the unhappy corollary of encouraging famine to be viewed, in policy terms, as something unto itself and, by extension, as something other than development. Development is a positive, famine a negative. Development is ongoing, famine is episodic. Development exalts professionalism; careers are built in its name. Famine exalts humanitarian mercy; here today, hopefully unnecessary tomorrow. With relief provided and lives saved, one can—even should—fold one's tent and go home. By contrast, one is in development for the long haul.

So powerful are these distinctions that organizations divide in their orientation, some emphasizing relief (for example, the Red Cross, United Nations Disaster Relief Organization, and the United Nations High Commissioner for Refugees), many more emphasizing development. An increasing number of organizations engage in both activities (U.S. Agency for International Development, United Nations Children's Fund, Save the Children, Catholic Relief Services, to identify just a few), but with a clear preference for development. Indeed, it is not uncommon within the same organization for relief and development to be separate responsibilities performed by different units with their own staffs and budgets, thereby institutionalizing the distinction itself. The bottom line is that development is the more rewarded focus. One turns to relief and relief workers when disaster strikes.

None of this is unreasonable, but it is counterproductive in the case of famine. One problem with the relief response to famine is that famine, a slow-onset disaster, is lumped together indiscriminately with such quick-onset disasters as earthquakes, floods, and typhoons. Because the latter happen suddenly, one has little option but to respond after the fact. Because they tend to be natural events of unusual force, there is not much one can do to prevent or mitigate them in advance; picking up the pieces (that is, relief) is about the only option.[17]

Three points are worth stressing in this regard. First, one opts for relief when nothing else is really possible, or when all else fails. Second, because—as noted above—famine is more man-made than a cruelty of nature, it is far more subject to manipulation than, say, a volcanic eruption or cyclone.

Third, and most important, famine's lengthy gestation offers the opportunity to intervene before relief becomes necessary; because famine is a slow-onset disaster, it is possible to chart the processes leading to it and to identify the critical indicators that a famine dynamic is underway (see Chapter 11 for an illustration). This is the promise of early warning systems. Similarly, with detection it becomes possible to respond early in the process and thereby, hopefully, to snuff it out. This is what has happened in India over the past 100 years (excepting 1943): Particularly during the colonial period, the authorities first declared famine and then responded to prevent its emergence.[18] (In Africa, by contrast, the tendency is to respond with relief after the worst has already happened.) By extension, it becomes possible to prepare for famine by planning for it in advance. Interventions can be designed and strategized, necessary materiel stockpiled, and personnel trained for the tasks to be performed. Again, India's experience is instructive (Berg 1973; Singh 1975; McAlpin 1983; Drèze 1990a).

Because prevention is possible, it makes no sense to confine the response to relief, especially inasmuch as famine entails such high human, social, economic, and political costs. Ironically, from a developmental perspective, the principal reason for treating famine as a development issue is to protect development. At the very least, a preventive famine policy is insurance against development being severely undermined. When integrated with development, a preventive famine policy has the potential to go beyond protecting the downside to include building the upside. This is because famine is a function of underdevelopment in a much broader sense than poverty alone. Famine thrives on poor transport, weak communications, market segmentation, and limited options for alternative employment and protection of income. It also thrives on governments whose operational capabilities do not allow for timely and effective intervention. (Despite its poverty, India has excellent transport, well-developed communications, integrated markets, and an official capacity to provide food and health care, launch public works, expand employment, protect income, and provide loans to farmers so that they can retain or replenish their productive assets.) All of these concerns are central to development, or at least to concepts of development that go beyond urban-centered industrialization.

In sum, the opportunity exists to make famine policy preemptive and not merely reactive. At the same time, it is possible to make preparation for famine an ally of development, indeed a core component of development, as against being an alternative to it. Greater international effort is called for to help the governments of famine-prone countries to think this way and act accordingly. Clearly, for donor agencies to help in this fashion they need to think this way and act accordingly themselves.[19]

There is a final linkage between famine and development. Preparedness planning and preventive efforts may fail to arrest the onset of famine, in which case relief becomes necessary if lives are to be saved and health restored. Unfortunately, the divorce between relief and development renders relief a discrete activity that is appropriately terminated when its immediate purposes have been served. (Alternatively, relief chugs along, especially in refugee camps, a holding pattern with no end in sight.) The problem is that even successful relief does little to rebuild the future; it makes a future possible, but relief itself does not make famine victims, particularly the uprooted, viable once again. In fact, it is a pervasive characteristic of famine that it leaves its surviving victims considerably worse off, economically and in other respects, than they were before. As Mellor and Gavian (1987, 541) note, "Famine conditions redistribute incomes away from the poor, dealing them a smaller proportion of a shrinking pie." Without asset regeneration famine has lasting effects.

Nor is rehabilitation a sufficient answer. Rehabilitation—return to land and home; recapitalization of herds, seeds, and implements; restoration of previous means of livelihood—simply recreates the status quo ante in most instances. That is better than relief alone, but it hardly addresses the vulnerability that pushed people over the brink the last time.

What it all comes down to is this: Famine relief should be seen as the first step back to development. It is not an end unto itself but the essential precondition for recapturing development and perhaps even redirecting development so that it explicitly and purposefully reduces vulnerabilities and creates new capacities (Taylor 1978; Independent Commission 1985; Anderson 1985; Anderson and Woodrow 1989). Only when relief is linked to development will people be better able to withstand future shocks disposing to famine and will governments be better able to intervene to help them do so. The linkage is more than sequential—relief, rehabilitation, development; it is iterative. How relief is organized and implemented, including provision of health care and uses of food aid, can themselves be shaped by the development goals to which they are tied (see, for example, Hay 1986 and Chapter 6, by Anderson and Woodrow, in this book).

In sum, the famine-development linkage is twofold. The development process best obviates the need for famine relief when it enhances productivity, builds market strengths, expands opportunities in society, strengthens income generation in rural areas, and provides basic services (nutrition, health, education) to all. In famine-prone countries, these processes are best supported and protected by having well-considered preemptive interventions available and the means with which to activate them. Famine prevention insulates development from acute accelerating stress. If famine conditions emerge anyway, their effects can be mitigated by these measures. Then, if relief is necessary, it can be tailored to promote a rapid return to development. So simple are these notions that the amazing thing is how rarely they are put into practice.

Relinking famine and development will both encourage and facilitate a more effective response when famine looms on the horizon. Just as there is a need in agriculture to reintegrate production and consumption, food and nutrition, so there is a need to incorporate famine policy into the mainstream of development.

Notes

This chapter is adapted from a larger paper, "Beyond Relief: A Developmental Perspective on Famine," presented at the Fourteenth International Congress of Nutrition, Seoul, Korea, 20–25 August 1989. Portions appear in "Famine: A Perspective for the Nutrition Community" *Nutrition Reviews*, 49 (May 1991): 145–153.

1. Chapter 11 elaborates on this observation. See also Drèze and Sen 1989 and Drèze 1990a and 1990b.

2. De Waal 1989 has challenged the notion that famine necessarily entails a surge in mortality, suggesting that widespread hunger and destitution constitute famine even when people do not die. See Devereux and Hay 1986 for an extensive discussion of the various ways in which famine has been defined.

3. The physiological effects of malnutrition and famine are analyzed in Rivers 1988; see also Scrimshaw 1987 and Dasgupta and Ray 1990.

4. This is a theme that recurs throughout this book. See especially Chapters 4 and 9–11. See also Walker 1989 and the several papers on early warning by Cutler referenced at the end of this chapter.

5. Cox 1981 calls starvation, social disruption, and disease the "triad of famine." All may be—and usually are—exceptional in scope; but of the three, only social disruption is distinctive. On the other hand, famine seldom victimizes everyone in the afflicted environment. Although it makes destitute many, famine can further enrich the relatively few—large landowners, wealthy herders, and entrepreneurs especially—who are able to acquire the assets sold or abandoned (Greenough 1982; Watts 1991).

6. Famine in modern times has become a major source of political instability. Following the Great West African Famine of 1968–74, for example, every national government in the Sahel excepting Senegal's fell in successful coups d'état, as did the regime of Emperor Haile Selassie in Ethiopia. Other factors were involved, to be sure; but famine significantly undermined the legitimacy of leaderships unwilling or unable to cope.

7. Renewed famine in the former USSR has been predicted by economist Vladimir Tikonov, a member of the last National Congress, unless radical changes in the economy are achieved (*New York Times*, 18 June 1989). Most analysts, however, believe that Russia's easy access to world grain markets should be adequate to compensate for deficiencies in domestic food production. On the other hand, logistical breakdowns in the procurement, storage, and distribution of food have become pressing concerns.

8. Concerning the latter three references, see Conquest 1986; Ashton et al. 1984; and Shawcross 1984.

9. The singular importance of transport in famine reduction has been noted by many analysts and is discussed at length in Hurd 1975 and McAlpin 1983. Vulnerability to famine is addressed by most of the authors cited in this chapter, but empirical assessment remains difficult. See also D'Souza 1988; Downing 1991.

10. A good critique of Malthus's theories about population appears in Devereux and Hay 1986.

11. For an alarmist argument to the contrary, see Paddock and Paddock 1967. The seriousness of population pressures on land as a factor enhancing vulnerability to famine is soberly assessed in Timberlake 1985 and many other sources. A good distillation appears in Devereux and Hay 1986.

12. Cox 1981 notes the existence historically of two famine belts, one stretching from Ireland across northern Europe to Siberia and China and the other extending from Africa across South and Southeast Asia. Famine seems to have been much less common in the Americas. Kates and his associates (1988) have discerned a fairly steady decline in the numbers of people victimized by famine during the last four decades. Although comforting, their assessment is influenced by the unusually large famine in China in the early 1960s and by the shift in famine's locus from Asia to Africa. On the other hand, one veteran observer (Dando 1988, 19) believes that "famines of the future will last for extended periods of time, cover broad geographical areas, including major metropolitan regions, encompass many nations and involve truly vast populations."

13. Bangladesh is a mixed case. Governmental capabilities to detect and respond to incipient famine are much improved (Cutler 1985; Clay 1985; Osmani 1991), but political will remains suspect and the country continues to be extremely prone to flooding and other disasters.

14. In his monumental study of the African poor, Iliffe (1987, 6) argues that famine mortality actually declined in Africa during the 1920s and 1930s as a result of socioeconomic and political development, with "epidemic starvation for all but the rich" giving way to "endemic undernutrition for the very poor." That famine reemerged in the modern period is explained by the growth of structural poverty in rural areas, by political conflict and warfare, and by drought. The most interesting explanation, theoretically, is the first because of what explains it. See, for example, Franke and Chasin 1980; Lofchie 1975; Bates 1981 and 1983; and Barker 1989.

15. Drought used to be considered the principal cause of famine. This is no longer the case (Lofchie 1975; Greenough 1976 and 1982; Sen 1981; Dando 1981; Timberlake 1985; Glantz 1987 and 1989; Drèze and Sen 1989). The role of drought as a trigger of famine and its reverberating consequences down to the level of individual nutrition is examined systematically in Teklu, von Braun, and Zaki 1991.

16. The concept *entitlement* is Sen's (1981; see also Drèze and Sen 1989 and 1990a). It is empirical, not normative, and refers to what different people can reliably command and expect to command in normal times. Entitlements to food are based on endowment, what people own and what they produce, as well as on what they are able to acquire in exchange for their employment and income, as mediated by prices. Following Sen, analysts of famine often refer to three types of entitlements: direct (endowment), exchange, and dependency, the latter referring to what children and other dependents can command in the social system.

17. The literature on disaster management does discuss preparedness and prevention quite prominently (see, for example, Stephens and Green 1979; Cuny 1983; and Comfort 1988); but except in the case of flooding, most preparedness for quick-onset disasters necessarily emphasizes relief.

18. India's approach to famine management is summarized in Chapter 11. See Greenough 1976 and 1982 concerning the special case of Bengal during World War II.

19. Parenthetically, it is a sad commentary on USAID's Famine Early Warning System (FEWS) project that its principal objective is to facilitate U.S. decisionmaking so as to trigger a more timely release of food aid. As worthy a concern as this is, it is steeped in a relief mentality and, moreover, does virtually nothing to build detection and response capacities in the participating African countries. Some movement in the right direction is evident in Phase II of the project.

References

Aird, John S. 1982. "Population Studies and Population Policy in China." *Population and Development Review* 8 (June): 85–97.

Alamgir, Mohiuddin. 1981 "An Approach Towards a Theory of Famine." In Robson, 19–40.

Anderson, Mary B. 1985. "A Reconceptualization of the Linkages Between Disasters and Development." *Disasters* 9, Harvard Supplement: 45–51.

Anderson, Mary B., and Peter J. Woodrow. 1989. *Rising from the Ashes: Development Strategies in Times of Disaster*. Boulder: Westview Press.

Arnold, David. 1988. *Famine: Social Crisis and Historical Change*. Oxford: Basil Blackwell.

Ashton, Basil, Kenneth Hill, Alan Piazza, and Robin Zeitz. 1984. "Famine in China, 1958–61." *Population and Development Review* 10 (December): 613–645.

Barker, Jonathan. 1989. *Rural Communities Under Stress: Peasant Farmers and the State in Africa*. Cambridge: Cambridge University Press.

Bates, Robert H. 1981. *Markets and States in Tropical Africa: The Political Basis of Agricultural Policies*. Berkeley: University of California Press.

Bates, Robert H. 1983. *Essays on the Political Economy of Rural Africa*. Berkeley: University of California Press.

Belli, Pedro. 1971. "The Economic Implications of Malnutrition: The Dismal Science Revisited." *Economic Development and Cultural Change* 20 (October): 1–23.

Berg, Alan. 1973. *The Nutrition Factor: Its Role in National Development*, Appendix A, 211–221. Washington D.C.: Brookings Institution.

Berg, Alan. 1981. *Malnourished People: A Policy View*. Poverty and Basic Needs Series, World Bank.

Bongaarts, John, and Mead Cain. 1982. "Demographic Responses to Famine." In Cahill, 44–59.

Cahill, Kevin M., ed. 1982. *Famine*. Maryknoll, N.Y.: Orbis Books.

Carlson, Dennis G. 1982. "Famine in History: With a Comparison of Two Modern Ethiopian Disasters." In Cahill, 5–16.

Clay, Edward. 1985. "The 1974–1984 Floods in Bangladesh: From Famine to Food Crisis Management." *Food Policy* 10 (August): 202–206.

Coale, Ansley J. 1981. "Population Trends, Population Policy, and Population Studies in China." *Population and Development Review* 7 (March): 267–297.

Comfort, Louise K., ed. 1988. *Managing Disaster: Strategies and Policy Perspectives*. Durham, N. C.: Duke University Press.

Conquest, Robert. 1986. *The Harvest of Sorrow: Soviet Collectivization and the Terror-Famine*. New York: Oxford University Press.

Cox, George W. 1981. "The Ecology of Famine: An Overview." In Robson, 5–18.

Cuny, Frederick C. 1983. *Disaster and Development*. New York: Oxford University Press.

Curtis, Donald, Michael Hubbard, and Andrew Shepherd, eds. 1988. *Preventing Famine: Policies and Prospects for Africa*. London and New York: Routledge.

Cutler, Peter. 1984. "Famine Forecasting: Prices and Peasant Behaviour in Northern Ethopia." *Disasters* 8, 1: 48–56.

Cutler, Peter. 1985. "Detecting Food Emergencies: Lessons from the 1979 Bangladesh Crisis." *Food Policy* 10 (August): 207–224.

Cutler, Peter. 1986. "Famine Warning, Famine Prevention and Nutrition." *Nutrition Bulletin* 46 (January): 23–28.

Cutler, Peter. 1987. "Early Warning of Famine: A Red Herring?" *Proceedings of the Nutrition Society* 46: 263–266.

Cutler, Peter. 1988. "Preparation for Early Response to Disasters." Paper presented at the WHO/ACC/SCN Conference on Nutrition in Times of Disasters, World Health Organization, Geneva, 27–30 September.

Dando, W. A. 1981. "Man-Made Famines: Some Geographical Insights from an Exploratory Study of a Millenium of Russian Famines." In Robson, 139–154.

Dando, W. A. 1988. "World Food and Regional Famines: Problems and Prospects."*Currents* 3: 11–19.

Dasgupta, Partha, and Debraj Ray. 1990. "Adapting to Undernourishment: The Biological Evidence and its Implications." In Drèze and Sen 1990a, 191–246.

Desai, Meghnad. 1988. "The Economics of Famine." In Harrison, 107–138.

Devereux, Stephen, and Roger Hay. 1986. *Origins of Famine: A Review of the Literature*. 2 vols. Oxford: Oxford University, Food Studies Group. Forthcoming as *Theories of Famine*, Harvester Wheatsheaf.

de Waal, Alexander. 1989. *Famine That Kills: Darfur, Sudan, 1984–1985*. Oxford: Clarendon Press.

Downing, Thomas E. 1991. *Assessing Socioeconomic Vulnerability to Famine: Frameworks, Concepts, and Applications*. FEWS Working Paper 2.1, Final Report the U.S. Agency for International Development, Famine Early Warning System Project, 30 January.

Downing, Thomas E., Kangethe W. Gitu, and Crispin M. Kamau, eds. 1989. *Coping with Drought in Kenya: National and Local Strategies.* Boulder: Lynne Rienner Publishers.

Downs, R. E., Donna O. Kerner, and Stephen P. Reyna, eds. 1991. *The Political Economy of African Famine.* Philadelphia: Gordon and Breach.

Drèze, Jean, 1990a. "Famine Prevention in India." In Drèze and Sen 1990b, 13–122.

Drèze, Jean. 1990b. "Famine Prevention in Africa: Experiences and Lessons." In Drèze and Sen 1990b, 123–172.

Drèze, Jean, and Amartya Sen. 1989. *Hunger and Public Action.* Oxford: Clarendon Press.

Drèze, Jean, and Amartya Sen. 1990a, eds. *The Political Economy of Hunger.* Vol. 1, *Entitlement and Well-Being.* Oxford: Clarendon Press.

Drèze, Jean, and Amartya Sen. 1990b, eds. *The Political Economy of Hunger.* Vol. 2, *Famine Prevention.* Oxford: Clarendon Press.

Drèze, Jean, and Amartya Sen. 1991, eds. *The Political Economy of Hunger.* Vol. 3, *Endemic Hunger.* Oxford: Clarendon Press.

D'Souza, Frances. 1988. "Famine: Social Security and an Analysis of Vulnerability." In Harrison, 1–56.

Eicher, Carl K. 1987. "Famine Prevention in Africa: The Long View." Reprint No. 3, MSU International Development Papers, Department of Agricultural Economics, Michigan State University.

Franke, Richard W., and Barbara H. Chasin. 1980. *Seeds of Famine: Ecological Destruction and the Development Dilemma in the West African Sahel.* Montclair, N.J.: Allenheld, Osmun.

Glantz, Michael H. 1987, ed. *Drought and Hunger in Africa: Denying Famine a Future.* Cambridge: Cambridge University Press.

Glantz, Michael H. 1989. "Drought, Famine and the Seasons in Sub-Saharan Africa." In Huss-Ashmore and Katz, 45–71.

Greenough, Paul R. 1976. "Famine Victimization in a Traditionally Famine-Free Region: Bengal 1943–44." Paper presented at the panel on Famines in South Asia: Theory, History and Policy, Twenty-eighth Annual Meeting of the Association for Asian Studies, Toronto, Canada, 19 March.

Greenough, Paul R. 1982. *Prosperity and Misery in Modern Bengal: The Famine of 1943–1944.* New York: Oxford University Press.

Harrison, G. Ainsworth, ed. 1988. *Famine.* New York: Oxford University Press.

Hay, Roger W. 1986. "Food Aid and Relief-Development Strategies." Occasional Papers 8, World Food Programme, Rome, 23 July.

Hay, Roger W. 1988. "Famine Incomes and Employment: Has Botswana Anything to Teach Africa?" *World Development* 16: 1113–1125.

Holm, John D., and Richard G. Morgan. 1985. "Coping with Drought in Botswana: An African Success." *Journal of Modern African Studies* 23: 463–482.

Hurd, John II. 1975. "Railways and the Expansion of Markets in India, 1861–1921." *Explorations in Economic History* 12 (July): 263–288.

Huss-Ashmore, Rebecca, and Solomon H. Katz, eds. 1989. *African Food Systems in Crisis.* Part 1, *Microperspectives.* New York: Gordon and Breach.

Iliffe, John. 1987. *The African Poor: A History.* Cambridge: Cambridge University Press.

Independent Commission on International Humanitarian Issues. 1985. *Famine: A Man-Made Disaster?* London: Pan Books.

Insel, Barbara. 1985. "A World Awash in Grain." *Foreign Affairs* 63 (Spring): 892–911.

Kates, Robert W., Robert S. Chen, Thomas E. Downing, Jeanne X. Kasperson, Ellen Messer, and Sara R. Millman. 1988. "The Hunger Report: 1988." The Alan Shawn Feinstein World Hunger Program, Brown University, August. Mimeo.

Kennedy, Eileen T., and Bruce Cogill. 1987. *Income and Nutritional Effects of the Commercialization of Agriculture in Southwestern Kenya.* International Food Policy Research Institute, Research Report 63, November.

Lappé, Frances Moore, and Joseph Collins. 1977. *Food First: Beyond the Myth of Scarcity.* Boston: Houghton Mifflin.

Leibenstein, Harvey. 1982. "Famine and Economic Development." In Cahill, 108–119.

Lofchie, Michael F. 1975. "Political and Economic Origins of African Hunger." *Journal of Modern African Studies* 13 (December): 551–567.

McAlpin, Michelle Burge. 1983. *Subject to Famine: Food Crises and Economic Change in Western India, 1860–1920.* Princeton: Princeton University Press.

Mellor, John W., and Sarah Gavian. 1987. "Famine: Causes, Prevention, and Relief." *Science* 235 (30 January): 539–545.

Moremi, Tswelopele C. 1988. "Transition from Emergency to Development Assistance: Botswana Experience." Paper presented at the WHO/ACC/SCN Conference on Nutrition in Times of Disasters, World Health Organization, Geneva, 27–30 September.

Morgan, Richard. 1988. "Drought-Relief Programmes in Botswana." In Curtis, Hubbard, and Shepherd, 112–120.

Newman, Lucille F., ed. 1990. *Hunger in History: Food Shortages, Poverty, and Deprivation.* Oxford: Basil Blackwell.

Osmani, S.R. 1991. "The Food Problems of Bangladesh." In Drèze and Sen 1991, 307–346.

Packard, Randall M. 1984. "Maize, Cattle and Mosquitoes: The Political Economy of Malaria Epidemics in Colonial Swaziland." *Journal of African History* 25, 2: 189–212.

Paddock, William, and Paul Paddock. 1967. *Famine 1975! America's Decision: Who Will Survive?* Boston: Little, Brown.

Pankhurst, Richard. 1966. "The Great Ethiopian Famine of 1888–1892: A New Assessment." *Journal of the History of Medicine and Allied Sciences* 21, April and July: 95–124 and 271–294.

Pinstrup-Andersen, Per. 1983. "Export Crop Production and Malnutrition." Washington, D.C.: International Food Policy Research Institute.

Ram, N. 1990. "An Independent Press and Anti-Hunger Strategies: The Indian Experience." In Drèze and Sen 1990a, 146–190.

Ravallion, Martin. 1987. *Markets and Famines.* Oxford: Clarendon Press.

Rivers, J. P. W. 1988. "The Nutritional Biology of Famine." In Harrison, 57–106.

Rivers, J. P. W., J. F. J. Holt, J. A. Seaman, and M. H. Bowden. 1976. "Lessons for Epidemiology from the Ethiopian Famines." *Annales société belge de médecine tropicale* 56, 4–5: 345–360.

Robson, John R. K., ed. 1981. *Famine: Its Causes, Effects and Management.* New York: Gordon and Breach.

Rotberg, Robert I. 1983. *The Journal of Interdisciplinary History* 16 (August): 199–534.

Scrimshaw, Nevin S. 1987. "The Phenomenon of Famine." *Annual Review of Nutrition* 7: 1–21.

Seaman, J., J. Holt, and J. Rivers. 1978. "The Effects of Drought on Human Nutrition in an Ethiopian Province." *International Journal of Epidemiology* 7 (March): 31–40.

Sen, Amartya. 1981. *Poverty and Famines: An Essay on Entitlement and Deprivation.* Oxford: Clarendon Press.

Sen, Amartya. 1987. "Food and Freedom." Third Sir John Crawford Memorial Lecture, World Bank, Washington, D.C., 29 October.

Shawcross, William. 1984. *The Quality of Mercy: Cambodia, Holocaust and Modern Conscience.* New York: Simon and Schuster.

Singh, K. Suresh. 1975. *The Indian Famine, 1967: A Study in Crisis and Change.* New Delhi: People's Publishing House.

Stephens, Lynn H., and Stephen J. Green, eds. 1979. *Disaster Assistance: Appraisal, Reform and New Approaches.* New York: New York University Press.

Taylor, Alan J. 1978. "Relief, Development and the Foreign Voluntary Aid Organization." Paper presented at the Workshop on Disaster Relief, Canadian Council on International Cooperation, Ottawa, Canada, 17–18 April.

Teklu, Tesfaye, Joachim von Braun, and Elsayed Zaki. 1991. *Drought and Famine Relationships in Sudan: Policy Implications.* Research Report 88. Washington, D.C.: International Food Policy Research Institute.

Timberlake, Lloyd. 1985. *Africa in Crisis: The Causes, the Cures of Environmental Bankruptcy.* London: Earthscan.

Vaughan, Megan. 1987. *The Story of an African Famine: Gender and Famine in Twentieth Century Malawi.* Cambridge: Cambridge University Press.

Walker, Peter. 1989. *Famine Early Warning Systems: Victims and Destitution.* London: Earthscan.

Watts, Michael. 1991. "Heart of Darkness: Reflections on Famine and Starvation in Africa." In Downs, Kerner, and Reyna, 23–68.

Wolde Mariam, Mesfin. 1984. *Rural Vulnerability to Famine in Ethiopia: 1958–1977.* New Delhi: Vikas.

Wolde Mariam, Mesfin. 1987. "The Social and Economic Origins of Famine in Ethiopia." Workshop on Famine and Famine Policy, Tufts University, 10 December. Transcript.

Woodham-Smith, Cecil. 1962. *The Great Hunger: Ireland 1845–49.* London: Hamish Hamilton.

Part II

National and International Responses to Famine

Introduction

It would be gratifying if people threatened with famine could cope on their own and thereby prevent a crisis from becoming a disaster. In all instances of famine and even potential famine, people do respond in ways that are eminently sensible. Very early in the process, many take steps to enhance their prospects for survival and to protect their productive assets so as to remain economically viable.

However, coping strategies at the household and community levels seldom succeed by themselves in averting famine. National and international responses are an essential complement to what people do on their own. Part II comprises four chapters on national and international responses to famine in the 1980s.

Chapter 2, by Leonard Berry and Thomas E. Downing, offers an overview of what happened in six African countries that experienced intense drought. Between 1980 and 1986, the rains failed at one point or another in Mali, Sudan, Ethiopia, Kenya, Mozambique, and Botswana, inflicting acute stress on millions of people, many of whom were already in the throes of civil strife. Berry and Downing compare the severity and impact of drought across the six countries and examine the factors influencing the effectiveness of each country's policy response. For reasons noted by the authors, the economies of Kenya and Botswana minimized the drought's impact, whereas the far weaker economies of Ethiopia, Sudan, Mali, and Mozambique went into tailspins from which they have yet to recover.

Pastoral nomads in the pastoral zone of Niger were among the less fortunate. Their plight in the severe drought of 1984 is the subject of Chapter 3 by J. Dirck Stryker. The government of Niger responded to the crisis with a range of policies and programs intended to preserve the rangeland, protect animals, and ensure adequate food supplies. It is clear from Stryker's account that some of these policies and programs worked well, others not so well. Especially interesting are instances in which the well-intentioned government did seemingly sensible things, only to have them misfire.

Whereas many analysts ask why famines happen, Peter Cutler's question in Chapter 4 is why famines are *allowed* to happen. His is a political question, which acknowledges that whether famine emerges or not depends ultimately—and critically—on the timeliness and effectiveness of intervention. Famine results when a process of destitution runs full course, producing widespread starvation, disease, and death. It is helpful to be reminded that the outcome is not inevitable. Cutler reviews how national governments, donor countries, intergovernmental agencies and private voluntary organizations typically deal with famine; and he identifies the political constraints faced by each type of institution that limits its ability to engage in preventive action. In dramatizing the intensely political nature of famine, Cutler implicitly challenges more agroclimatological and technical perspectives. He also calls into question the current enthusiasm for famine early warning systems, which seem to assume that detection is the key to action.

Part II concludes with Chapter 5 by Jack Shepherd, who documents the reluctance of the Reagan administration to send food relief to government-controlled areas of Ethiopia even while vigorously pursuing a sizable covert operation of food shipments into rebel-held territory. This chapter provides a dramatic account of the administration's manipulation of famine for political advantage and a compelling illustration of Cutler's thesis concerning the primacy of politics in famine response.

Chapter 5 makes clear that the failure to provide food assistance to government-controlled areas of Ethiopia did not reflect uncertainty concerning the reality of the situation, but rather a desire to destabilize that country's Marxist government. Following television's disclosure of a sea of suffering humanity in Korem in October 1984, the American public's attention focused on famine with telling effect. Feeding starving people, regardless of where they live and the politics involved, became an imperative. A major task for those concerned with famine is to make a humanitarian response to famine politically necessary. Then maybe we can move on to a developmental and preemptive approach, themes addressed in Parts III and IV.

2

Drought and Famine in Africa, 1981–86

A Comparison of Impacts and Responses in Six Countries

Leonard Berry and Thomas E. Downing

The early 1980s were marked by drought in large areas of Africa. Most countries experienced extended drought lasting over a year or recurrent drought several times during the first half of the decade. The causes of drought in Africa have been reviewed at a continentwide level and for specific localities. Even though there were spatial variations in rainfall shortage, meteorological factors were the primary precipitating causes of the drought (Degefu 1987; Dennett, Elston, and Rodgers 1985; Farmer and Wigley 1985; Kerr 1985; Lamb 1982, 1983; Nicholson 1985, 1989; Ogallo and Anyamba 1985; Rasmusson 1987; World Meteorological Organization 1985). More fundamental causes of famine have been documented in the environmental, development, and economic history of Africa. These include soil erosion (Berry 1984; Lal 1987); deforestation (Timberlake 1985); overgrazing (Ibrahim 1984); disruption of traditional social and economic relationships due to colonialism, the spread of capitalism, population growth, and international economic relations (Berry 1984; Hart 1982; Lofchie 1975, 1987; Watts 1983); marginalization of rural smallholders and pastoralists (Horowitz and Little 1987; Wisner 1977); failure of agricultural research (Lipton 1985); degree of articulation and integration of the market economy (Mellor and Gavian 1987; Hyden 1983); food entitlement through market exchanges (Sen 1981); and civil strife and refugees (World Bank 1984; Young 1985).

The impact of drought and the ability of local, national, and international organizations to respond effectively vary substantially among and within countries. Factors that have been cited as instrumental in ameliorating the impact of drought include the capabilities of government and international organizations (Payne, Rummel, and Glantz 1987), the state of preparedness and warning (Borton and Clay 1986; Borton and Stephenson 1984; Borton 1984; Cutler and Stephenson 1984), and local response capabilities (York 1985).

This chapter originated as a review of the U.S. response to the African drought of the early 1980s and draws substantially from that report (Downing et al. 1987). Six countries were selected from those affected by drought in Africa between 1980 and 1985: Botswana, Ethiopia, Kenya, Mali, Mozambique, and Sudan. Drought within each country varied in its pattern, impacts, and responses; but as far as we can measure, the meteorological drought in each country was of comparable intensity. The marked variations among the six countries are in the effects of the drought. The success of Botswana and Kenya in preventing famine stands out in stark contrast to the inadequate responses in the other four countries.

This chapter presents a comparative assessment of the impacts and responses in each country, beginning with an analysis of rainfall shortage as the precipitating cause. We focus on the response to the food crisis rather than on an exposition of the long-term historical trends that underlie the progression of rainfall shortage into drought and famine. The nature of the meteorological drought and its impacts in each country on agriculture, population, and economy are reviewed next. Responses to the drought are compared, focusing on preparedness and warning, internal responses, and international assistance. The conclusion suggests that civil strife and disorder are the major factors preventing effective responses to drought. However, further improvements in preparedness, early warning, and food policy should enable governments to cope with a variety of fluctuations in food supplies and entitlements.

Rainfall Patterns

The 1980s drought in Africa, in a meteorological sense, had two distinct patterns. In West Africa, particularly in the Sudano-Sahelian zone, a decline in seasonal rainfall has been documented since at least the 1970s, and drought has become a recurrent problem over the period 1970–85 (Farmer and Wigley 1985). In the rest of Africa, there is no evidence of a long-term trend in rainfall, and droughts are sporadic episodes in the climatic record (Farmer and Wigley 1985; Tyson 1986).

Parts of Africa experienced moderate or severe drought beginning in 1980, particularly in eastern and southern Africa. Conditions were better the following year in most of the continent, but worse in the Sahel, including Sudan (Figure 2.1). In 1982, the beginnings of the

Figure 2.1 Drought Patterns, 1981–84

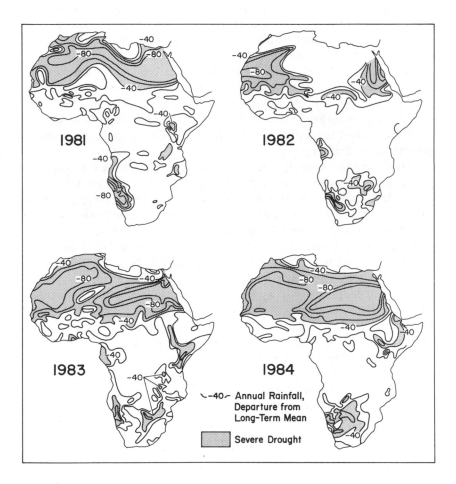

The isolines are annual rainfall as a percentage departure from the long-term mean. Wet areas, over 20 percent greater than average, are not shown. The Sahel, Horn of Africa, Kenya, and parts of southern Africa experienced severe drought, less than 40 percent of the long-term average, while moderate drought, 20 to 40 percent of average, extended the effect of the drought in many countries.
Source: S. E. Nicholson, "Land Surface Atmosphere Interaction: Physical Processes and Surface Changes and Their Impact," *Progress in Physical Geography* 12,1 (1988): 36–65.

African drought of the 1980s were apparent, at least in retrospect. Rainfall was particularly deficient in southern Africa. The most extensive and severe drought conditions occurred in 1983 in West Africa and 1984 in East Africa. The drought in southern Africa continued from 1982 to 1984. In contrast, rainfall in 1985 and 1986 was near or above average in most of the continent, although the impacts of the drought lingered in many areas.

An index of drought was computed from 1980 to 1986 for each of the six countries (Table 2.1). The index is the sum of the percentage area affected by drought (with severe drought given twice the weight of moderate drought) divided by the maximum possible score. The index combines intensity and duration of drought to gauge the geographic area of drought impact.

This drought severity index divides the six countries into two groups. In the more severely affected group, Mali and Sudan experienced drought in each year and Botswana in every year but one. All three had two to four years of severe drought. Among the less affected countries, Ethiopia and Mozambique had persistent drought in the early 1980s, and Kenya had two peak years. These latter three had several years without any drought. The index is based on each country's entire area, meaning that drought confined to agricultural lands is not weighted as heavily as its impacts would warrant. For example, the index may underestimate the severity of the 1984 drought in Kenya and overestimate the widespread moderate droughts in Sudan. In terms of coping with drought, severe but short-lived droughts are more manageable than prolonged episodes that may vary in intensity. However, each country experienced severe drought at some time in the 1980s, and each required emergency interventions to prevent famine. The timeliness and success of those interventions depended on factors other than the meteorological nature of drought itself.

Impacts of the Drought

Agricultural Production

The major direct impact of the rainfall shortages was on agricultural production. Data on cereal production and per capita consumption indicate that 1984–85 was the worst year of drought for Ethiopia, Kenya, Mali, and Sudan, that 1983–84 was the worst year in Mozambique, and that Botswana suffered prolonged drought after the bumper year of 1981–82. The effect of population growth, in per capita cereal consumption data, highlights the erosion of agricultural production. Sharp recoveries after the drought occurred in Kenya, Mali,

Table 2.1 Drought Index, 1980–86

	Percent of Country Affected in 1980–86							Weighted Score	Rank
	1980	1981	1982	1983	1984	1985	1986		
Botswana	30	0	90	90	70	80	40	48	3
Ethiopia	60	30	50	30	80	0	0	36	6
Kenya	100	70	40	0	70	0	0	40	5
Mali	10	80	80	100	100	20	20	65	1
Mozambique	10	50	50	60	60	0	0	40	4
Sudan	70	60	80	60	80	10	20	56	2

Source: See Downing, J., et al. 1987 for the original maps and sources.
Note: The spatial extent of moderate and severe drought in each country was mapped based on available sources. The percentage of each country affected, computed by tenths, includes both moderately and severely affected areas. The weighted score is the sum of the severe drought area (times 2) and moderate drought areas, divided by 1,400, the maximum possible score.

and Sudan. These data are corroborated by the Food and Agriculture Organization (FAO) indices of total food production (Benson and Clay 1986). Total food production in Mali, Mozambique, and Sudan fell below the 1976–78 average during the drought. National totals are important in determining the context of coping with the impacts of drought, although they mask more severe regional shortages. Indeed, the relatively small changes in per capita consumption indicate the sensitivity of national food systems to disruption.

There were also important changes in the components of the total food supply. In 1984–85, wheat production in Kenya was a third less than the recent average (Borton 1989), and in Sudan sorghum production was about half the average (Food and Agriculture Organization 1986). In each country, almost no production was realized in some parts of the country during the drought (for example, Eastern Province in Kenya and northern Ethiopia). Wheat production at the Gezira irrigation scheme in Sudan was suspended during the 1984–85 season due to water shortages.

Data on the aggregate effect of the 1980s drought on livestock are even less reliable than for agricultural production. Estimates for the Sahel suggest that about a third of the livestock were sold or died, about the same magnitude as in the 1970s drought (USDA/ERA 1986a). In Mali, livestock losses were 40–50 percent (Somerville 1986), and 40–60 percent of livestock were lost in affected areas in Kenya (Field and Njiru 1985; Potter 1988). Rebuilding herds will take a decade if the process is left to natural increase alone.

Population Affected

Declining per capita food consumption levels in the years before the 1982–84 drought resulted in nutritional levels that were already marginal among vulnerable groups in some countries (especially Mali, Sudan, Mozambique, and Ethiopia). The typical pattern of low and uneven food consumption, combined with large variations in food production and availability, made sub-Saharan Africa particularly vulnerable to a food emergency and resultant malnutrition in the 1980s (USDA/ERS 1986a).

The food crisis in sub-Saharan Africa reached its height (or nadir) in late 1984 and early 1985, when some twenty-five million people were estimated to be severely affected. Estimates of the number of people affected in each of the six countries vary considerably, related not only to the extent of the drought but also to the imprecise definition of population affected (Table 2.2). The lowest percentage of population vulnerable to hunger was in Kenya, but one and a half million people were involved. The highest was in Botswana, where nearly all the population was reported to be vulnerable. While these extremes may be due to different definitions, even a rate of 10–30 percent represents a large number of people. Although the situation in Ethiopia was most publicized and certainly traumatic, Sudan had not only a larger population affected (over eight million), but a larger proportion as well.

Table 2.2 Drought-Affected Population, 1983–85

Country	1983	1984	1985	Total	Ratio
Botswana	410	1,037	880	1,150	96
Ethiopia	2,000	5,000	7,750	44,790	17
Kenya	—	1,575	835	21,480	7
Mali	—	1,500	1,500	8,300	18
Mozambique	4,000	4,750	2,466	14,340	33
Sudan	40	1,000	8,400	23,780	35

Source: U.S. Office of Foreign Disaster Assistance 1987, DH&SMC 1985 for Kenya.
Notes: Population in 1,000s. Ratio is percentage of total population affected in worst year. Definition of population varies for each country.

In November 1984, between six and ten million people were in danger of starvation in Ethiopia, and perhaps half were in immediate life-threatening jeopardy. Korem, a much publicized feeding camp in Wollo, was one of the worst scenes of devastation and death from famine and epidemics (King 1986). In Sudan, the malnutrition rate of displaced persons was estimated to be at least five times higher than normal in 1984–85. Out of a population of 6.3 million in Darfur and Kordofan, 4.2 million were at risk and two million were seriously at risk, comprising almost one-third of the population of the two regions (Brown et al. 1985). The El Geneina area was affected the most, with 77 percent of all children one to five years old suffering from malnutrition. Many people in Mali experienced severe malnutrition in some regions; some were eating wild grasses, roots, and flowers growing along the Niger river. There was widespread malnutrition in drought- and flood-affected provinces of Mozambique in 1983. Malnutrition continued to increase in some areas, causing an urgent need for supplementary feeding programs toward the end of 1985 (United Nations Office for Emergency Operations in Africa 1985).

The number of malnourished people in Kenya and Botswana never approached the levels in Ethiopia, Sudan, Mozambique, and Mali. Nevertheless, the drought in Kenya was said to be the worst in living memory. A study in Embu District in Kenya noted that approximately

30 percent of the population was severely affected and 30 percent moderately affected by famine. Six percent of toddlers were severely malnourished and 28 percent moderately malnourished (Neumann et al. 1989). In Botswana, national rates of malnutrition (percentage of children less than 80 percent of weight-for-age) in the drought years of 1982–83 were 27–31 percent, compared to 24–29 percent for the non-drought years of 1978 and 1980–81 (Mason et al. 1987).

Migration is an indicator of the acuteness of drought and the failure of other traditional coping strategies (Cutler 1984). Migration is not always a clear indicator, however, because of high levels of seasonal migration. Large-scale migration flagged the onset of famine in Sudan, where 900,000 Sudanese were estimated to have migrated from North to South Darfur (D'Silva 1985). Concurrently, refugees from Chad and Ethiopia arrived in Sudan. In Ethiopia, famine caused vast out-migration from the northern, rebel-controlled provinces into eastern Sudan. Despite a program to provide food relief to Ethiopia across the Sudanese border, 300,000 refugees left Ethiopia in search of food in 1985, flooding camps in Sudan. By April 1986, there were 852,000 Ethiopians in Sudan (U.S. Congress, Senate Committee on the Judiciary 1986). In Mali, much of the population of the northern regions moved south into areas where food, water, and other aid were available. There were several hundred thousand displaced persons in Mali in late 1985, comprising 3 percent of the population (Somerville 1986). Males often migrated to urban areas in search of work, leaving the women and children behind and even more vulnerable. In Mali and Sudan, there was fear that males would not return to their families after three years of drought. However, with the onset of the rains in 1985, return movements multiplied. Migration in Mozambique was most notably to escape the devastation created by the insurgents, the Mozambique National Resistance (MNR). There were an estimated 300,000 displaced persons in 1985, two years after the worst drought year (U.S. Agency for International Development 1985).

In Botswana, despite the large percentage of the population affected by drought, the displacement of people to camps was averted as a result of drought preparedness coordinated by the Inter-Ministerial Drought Committee (Borton and Clay 1986). In Kenya, migration was also of minor significance, though there were movements of nomads from the northern areas toward major cities and the wetter coast (Downing, Gitu, and Kamau 1989).

Economic Impacts

Drought affected the economy of each country, but the impacts were either ameliorated or compounded by external factors (see Table 2.3).

Table 2.3 Economic Indicators, 1984–85

Country	GNP Per Capita[a]		Bal. of Payments[b]		Debt Service (%)		Foreign Exchange[c]		Export Sector
	$	Growth (%)	1984	1985	1984	1985	1984	1985	
Botswana	840	8.3	-33	162	3.5	5.2	474	783	diamond, livestock exports
Ethiopia	110	0.2	-511	-660	13.6	19.4	44	148	coffee boom in early 1980s
Kenya	290	1.9	-444	-485	21.5	n.a.	390	391	coffee and tea boom in early 1980s
Mali	150	1.4	-164	-293	7.5	15.0	27	23	cotton stable, groundnuts collapsed
Mozambique	160	n.a.	-444	-347	n.a.	n.a.	n.a.	n.a.	cashew, cotton, tea decreased since independence
Sudan	300	0.0	-81	-135	6.3	9.0	17	12	groundnuts, gum arabic, sorghum decreased in 1980s, cotton variable

Sources: World Bank, *World Development Report, 1987* (New York: Oxford University Press, 1987); Economist Intelligence Unit (London) reports: *Guinea, Mali, Mauritania Country Report, No. 3* (1989), *Kenya Country Report, No. 3* (1989), *Namibia, Botswana, Lesotho, Swaziland Country Report, No. 2* (1989), *Sudan Country Report, No. 2* (1989), *Tanzania, Mozambique Country Report, No. 2* (1989), *Uganda, Ethiopia, Somalia, Djibouti Country Report, No. 2* (1989), *Country Report: Kenya, Nos. 2–4* (1984), *Country Report: Kenya, Nos. 1–4* (1985), *Country Report: Kenya, No. 3* (1986), *Country Report: Kenya, 1986–87* (1986); U.S. Department of Agriculture/Economic Research Service, *World Food Needs and Availabilities, 1984/85* (Washington, D.C.: USDA/ERS, 1984); U.S. Department of Agriculture/Economic Research Service, *Sub-Saharan Africa: Situation and Outlook Report*, Report No. RS-96–9 (Washington, D.C.: USDA/ERS, 1986); B. C. D'Silva, *Sudan: Policy Reforms and Prospects for Agricultural Recovery After the Drought*, Economic Research Service Staff Report No. AGES-850909 (Washington, D.C.: USDA/ERS, 1985).

Notes: [a] For 1985, in million U.S. dollars; growth is average annual growth rate (1965–85).
[b] Exports minus imports, in million U.S. dollars. [c] Excluding gold; in million U.S. dollars.

Botswana and Kenya had strong export economies and foreign exchange reserves, while Kenya and Ethiopia benefited from a temporary rise in the value of coffee exports. Botswana is a leading producer of diamonds, earning over $600 million in 1985. Beef, copper, and nickel are also important exports. Botswana has one of the highest GNPs in Africa, with impressive foreign reserves to fund a variety of development activities. The government paid for 94 percent of the nonfood cost of the drought in 1984–85, indicating the limited impact of the drought on the economy (Holm and Morgan 1985). Kenya was in a somewhat similar economic situation. Coffee exports and earnings increased due to the rise in coffee prices and collapse of international coffee price controls. Kenyan coffee exports peaked at 9,750 metric tons per month in the fourth quarter of 1984, with earnings over $16 million for the year. Tea exports and earnings also rose considerably in the early 1980s, as India withdrew from exports for a year. Commercial food imports cost over $60 million, and the debt service ratio increased from 16.5 percent in 1981 to 21.5 percent in 1985. High reserves of foreign exchange, primarily from coffee and tea, along with easy access to international food aid, enabled a rapid decision to import food and limited the economic impact of the drought.

Ethiopia also benefited from the coffee boom. Exports reached 98,000 metric tons and 99,000 metric tons in 1983–84 and 1985–86, compared to 88,000 metric tons in 1980–81 and 69,000 metric tons in 1984–85 (USDA/ERS 1986a). Ethiopia's balance of payments deficit increased from $295 million in 1980 to $620 million in 1987, with a debt service of 19.4 percent in 1985 (USDA/ERS 1986b; Economist Intelligence Unit 1989b), indicating that the coffee boom and international aid failed to compensate for the effects of drought and continued deterioration of the Ethiopian economy.

The disastrous economies of Mali, Sudan, and Mozambique were worsened by the drought. Mali, one of the poorest countries in the world, had few external reserves to cope with a severe or extended drought. Exports were not greatly affected by the 1980s drought; balance of payments deficits varied from $62 million to $124 million and the debt service from 8 to 17 percent. Cotton production was maintained during the 1980s at near 50,000 metric tons, but low prices limited revenues. Groundnut production was severely affected by a variety of factors, declining from 205,000 metric tons in 1975–76 to less than 10,000 metric tons in 1983–84.

Exports had declined in Sudan since the 1970s. Balance of payments deficits reached $135 million in 1985, and the debt service ratio increased from 6.3 percent in 1984 to 9.0 percent in 1985 (Economist Intelligence Unit 1989f). Declines in gum arabic, groundnut, and cereal production and viable returns from cotton contributed to Sudan's poor economic performance and exacerbated the drought's impacts.

The economy of Mozambique had been destabilized by civil strife (supported by South Africa), natural disasters, and restrictive government policies. The balance of payments was negative throughout the 1980s, reaching $607 million in 1982. Cashew, cotton, and tea production declined dramatically due to economic disruption after independence and the impact of the drought. For example, cashew production was 196,000 metric tons in 1973, 90,000 metric tons in 1981, and 18,100 metric tons in 1983 (Economist Intelligence Unit 1986c).

Comparison of Responses to the Drought

The meteorological drought and its impacts in each country varied but required urgent action by local, national, and international organizations as imports reduced national food deficits and a variety of programs increased consumption. The country comparison that follows seeks to identify the factors influencing each country's effectiveness in responding to the drought (Table 2.4). The degree of success in coping is measured by the number of people affected and the extent of social disruption. The discussion is grouped according to three major elements conditioning success: preparedness and warning, each country's policy response, and the international situation.

Preparedness and Warning

Infrastructure, economy, and institutions. A prerequisite of adequate preparedness to respond to a drought emergency is sufficient infrastructure to allow communication of information and transport of food and supplies. In all three countries severely affected by the drought, terrain and distance greatly hampers movement of people and materials. In Ethiopia, deep gorges and steep escarpments divide the country. In Sudan, the lack of surfaced roads cuts off large areas during the rainy season, and the long distances involved create major marketing and movement problems. In Mozambique, the lack of north-south highways and access roads to interior areas makes the movement of goods to population centers difficult.

The prevailing economic conditions were also not conducive to an effective drought response. Sudan had a national debt of over $9 billion (1985) and a severe shortage of foreign exchange. The economy of Mozambique was affected by labor restrictions in South Africa and internal strife. The Ethiopian economy, quite apart from the drought, had experienced declining production and export of the major cash

Table 2.4 Comparative Assessment of Drought Impacts and Responses

Country	Drought & Impacts	Preparedness & Warning	Internal Responses	International Situation
Botswana	1982–85 severe & prolonged, normal nutritional situation	exemplary, built upon existing capabilities	food- and cash-for-work supplementary feeding	high foreign exchange reserves, high foreign aid
Ethiopia	1980, 1982, 1984 varied, recurrent, severe large-scale famine	extensive capabilities, inadequate use of available information	marginal response to increasing crisis, political & military constraints, civil strife, lack of infrastructure, stringent trade restrictions	reluctance of donors, disbelief of information, lack of foreign exchange
Kenya	1981, 1984 severe, short-lived, nutritional deterioration	uncoordinated, lack of detailed plans, data collected but not validated, not timely	ad hoc committees, drawing upon existing staff, market & commercial imports, food-for-work, public distribution	high foreign exchange reserves, high presence & response from donors
Mali	1981–84 prolonged, moderate to severe, famine in several areas	limited capabilities from 1970s	backlogs in ports	lack of information and political factors delayed assistance
Mozambique	1981–84 prolonged, moderate, locally severe, cyclones, serious nutritional emergency	institution in place, poor preparedness	hindered by civil strife & lack of infrastructure	Western assistance delayed but substantial
Sudan	1980–84 prolonged, moderate to severe large-scale famine	limited institutional capabilities, suppressed information	hindered by civil strife, lack of infrastructure, coup, refugees	visible donor presence & assistance

Sources: Drawn from references in text; see also J. Drèze, *Famine Prevention in Africa*, Monograph No. 3, Development and Economic Research Programme, London School of Economics, January 1988, and F. D'Souza, *Famine and the Art of Early Warning: The African Experience*, Report prepared for the Overseas Development Administration–Economics and Social Research Division (Oxford: Department of Biological Anthropology, University of Oxford, 1989).

crop, coffee. In each case, there were little or no reserves of convertible exchange to pay for large quantities of imported foodstuffs. In contrast, Kenya and Botswana had sufficient foreign exchange and credit to facilitate commercial imports.

Institutional capacity was most developed in Kenya and Botswana and severely limited in Mozambique and Sudan.

Drought preparedness. Each country's drought preparedness and warning capabilities varied considerably. In Botswana, Ethiopia, Mali, and Mozambique there were established government committees empowered to collect information and coordinate activities addressing drought and famine. The government's response to drought in Botswana was decentralized. Districts were the focus of an elaborate early warning system and of coordinated drought-response mechanisms headed by the Inter-Ministerial Drought Committee. The response was effective due in large part to the government's willingness and foresight to establish a strong crisis prevention and response infrastructure within the country (Borton and Clay 1986). The Relief and Rehabilitation Commission (RRC) in Ethiopia was well staffed, ambitious, and capable of administering drought-relief programs. The effectiveness of the RRC, however, was curtailed by a lack of cooperation from other government agencies. The RRC's early warnings of the drought were not given credence by other agencies within Ethiopia and were ignored by the international community. Mali had assimilated certain political and administrative lessons learned as a result of the drought in the 1970s. The institutional changes included the creation of a drought policy committee (CNVAS) and a food distribution body (OPAM). However, these two agencies were often unable to coordinate their activities in a productive manner. Mozambique also had drought-relief institutions in place, and the government was committed to developing an effective national response to drought. The Mozambican authority responsible for administering relief measures, the Department for the Prevention and Control of National Calamities (DPCCN), demonstrated its potential, albeit belatedly, in 1985 when CARE began assisting in the transportation and distribution of food.

In Sudan, despite large semi-arid areas, drought had previously been dealt with regionally and by traditional means. Consequently there was no effective national organization. The role of Sudan's Food Aid National Administration (FANA) was limited to the monitoring of food aid deliveries and distribution. FANA's small staff was unable to manage the administrative needs of the relief effort.

Although emergency institutions and procedures were not in place in Kenya prior to the drought, the mobilization of the administration was quick and appropriate to the scale of the crisis. The hierarchy of government from national to local levels facilitated the collection of information and distribution of food aid. The Task Force on Food Supply and Distribution coordinated the emergency responses of individual ministries (Cohen and Lewis 1987; Borton 1989; Downing 1990).

Early warning of the 1980s drought. The timeliness, accuracy, and credibility of information available to government, NGOs, and donors are difficult to assess. In most of the countries, it appears that adequate information was available and that the emerging food shortages could have been confirmed well in advance of a crisis. Perhaps more critical than information were the levels of response and use of available information (Cutler 1985).

Botswana, Ethiopia, and Kenya have extensive food monitoring capabilities. Botswana has the best-developed early warning system in Africa. Likely harvests are forecast up to four months before the start of the annual relief program. This allows the government to gear up and request external assistance if required (Borton and Clay 1986; Morgan 1985). The Relief and Rehabilitation Commission in Ethiopia is a large agency with field staff throughout the country. The Ethiopian crisis did not result from failure of the RRC to warn of the impending situation. Rather, the government and donors did not heed the warnings due to other concerns (civil war, revolutionary celebrations, other food crises) and an inability to confirm the warnings (related to a lack of food statistics and skepticism regarding the RRC's credibility). The lack of food statistics in Ethiopia is exemplified by FAO data for 1983. The population was estimated to be 33.7 million, whereas the 1984 census reported 42 million (FAO 1983). This severely distorted the national food balance sheets used as a reference to gauge the extent of food shortage (Borton and Clay 1986). In Kenya, the government response was primarily motivated by the surge in sales of maize from the National Cereals and Produce Board, the grain marketing parastatal, while dry conditions were apparent in the vicinity of Nairobi and confirmed by the Meteorological Department (Borton 1989; Downing 1990). Little statistical data were available in the early stages of the drought crisis, although the Ministry of Agriculture was able to report which areas of the country were most affected.

Famine early warning systems were less capable in Mali, Mozambique, and Sudan. Mali participates in the West Africa regional organization Agrohydromet, which monitors crop and weather conditions, but it is not clear when and how this information is used. Agricultural statistics, as in Ethiopia, are deficient or not credible. The U.S. Agency for International Development (USAID) mission in Mali waited three months until the harvest estimates of 1983 were confirmed by a multidonor mission before forwarding a request for food aid to Washington (Downing et al. 1987). Mozambique probably had the least reliable data on food supplies and requirements. In the midst of civil war, the infrastructure for collecting data was not adequate. However, the magnitude of the food crisis was clear, particularly as the drought extended into 1984. Sudan had little history of major food crises and few institutions in the early 1980s capable of monitoring conditions throughout the country (Cutler and Shoham 1985). The Relief and Rehabilitation Commission in Sudan had a staff of ten, compared to ten thousand in Ethiopia.

The ability of international agencies to secure reliable and convincing data on the drought crisis was extremely important in expediting their responses. Information was critical in Mali and Ethiopia, where donors felt the need to gather additional data to substantiate government statistics. USAID and various private voluntary organizations (PVOs) worked jointly to generate their own surveys of drought and food conditions in Mali. The weak Western presence in Mozambique and Ethiopia in the early 1980s and the unreliable data available to relief organizations at that time demonstrate the need for in-country surveys by international agencies. In contrast, the large USAID agriculture section in Kenya enabled it to take the lead in coordinating donor responses to the drought.

Internal Responses

Food aid and imports. Total food aid in 1984–85 was highest in Botswana (46 kilograms per capita) and Sudan (40 kilograms per capita), compared to 18 kilograms per capita in Kenya. Most of the food aid was cereals, supplemented with dried skim milk and oil. Cereal imports (both commercial and food aid) in 1984–85 were substantial, ranging from 105,000 metric tons in Botswana to 1,595,000 metric tons in Sudan. Cereal imports as a percentage of national production and stocks highlight the different food situations in each country. In Ethiopia, Kenya, and Mali, cereal imports at the height of the crisis were less than 50 percent of national supplies. In contrast, Botswana and Mozambique were much more dependent on cereal imports throughout the 1980s, as was Sudan in 1984–85.

The approaches adopted to avert famine varied. In Botswana, there was an emphasis on household entitlements, and most of the food aid was distributed through various food- or cash-for-work schemes. In Kenya, about 80 percent of the imported food was distributed through normal market channels. Free food distribution and food-for-work schemes were an important but relatively minor component of ensuring adequate supplies at the household level. Famine relief camps and free food distribution were prevalent in Ethiopia, Mali, Mozambique, and Sudan.

Political response to drought. Critical at the national level in responding to the drought was the political will of the government to avoid a crisis or accept its existence and appeal for humanitarian assistance. In Botswana, drought is an accepted phenomenon, and the political system was active in ensuring an adequate response. In Kenya, the drought affected two of the largest ethnic groups at a time when the government was trying to consolidate its control of the country. A concerted effort to avoid political unrest was required, although the government's response was politically sensitive and not openly debated. Under Nimeiri, the government of Sudan was preoccupied with internal political and military conflict. The Nimeiri regime essentially left farmers and pastoralists to respond on their own according to indigenous methods. The coup in 1985 further complicated the response and greatly delayed the government's ability to implement relief programs. As in Sudan, the government of Mali was hesitant and politically unwilling to mobilize the necessary institutional resources to combat the effects of drought.

Household coping strategies. Traditional household coping strategies in the face of drought include sharing food among related households, diet diversity and consumption of famine foods, food preservation and storage, social organization and support networks, farming systems that use different ecological zones, mobility of livestock, diversification of livestock herds, and migration of family members or entire households (Akong'a and Downing 1988; Corbett 1988; Flueret 1986; McCabe and Ellis 1987). These traditional adaptations are common in many African countries. And yet in many countries these traditional coping strategies seem to have broken down in the 1980s. The duration and pervasiveness of drought during the 1970s and the 1980s prevented people in the Sahel from relying upon traditional fall-back desert economies (Somerville 1986). Modern responses, on the other hand, are generally market oriented and to be effective require a fairly well-articulated and integrated market system, as exemplified most clearly in Kenya and Botswana. In these countries, household-level responses are more integrated into the national political economy. Most households in Kenya rely on local markets for a significant amount of their food supply and have access to cash during periods of drought. In Botswana, rural households are incorporated into the national drought preparedness plan and are provided for through a variety of programs, including food for work and cash for work. Botswana is a rich country by African standards and utilizes this wealth during times of drought.

In western Sudan, adaptation took place in two stages (see Asher 1986; de Waal and Amin 1986: Ibrahim 1988; Omer 1988). During the first two years, 1981–83, the Sudanese relied heavily on traditional institutions and on local political leaders. But as the drought continued into 1984 and resources diminished, a second, more desperate stage was reached. Farmers had used their grain reserves and sold their jewelry and household belongings, and by 1984–85 more drastic measures were required. Men left their families and migrated to urban areas in search of work, which became increasingly scarce. Many did not return after two or three years and some not at all.

One survey in the Segu region of Mali found that only 1 percent of the households used famine foods in the 1980s drought, compared to about 12 percent in the 1970s (Cole, R., personal communication, 1987). Traditional coping strategies were being replaced by more effective farming practices, especially crops with shorter cycles and cash cropping.

International Situation

Donor assistance. International assistance played a key role in the response to Africa's drought and famine crisis. The international response came in answer to requests for assistance due to deteriorating economic and agricultural conditions. In contrast to the national response, international efforts placed little emphasis on the early detection of crop failure and preemption of famine. Initially, assistance was oriented primarily toward relief. Once the drought ended, however, many agencies placed more emphasis on early detection of famine. In addition to the topics discussed above, the successes and failures of international organizations in providing assistance to drought-stricken African countries were influenced by the following factors:

Political compatibility. In each of the countries examined, aid was most easily administered when the donors and recipient government shared similar ideologies and political goals. For USAID, in particular, the political orientation of the governments of Ethiopia and Mozambique impeded the development of an effective U.S. response. For the Western-leaning governments of Kenya and Botswana, the United States was able to formulate a more timely and coordinated response. Political compatibility played a less significant role for PVOs, which were able to work with a greater degree of political autonomy.

In-country presence. The in-country presence of the donor facilitated the agency's relief efforts. Foreign agencies with personnel and facilities in the country were better equipped to formulate plans, implement relief programs, and conduct evaluations than were agencies that managed relief programs indirectly or from overseas bureaus.

Donor country political atmosphere. Differing political forces within each donor country interacted to produce a response to the crisis in Africa. For donor governments, the extent of their commitment to assistance programs depended on their political willingness to undertake such an effort. In the United States, for example, the political atmosphere for assistance was formed from media portrayals of the crisis, government legislative and foreign policy agendas, the interests of farmers, and internal cultural and humanitarian perspectives. These conditions account for the significant role played by domestic religious and private organizations in meeting the African crisis; they are a testimony to the favorable political environment in the United States for private sector foreign assistance. In Mozambique and Ethiopia, Marxist-oriented governments were not viewed favorably by the United States (see Chapter 5), although the relationship with Mozambique became more cooperative over time. This was not the case with Ethiopia, although relations with the United Nations were more cooperative.

The success of donor assistance in each country was highly dependent on the donor's willingness to provide financial and technical support to bolster deficient physical infrastructure. In Sudan, USAID and the European Community effectively coordinated the prepositioning of food to isolated and inaccessible areas through their respective airlift operations.

Civil strife. Three of the countries were torn by ongoing insurgencies. In Ethiopia, the Eritrean People's Liberation Front and other groups had been fighting for secession for nearly two decades. The government was not effectively in control of rural areas in the north of the country. The Sudan People's Liberation Army and Anyangya groups in southern Sudan had been fighting the northern government intermittently for fifteen years, while refugees from Ethiopia, Uganda, and Chad and a successful coup further complicated the drought response. In Mozambique, the MNR, supported by South Africa, made replanting of crops and delivery of food aid dangerous in some areas and impossible in others.

Conclusion

The six countries chosen for this study all experienced severe and, in most cases, paralyzing drought in the early 1980s. In each country there was a significant reduction in crop production and major losses of livestock. Because the economy of each country is heavily dependent on agricultural and livestock production, the effects of the drought were national even though not all parts of the country directly experienced drought.

The responses to the drought and the effectiveness of the responses, however, were very different. Ethiopia, Mozambique, and Sudan had major problems dealing with the drought. Kenya and Botswana had the most effective responses, and Mali was in an intermediate category. In Ethiopia, Mozambique, and Sudan the major constraints appeared to be civil strife and political factors, together with a lack of infrastructure for communication and transportation.

The effective national responses in Kenya and Botswana offer different models of drought-relief organization, preparation, and implementation. The ad hoc approach adopted in Kenya worked well in a situation where the drought was easily identified and monitored, foreign exchange and assistance were readily available, and a stable government administration was able to manage the crisis. These factors might change in the future, and more thorough preparedness planning is warranted. Botswana stands out as the best African model of drought preparedness. The underlying factors for Botswana's success include internal stability, a wealthy economy, strong commitment by the government, significant assistance from Western donors, the comparatively small size of the country's population, a well-developed regional transport system, and recurrent experiences with drought (Borton and Clay 1986).

The single most effective policy to prevent catastrophic famine in Africa is to promote internal stability and reconciliation of civil strife. Enforcing the Geneva Convention prohibiting the use of food as a weapon, although difficult, would certainly help. A corollary is to support investment in the transport and marketing sectors, leading to greater integration of rural areas and national food markets.

In the longer run, each country needs to develop a drought policy that is understood by the ministries and donors. Coordinating mechanisms within governments are essential to an effective response. Given a stable government and the infrastructure to allow timely flows of communication and supplies, early warning and monitoring systems are a high priority. Information is a vital factor in all circumstances. Information is most credible when all parties have confidence in it. Thus, in developing information systems it is important that governments and agencies jointly collect, analyze, and act on the information. With the increased sophistication of remote sensing in monitoring crop production, information on basic agricultural production is no longer entirely within the domain of national governments, and the information should be accessible to the relevant agencies.

Large-scale commercial food purchases on the world market were not an option during the "World Food Crisis" of the 1970s and may not be a reliable coping strategy in the future (Borton and Clay 1986). For countries where drought is expected to recur, preparedness planning is essential. Ad hoc responses are simply not reliable.

The 1980s African drought has reinforced the need for research on famine and food systems. The broadest requirement is to learn from experience—to document drought responses at the household, agency, national, and international levels. As part of emergency drought-response plans, personnel should be designated as drought historians and studies should be initiated immediately after the emergency phase to document the chronology of events. This is an initial requirement to understanding the effectiveness of different responses to drought and to ensuring adequate training of future managers and preparedness for future crises. Where internal conflict continues, however, all of these recommendations are almost impossible to implement.

References

Akong'a, J., and T. E. Downing. 1988. "Smallholder Vulnerability and Response to Drought." In *The Impact of Climatic Variations on Agriculture,* edited by M. L. Parry, T. R. Carter, and N. T. Konijn, 221–248. Dordrecht, Netherlands: Kluwer.

Asher, M. 1986. *A Desert Dies.* New York: St. Martin's Press.

Benson, C., and E. Clay. 1986. "Food and Food Crisis in Sub-Saharan Africa: Statistical Trends and Implications." *Disasters* 10, 4: 303–316.

Berry, S. S. 1984. "The Food Crisis and Agrarian Change in Africa: A Review Essay." *African Studies Review* 27, 2: 59–112.

Borton, J. 1984. *Disaster Preparedness in Botswana.* London: Relief and Development Institute.

Borton, J. 1989 "Overview of the 1984–85 National Drought Relief Program." In *Coping with Drought in Kenya: National and Local Strategies,* edited by T. E. Downing, K. W. Gitu, and C. M. Kamau, 24–64. Boulder: Lynne Rienner Publishers.

Borton, J., and E. Clay. 1986. "The African Food Crisis of 1982–1986." *Disasters* 10, 4: 258–272.

Borton, J., and R. Stephenson. 1984. *Disaster Preparedness in Kenya.* London: Relief and Development Institute.

Brown, V. W., S. S. Stolba, R. C. Walker, and D. H. Wood. 1985. *Evaluation of the African Emergency Food Assistance Program 1984–85: Sudan.* Prepared for the U.S. Agency for International Development. Washington, D.C.: Devres, Inc.

Cohen, J. M., and D. B. Lewis. 1987. "Role of Government in Combatting Food Shortages: Lessons from Kenya 1984–85." In *Drought and Hunger in Africa,* edited by M. H. Glantz, 269–296. Cambridge: Cambridge University Press.

Corbett, J. 1988. "Famine and Household Coping Strategies." *World Development* 16, 9: 1099–1112.

Cutler, P. 1984. "Famine Forecasting: Prices and Peasant Behaviour in Northern Ethiopia." *Disasters* 8, 1: 48–56.

Cutler, P. 1985. *The Use of Economic and Social Information in Famine Prediction and Response.* Report prepared for the Overseas Development Administration. London: Overseas Development Administration.

Cutler, P., and J. Shoham. 1985. *The State of Disaster Preparedness in the Sudan.* Report prepared for the Ford Foundation. London: Relief and Development Institute.

Cutler, P., and R. Stephenson. 1984. *The State of Food Emergency Preparedness in Ethiopia.* London: Relief and Development Institute.

Degefu, W. 1987. "Some Aspects of Meteorological Drought in Ethiopia." In *Drought and Hunger in Africa*, edited by M. H. Glantz, 23–36. Cambridge: Cambridge University Press.

Deloite, Haskins, and Sells Management Company. 1985. *Final Report on the USAID/GOK Food Relief Monitoring and Evaluation*. Nairobi: USAID/Kenya.

Dennett, M. D., J. Elston, and J. A. Rodgers. 1985. "A Reappraisal of Rainfall Trends in the Sahel." *Journal of Climatology* 5, 4: 353–362.

de Waal, A., and M. M. Amin. 1986. *Survival in Northern Darfur 1985–1986*. Report of the SCF Survey Team, Northern Darfur, October–December 1985. London: Save the Children Fund.

Downing, J., L. Berry, L. Downing, T. E. Downing, and R. Ford. 1987. *Drought and Famine in Africa, 1981–1986: The U.S. Response*. Worcester, Mass.: Clark University.

Downing, T. E. 1990. "Monitoring and Responding to Famine: Lessons from the 1984–85 Food Crisis in Kenya." *Disasters* 14, 3: 204–229.

Downing, T. E., K. W. Gitu, and C. M. Kamau. 1989. *Coping with Drought in Kenya: National and Local Strategies*. Boulder: Lynne Rienner Publishers.

Drèze, J. 1988. *Famine Prevention in Africa*. Monograph No. 3, Development and Economic Research Programme, London School of Economics.

D'Silva, B. C. 1985. *Sudan: Policy Reforms and Prospects for Agricultural Recovery After the Drought*. Economic Research Services (ERS) Staff Report No. AGES-850909. Washington, D.C.: USDA/ERS.

D'Souza, F. 1989. *Famine and the Art of Early Warning: The African Experience*. Report prepared for the Overseas Development Administration-Economics and Social Research Division. Oxford: Department of Biological Anthropology, University of Oxford.

Economist Intelligence Unit 1984. *Country Report: Kenya*. Nos. 2–4. London: Economist Intelligence Unit.

Economist Intelligence Unit. 1985. *Country Report: Kenya*. Nos. 1–4. London: Economist Intelligence Unit.

Economist Intelligence Unit. 1986a. *Country Report: Kenya*. No. 3. London: Economist Intelligence Unit.

Economist Intelligence Unit. 1986b. *Country Report: Kenya, 1986–87*. London: Economist Intelligence Unit.

Economist Intelligence Unit. 1986c. *Country Report: Mozambique*. Nos. 1–4. London: Economist Intelligence Unit.

Economist Intelligence Unit. 1989a. *Guinea, Mali, Mauritania Country Report*. No. 3. London: Economist Intelligence Unit.

Economist Intelligence Unit. 1989b. *Kenya Country Report*. No. 3. London: Economist Intelligence Unit.

Economist Intelligence Unit. 1989c. *Namibia, Botswana, Lesotho, Swaziland Country Report*. No. 2. London: Economist Intelligence Unit.

Economist Intelligence Unit. 1989d. *Sudan Country Report*. No. 2. London: Economist Intelligence Unit.

Economist Intelligence Unit. 1989e. *Tanzania, Mozambique Country Report*. No. 2. London: Economist Intelligence Unit.

Economist Intelligence Unit. 1989f. *Uganda, Ethiopia, Somalia, Djibouti Country Report*. No. 2. London: Economist Intelligence Unit.

Farmer, G., and T. M. L. Wigley. 1985. *Climatic Trends for Tropical Africa*. Norwich, U.K.: Climatic Research Unit, University of East Anglia.

Field, C. R., and G. K. Njiru. 1985. *Conclusions and Urgent Recommendations Concerning Famine Relief Requirements in Six Districts of the Arid Zone of Kenya.* Nairobi: United Nations Educational, Scientific and Cultural Organization, Integrated Project in Arid Lands.

Flueret, A. 1986. "Indigenous Responses to Drought in Sub-Saharan Africa." *Disasters* 10, 3: 224–229.

Food and Agriculture Organization (FAO). 1983. *Food Production Year Book.* Rome: FAO.

Food and Agriculture Organization (FAO). 1986. *Food Production Year Book.* Rome: FAO.

Hart, K. 1982. *The Political Economy of West African Agriculture.* Cambridge: Cambridge University Press.

Holm, J. D., and R. W. Morgan. 1985. "Coping with Drought in Botswana: An African Success." *Journal of Modern African Studies* 23, 3: 463–482.

Horowitz, M., and P. Little. 1987. "African Pastoralism and Poverty: Some Implications for Drought and Famine." In *Drought and Hunger in Africa,* edited by M. H. Glantz, 59–82. Cambridge: Cambridge University Press.

Hyden G. 1983. *No Shortcuts to Progress: African Develpment Management in Perspective.* London: Heinemann.

Ibrahim, F. N. 1984. "Ecological Imbalance in the Republic of Sudan—with Reference to Desertification in Darfur." *Bayreuther Geowissenschaftliche Arbeiten.*

Ibrahim, F. N. 1988. "Causes of Famine Among the Rural Population of the Sahelian Zone of the Sudan." *GeoJournal* 17, 1: 133–141.

Kerr, R. A. 1985 "Fifteen Years of African Drought." *Science* 227: 1453–1454.

King, P. 1986. *An African Winter.* Middlesex, U.K.: Penguin Books.

Lal, R. 1987. "Managing the Soils of Sub-Saharan Africa." *Science* 236: 1069–1076.

Lamb, P. J. 1982. "Persistence of Subsaharan Drought." *Nature* 299: 46–47.

Lamb, P. J. 1983. "Subsaharan Rainfall Update for 1982: Continued Drought." *Journal of Climatology* 3, 4: 419–422.

Lipton, M. 1985. *The Place of Agricultural Research in the Development of Sub-Saharan Africa.* Discussion Paper 202. Brighton, U.K.: Institute of Development Studies, University of Sussex.

Lofchie, M. F. 1975. "Political and Economic Origins of African Hunger." *Journal of Modern African Studies* 13, 4: 551–567.

Lofchie, M. F. 1987. "The Decline of African Agriculture: An Internalist Perspective." In *Drought and Hunger in Africa,* edited by M. H. Glantz, 85–109. Cambridge: Cambridge University Press.

Mason, J. B., J. G. Haaga, T. O. Maribe, G. Marks, V. J. Quinn, and K. Test. 1987. "Using Agricultural Data for Timely Warning to Prevent the Effects of Drought on Child Nutrition in Botswana." *Ecology of Food and Nutrition* 19: 169–184.

McCabe, J. T., and J. E. Ellis. 1987. "Beating the Odds in Arid Africa." *Natural History* 96, 1: 32–41.

Mellor, J. M., and S. Gavian. 1987. "Famine: Causes, Prevention, and Relief." *Science* 235: 539–545.

Morgan, R. W. 1985. "From Drought Relief to Post-Disaster Recovery: The Case of Botswana." *Disasters* 9, 1: 44–50.

Neumann, C. G., N. O. Bwibo, E. Carter, S. Weinberg, A. A. Cattle, D. Ngare, M. Baksh, M. Paolisso, A. H. Coulson, and M. Trostle. 1989. "Impact of the

1984 Drought on Food Intake, Nutritional Status and Household Response in Embu District." In *Coping with Drought in Kenya: National and Local Strategies,* edited by T. E. Downing, K. Gitu, and C. Kamau, 231–244. Boulder: Lynne Rienner Publishers.

Nicholson, S. E. 1985. "Sub-Saharan Rainfall, 1981–1984." *Journal of Climate and Applied Meteorology* 24: 1388–1391.

Nicholson, S. E. 1988. "Land Surface Atmosphere Interaction: Physical Processes and Surface Changes and Their Impact." *Progress in Physical Geography* 12, 1: 36-65.

Nicholson, S. E. 1989. "Long-Term Changes in African Rainfall." *Weather* 44, 2: 46–56.

Ogallo, L. J., and E. K. Anyamba. 1985. *Drought of Tropical Central and Eastern Africa, July–November, Northern Springs of 1983–1984.* Nairobi: Kenya Meteorological Department.

Omer, M. M. el-J. 1988. "Environmental Management: Traditional Versus Modern (Case Study: Um-Ruaba District, Sudan)." Ph.D. diss., Clark University, Worcester, Mass.

Payne, R., L. Rummell, and M. H. Glantz. 1987. "Denying Famine a Future: Concluding Remarks." In *Drought and Hunger in Africa,* edited by M. H. Glantz, 433–444. Cambridge: Cambridge University Press.

Potter, H. L. 1988. "The Effects on Livestock Production." In *The Impact of Climatic Variations on Agriculture,* edited by M. L. Perry, T. R. Carter, and N. T. Konijn, 209–220. Dordrecht, Netherlands: Kluwer.

Rasmusson, E. M. 1987. "Global Climate Change and Variability: Effects on Drought and Desertification in Africa." In *Drought and Hunger in Africa,* edited by M. H. Glantz, 3–22. Cambridge: Cambridge University Press.

Sen, A. 1981. *Poverty and Famines: An Essay on Entitlement and Deprivation.* Oxford: Clarendon Press.

Somerville, C. M. 1986. *Drought and Aid in the Sahel: A Decade of Development Cooperation.* Boulder: Westview Press.

Timberlake, L. 1985. *Africa in Crisis: The Causes, the Cures of Environmental Bankruptcy.* London: Earthscan.

Tyson, P. D. 1986. *Climate Change and Variability in Southern Africa.* Cape Town: Oxford University Press.

U.N. Office for Emergency Operations in Africa (UNOEOA). 1985. *Sudan Quarterly Review.* 15 July–15 October. Khartoum: UNOEOA.

U.S. Agency for International Development (USAID). 1985. *Disaster Case Reports.* Washington, D.C.: USAID Office of Foreign Disaster Assistance.

U.S. Congress, Senate Committee on the Judiciary. 1986. *Ethiopia and Sudan One Year Later: Refugee and Famine Recovery Needs.* 99th Cong., 2d sess. (April).

U.S. Department of Agriculture/Economic Research Service (USDA/ERS). 1984. *World Food Needs and Availabilities, 1984/85.* Washington, D.C.: USDA/ERS.

U.S. Department of Agriculture/Economic Research Service (USDA/ERS). 1986a. *Sub-Saharan Africa: Situation and Outlook Report.* Report No. RS-96-9. Washington, D.C.: USDA/ERS.

U.S. Department of Agriculture/Economic Research Service (USDA/ERS). 1986b. *World Food Needs and Availabilities, 1986/87: Fall Update.* Washington, D.C.: USDA/ERS.

U.S. Department of Agriculture/Economic Research Service (USDA/ERS). 1987. *World Food Needs and Availabilities, 1987/88.* Washington, D.C.: USDA/ERS.

U.S. Office of Foreign Disaster Assistance (OFDA). 1987. *The Disaster History: Significant Data on Major Disasters Worldwide, 1900–Present.* Washington, D.C.: USAID/OFDA.

Watts, M. 1983. *Silent Violence: Food, Famine and Peasantry in Northern Nigeria.* Berkeley: University of California Press.

Wisner, B. J. 1977. *The Human Ecology of Drought in Eastern Kenya.* Ph.D. diss., Clark University, Worcester, Mass.

World Bank. 1984. *Toward Sustained Development in Sub-Saharan Africa: A Joint Program of Action.* Washington, D.C.: World Bank.

World Bank. 1987. *World Development Report, 1987.* New York: Oxford University Press.

World Meteorological Organization (WMO). 1985. *The Global Climate System: A Critical Review of the Climatic System During 1982.* Geneva: WMO.

York, S. 1985. "Report on a Pilot Project to Set Up a Drought Information Network in Conjunction with the Red Crescent Society in Darfur." *Disasters* 9, 3: 173–178.

Young, L. 1985. "A General Assessment of the Environmental Impact of Refugees in Somalia with Attention to the Refugee Agricultural Programme." *Disasters* 9, 2: 122–133.

3

Drought and Famine in the Pastoral Zone of the Sahel

The 1984 Drought in Niger

J. Dirck Stryker

Following three years of declining rainfall, the Sahelian area of West Africa was hit by devastating drought in 1984. Within the pastoral zone,[1] this was said to be the worst drought in living memory, due both to the low level of rainfall, which rivaled the unusually dry years of 1972 and 1973, and to its poor timing.

The herders who inhabit this zone reacted as they always do in times of stress by employing various strategies to sustain themselves and preserve their herds. Nevertheless, the severity of the drought was such that many animals died or were sold at very low prices. Large numbers of herders were thus impoverished and forced to seek relief at camps, irrigated garden sites, and other food distribution points.

The governments of the Sahelian countries, assisted by donor agencies, undertook a number of actions designed to lessen the effects of the drought. They tried to encourage the movement of herders and their animals out of the pastoral zone, to provide relief to those unable to move, and to assist in the reconstitution of herds after the rains returned in 1985. Some of these actions were effective; others were not.

During the entire period of the drought and its immediate aftermath, the staff of the Niger Integrated Livestock Project (NILP) was present in the pastoral zone of the Republic of Niger. This NILP staff made every effort to assist herders and at the same time to record the physical manifestations of the drought, the response of herders to its effects on the rangeland, and the impact of government measures designed to mitigate its influence. Rainfall and biomass production were monitored, herders were surveyed, market information was gathered, data on health and nutritional status were collected, financial analyses were undertaken, and observations regarding the efficacy of government actions were noted. Much of this information has now been analyzed, and the conclusions of this analysis are the main subject of this chapter.

The opportunity to observe closely the impact of drought and the efforts to mitigate its effects was vitally important in view of the controversy that exists regarding the long-term viability of the pastoral zone. The next section elucidates the major elements of this controversy. This is followed by a description of the impact of drought in the Sahel and herder response to it, both generally and within the context of the 1984 drought. Next is a discussion and evaluation of the effectiveness of actions taken by the Government of Niger to dampen the impact of the drought. The final section draws together some conclusions for Sahelian government and foreign donor policy regarding the pastoral zone.

The Viability of the Pastoral Zone

A considerable controversy has existed for a number of years regarding the long-term viability of the pastoral zone. On the one hand, the resources of the Sahelian rangeland are seen as a valuable complement to the limited agricultural potential of the adjacent semi-arid region. On the other hand, these rangeland resources are thought to be rapidly deteriorating under the combined impact of growing population, increased opportunities for livestock marketing, introduction of new technology for improved animal health and water development, and displacement of local political authorities by national governments (Stryker 1989).

There is little doubt that the pastoral zone is very important for the economies of the Sahel. It is the major breeding area for most of the region's cattle, camels, sheep, and goats. About seven million people, or 17 percent of the total population of Sahelian countries, inhabit this zone. Others, who normally live in the semi-arid lands farther south, make use of the zone during the rainy season.

The major traditional economic activity in the zone is pastoral nomadism. Given the low labor wage rates and high capital costs associated with poverty in the Sahel, spatial and temporal variations in rainfall are accommodated by animal movements requiring intensive use of labor.[2] The most important of these movements is the seasonal transhumance, which takes advantage of fresh pasture generated during the rainy season. This is the most efficient way in which rangeland resources can be exploited.

The principal problem associated with pastoral nomadism is that the rangeland is held in common rather than owned by individuals.

An important reason for this is that the resource base is adequate to support only a low density of population, while the need to move animals implies that this population is seldom stationary. As a result, the cost of establishing and enforcing land use rights tends to be high. This leads to a "tragedy of the commons" situation in which individual herders overgraze their animals because they do not take into account the effects this grazing has on the total quantity and quality of available pasture.

Those who claim that the rangeland resource base is rapidly deteriorating in the pastoral zone argue that growing population pressure has severely complicated the establishment and enforcement of land use rights. Furthermore, rising animal prices have encouraged an expansion of commercial activity and facilitated the transfer of animal ownership to traders, civil servants, and others not subject to traditional forms of land control. This transfer has not been accompanied by a more settled ranching mode of production, which might reduce the problem of overgrazing, but by the herders tending the animals of absentee owners who are not very concerned with good range management. At the same time, the introduction of vaccination against rinderpest and other animal health measures, as well as the development of boreholes and other water resources, has placed additional pressure on the rangeland. The impact of these forces might be mitigated through better management by local authorities of the rangeland resources, but the power of these authorities has been severely eroded by national governments (Stryker 1989). Finally, the pressure on rangeland resources and the tendency to overuse them are greatly exacerbated in times of drought because of the general shortage of pasture.

The long-term viability of the pastoral zone thus depends on two essential factors. The first is to restore to local political authorities the power to manage the rangeland. The second is to find a way to encourage the movement of animals out of the zone in time of drought.

Drought and Herder Response

The Impact of Drought

Drought is the normal condition of the Sahelian pastoral zone. Each year the northward movement of the intertropical convergence zone brings no more than four months of erratic rainfall. In some years this movement is arrested and the rains fail. When this occurs several years in a row, the impact of drought is especially severe.

The herders who inhabit the pastoral zone have learned how to adapt to these variable conditions. The essence of their adaptation is movement and diversity. When the rains come, herds are moved from their dry season habitats in the south into drier areas to the north where nutritious vegetation is newly produced by the rain. In drought years, when rainfall is inadequate, this pattern is broken. Herds are moved either to the few areas within the pastoral zone where there is vegetation or to the more humid region to the south. When the herds cannot be moved, the risk is high of being trapped without adequate feed.

Diversification is also important in enabling herders to survive in this environment. Species diversification permits exploitation of different kinds of vegetation, which often fare differentially in a drought year. Late rains in September 1984, for example, permitted some growth of perennial trees and shrubs, which benefited camels and goats as browsers even though the growth of pasture for cattle and sheep was very poor. Diversified sources of income also permit herders to buy supplementary feed and to escape having to sell their animals at desultory prices in order to buy grain.

The ability of herders to diversify their sources of income has decreased markedly over the past seventy-five years. Commerce is a much less important activity for herders than it used to be, and the fruits of military conquest are no longer available. In addition, population growth in the agricultural areas to the south has resulted in increased pressure on the rangeland. This has not only decreased the importance of cultivation as a supplementary source of food production for herders; it has also reduced the availability of dry season pasture.[3] For a while this loss of income was compensated by an increase in opportunities for wage employment in the cities and coastal countries to the south, but the slackening of economic growth in these areas has lessened the importance of this alternative.

The decrease in the diversity of income sources was accompanied for some time by a secular increase in the relative prices of animals being exchanged for cereals. This was especially important for cattle and sheep, the demand for which expanded strongly outside the pastoral zone during the 1950s, 1960s, and 1970s. This encouraged specialization in the herding of these animals at the expense of camels and goats. The result was a decrease in species diversity and an increased dependence on the animals that are most susceptible to drought. This also made herders highly dependent on the market economy, and especially on livestock sales used to finance the purchase of cereals. Among the Wodaabe (nomadic Fulani), for example, sales of livestock at the end of the 1970s constituted 90 to 95 percent of total cash income, while cereals comprised about three-quarters of total caloric consumption (Sollod et al. 1987).

During a severe drought year, the prices of animals sold on the market plummet at the same time that the prices of cereals rise sharply. Animal prices fall because herders are forced to sell if their animals are unlikely to survive, or if they need the cash to buy food. At the same time, demand for animal products slackens because of the impact of the drought on income. Cereal prices, on the other hand, increase with the decline in production resulting from the drought.

Animal prices in the Department of Tahoua during December 1984 were one-half their real, long-term average from 1970 to 1983. During the same month, cereal prices were almost double their level twelve months earlier. The terms of trade (prices of animals divided by prices of cereals) remained highly unfavorable for herders until July 1985, when the rains returned and animal prices started to rise (Sollod et al. 1987). As these prices continued to increase during 1985 and 1986, herders who had been impoverished by the drought found it difficult to purchase animals with which to reconstitute their herds. On the other hand, wealthier traders, farmers, civil servants, and herders possessing the resources to buy animals at low prices and to maintain them with purchased feed during the drought were able to benefit substantially from these price movements, resulting in greater inequality within the pastoral zone.

During a drought, animal losses and decreased productivity, coupled with adverse movements in the terms of trade, lead to a deterioration in the health and nutritional status of the herder population. This group is already the most nutritionally at-risk in the Sahel, even in nondrought years.[4] Furthermore, rates of malnutrition vary spatially and temporally within the pastoral zone. Especially high rates of malnutrition during the dry season, in particular, are explained by high temperatures, lack of water, long distances between camp and water due to increasingly scarce pasture, strenuous work involved in digging and maintaining wells and in drawing water for animals, the need to reserve limited milk supplies for young animals, and adverse terms of trade between the prices of animals in poor condition and those of cereals (Loutan and Lamotte 1984).

Herder Response

Herder response to drought varies depending upon ethnic group and social class. Twareg nobles, for example, can redirect their labor force between livestock, crops, commerce, transportation, and crafts. During the very severe drought that occurred in 1972 and 1973, however, they abandoned much of their labor force to conserve food for themselves. Those less fortunate had no choice but to flee toward more humid areas farther south (Starr 1986).

As the political, social, and economic organization of the Twareg weakened during the colonial period, Wodaabe herders from northern Nigeria, specializing largely in cattle, migrated into the pastoral zone of Niger. Because of their close relationships with farmers in the south, the Wodaabe were for a while able to move relatively easily into more humid areas in times of drought. This practice has become more difficult, however, as social ties have weakened and demographic pressures have intensified with the passage of time (Sollod et al. 1987).

In Niger many of the Twareg remained in the pastoral zone in 1984 but engaged in activities such as handicrafts and irrigated gardening. They also sold animals in order to buy grain and supplemental feed for the animals they retained. A survey of sixty Twareg families found, in fact, that the herders who remained within the zone and were most successful in surviving the drought reduced substantially their animal holdings, especially of sheep and cattle, when the rains first failed. They thus were better able to protect the animals remaining in their herds, through supplementary feeding and other measures, until the rains returned (Cord, El Inguini, and Stem 1986).[5]

To protect themselves during the drought, some herders sold sheep and cattle, which are especially dependent on pasture, in order to buy goats and camels, which rely instead on the more abundant browse.[6] Market presentations of sheep and cattle in the Tahoua Department peaked in January 1985, whereas sales of goats and camels increased to a much lesser extent and reached a maximum only in April of that year. After the drought, sheep and goats were in heavy demand because of their relatively low cost and high reproduction rates (Sollod et al. 1987).

Out-migration was also a common strategy in Niger during 1984–85, especially among the Wodaabe, because of the susceptibility of their cattle to drought. The Twareg, on the other hand, often remained in their customary dry season habitats, located in low-lying areas that support perennial trees and shrubs. When they did migrate, this was usually because they had lost most of their animals and needed to seek food relief or employment in urban areas (Sollod et al. 1987).

Herders who migrated south with their animals early during the drought fared reasonably well. A survey during June 1985 of the livestock markets within and to the south of the NILP zone reported that over one-half of the herders in the markets were able to support themselves through animal sales. This was in contrast to another survey of herders at gardening sites in the north, who were heavily dependent on government assistance (Metzel and Haymond 1985). These results may be biased, however, since herders at the gardening sites were there primarily to receive food relief.

The surveys also showed that both cattle and Wodaabe herders were found much more frequently in the south than in the north. In contrast, herders in the north, whether in the markets or at the garden sites, were more likely to be Twareg and to have camels rather than cattle. Regardless of location, animal health problems were reported to be greater at the garden sites than near the markets, suggesting the dangers of excessive animal concentrations (Metzel and Haymond 1985). On the other hand, Wodaabe herders returning to the pastoral zone after the rains reported heavy losses of cattle due to disease in the more humid areas of the south, especially in Nigeria. This was off-set, to some extent, by the greater availability and lower price of feed.

Government Actions in Niger

Government actions to mitigate the effects of drought in the pastoral zone aim at preserving the rangeland and animal resources and at ensuring adequate supplies of food for the population. In Niger during the 1984 drought, the relative success of different efforts varied substantially.

The Government of Niger was strongly committed from the beginning to ensuring the availability of food sufficient to avoid severe malnutrition and starvation. In September 1984, it officially requested food aid from the donors and established an interministerial committee to coordinate its receipt and distribution. Primary delivery of food was to be the responsibility of the army, relying for logistical support on the Niger Office for Food Products (OPVN) and the Ministry of Transport and Commerce. Limited amounts of food and medical supplies were also distributed directly by international relief agencies (Sollod et al. 1987).

Initially, the government did not want to establish camps to facilitate the distribution of food. Dry season garden sites were created instead, where herders who remained in the pastoral zone could settle and receive food relief as long as they also worked to feed themselves. Wells were dug, and families were given small plots of land, seeds, and tools. The objective over the longer run was to make the herders less vulnerable to variations in rainfall and to sedentarize the nomadic population.

As the year wore on, the problem of ensuring adequate supplies of food became intense. Having delivery handled by the military facilitated coordination; but the army was inexperienced compared with the private voluntary organizations (PVOs), and much of the food arrived late.[7] Nutrition surveys, for example, suggested that about 70 percent of the children in some areas were malnourished in the month of May 1985, following a measles epidemic; but large deliveries of food did not arrive until June and July. By this time, the relief camps, which had grown in size during the hot dry season despite the government's wishes, had begun to disperse with the return of the rains.

The major thrust of the government's approach to saving animals and preserving the rangeland during the drought was to move animals out of the pastoral zone. A public information campaign was initiated to encourage out-migration. Arrangements were made for trucks going south to haul animals for a small fee, and border crossings by Nigerien herds into neighboring countries were facilitated through relaxation of export regulations, temporary removal of Nigerian import restrictions, and an early start for the vaccination campaign. More could have been done, however, to provide veterinary services along transportation routes and in the south, where the incidence of disease was high. Nor was anything done to extend vaccination coverage and to provide vitamins and other veterinary products during the critical 1985 hot season (Sollod et al. 1987).

Because government ranches were no more able to support their animals than were private herders, these ranches were destocked at the beginning of 1985, depressing already low prices and discouraging destockage by herders. At the same time, to help support animal prices, the government launched a dried meat program. Under this program, moribund animals were purchased at subsidized prices and slaughtered to provide a source of protein for the relief camps. Within the Tahoua Department, however, the animals purchased under the program accounted for only 0, 1, 4, and 8 percent respectively of market presentations of goats, cattle, sheep, and camels. The dried meat program purchased 4,964 head of cattle, overall, whereas the ranches sold 10,881 head (Sollod et al. 1987). The animals purchased by the dried meat program were in very poor condition and fetched a very low price even at the subsidized rate, whereas the ranches sold animals in much better condition at much higher prices. The combined effect of these actions, therefore, was to reduce cattle prices in the market.

Another effort to support animal prices and to ensure a supply for herd reconstitution after the drought (Opération Sauvetage des Femelles) involved purchasing females, holding them in the zone during the drought, feeding them supplements, and selling them to herders through a subsided credit scheme after the drought. A financial analysis of this operation, undertaken by the NILP staff, showed it to be highly unprofitable. This was principally because supplementary feed had to be purchased in the south and shipped north at high cost (Shaw 1985). The study suggests that it would have been more profitable to move animals to the feed, which is what the herders generally do, rather than to transport large amounts of feed to the animals. In addition to buying and feeding animals, the government also purchased and sold to herders cottonseed and occasionally wheat bran at subsidized prices. Supplies were severely limited, however, and shortages were reflected in high prices on the private market. The differences between the official selling price and private market prices were such that substantial profits went to those able to purchase this scarce feed at the lower, subsidized price.

Since the 1984 drought, the government has developed an early warning system to provide objective indicators of future drought. Biomass left standing on the rangeland at the end of the rainy season is measured to provide an estimate of the number of animals that could be sustained in the zone during the year. This biomass is measured using a combination of satellite imagery and verification on the ground. Market prices are also monitored for any indication of a deterioration in the herder's terms of trade following the rains, when these terms should normally improve. Such a deterioration would be an indication of distress sales necessitated by the poor condition of animals and the herder's need for grain. The overall goal of the early warning system is to estimate in a timely way the likely impact of the drought in order to quantitatively indicate the need for food relief.

While laudable, the early warning system suffers from some limitations. The most important of these is the integration of the system into a decisionmaking framework that translates need into action. Furthermore, the program is focused on conditions of highly deficient rainfall and does not adequately take into account the normal climatic variability of the zone. There is a need for a system that supplements existing mechanisms for the transmission of information on drought-related conditions to herders, farmers, traders, local officials, national decisionmakers, and foreign donors. This would facilitate the movement of animals, improve the efficiency of markets, help to provide better animal health coverage, and provide timely notice of the need for food relief in the event of severe drought.

Lessons

Much has been learned from the Niger experience about herder behavior in time of drought and about the effectiveness of government efforts to mitigate its effects. Some of the lessons are essentially negative, suggesting that there are certain actions the Nigerien government took in 1984–85 that did not contribute to its objectives. Others are positive and suggest directions in which the development of a drought strategy should move.

Among the negative lessons, the most important is that government ranches have a destabilizing effect on market prices because of the need to destock them at a time when market prices for animals are already falling. The suggestion has been made that these ranches should be turned into security reserves, or fodder banks, which could be used to furnish feed in drought years. In good years, on the other hand, hay could be harvested and sold to local animal feeders (Sollod et al. 1987). The economic feasibility of doing this needs to be studied.

It is also clear that government efforts to purchase female animals and provide them with feed transported from the south is not economically viable. More beneficial are efforts to facilitate the movement of animals out of the pastoral zone by subsidizing truck transport and easing trade restrictions. Ideally, Sahelian governments should eliminate, on a permanent basis, all restrictions on cross-border trade in livestock and institute a policy for subsidizing truck transport in years of severe drought.

Despite efforts to move animals out of the zone, some will always be left behind. If these survive, they are very useful in helping to reconstitute herds following the drought. This may require some subsidization of the cost of transporting high-value feed supplements, such as cottonseed, from the south. The subsidy could be justified by the fact that herders have little access to capital markets and are therefore in a poor position to retain or purchase the animals necessary to take advantage of the range resources that are available once the rains return. The main issue requiring investigation is whether this subsidy would encourage keeping too many animals in the zone and not allow adequate relief from grazing pressure following the drought.

It might be argued that a subsidy on the transport of feed supplements would aid transporters and merchants more than poor herders. This is unlikely to the extent that there is competition in the transportation industry since the savings in costs would be passed on to those purchasing the supplements. In any event, this subsidy, if it were available without restriction, would be much more equitable than if the government were to sell feed supplements at highly subsidized prices in very limited quantities, as was the case in Niger during 1984–85.

The dried meat program in Niger consumed a great deal of the time and energy of government officials and probably had very little effect on animal prices. Much more useful would have been a similar effort to extend veterinary services and increase the flow of vitamins and other veterinary products. This would have decreased animal losses and contributed to the maintenance of the herders' capital.

The need for good quantitative information is evident in the pastoral zone at all times, and particularly during years of severe drought. In Niger, much of that information is currently being gathered, but collection needs to be integrated with analysis and dissemination in a total information package. This should include data on the distribution of rainfall, pasture conditions, market prices, and animal health problems. Analysis and dissemination must be timely to be useful. Microcomputers and radios at the department level have an important role to play. The data would also assist donors and national governments in getting food aid delivered more quickly. The information system, however, must be fully integrated into institutional arrangements for decisionmaking during drought emergencies. A start has been made in Niger, but much remains to be done.

Over the longer term, anything that can be done to diversify sources of herder income and to increase their range of options is likely to lessen the adverse consequences of drought. This might occur by strengthening market and financial institutions and by increasing opportunities for employment in handicrafts and local industrial activities. Better markets help to avoid steep price declines when herders are forced to sell their animals. Improved financial institutions enable herders to keep their cash from the sale of animals in interest-earning deposits and to borrow at the end of the drought to rebuild their herds (Metzel and Stem 1984). Finally, income from sources other than livestock permits herders to purchase cereals without selling their animals in a depressed market.

In the very long run, the viability of the pastoral zone depends to a large extent on the ability of herders, national governments, and foreign donors to deal with drought. A critical element is the problem of overgrazing and efforts to deal with it through common property management. There is some evidence that organized grazing schemes have worked reasonably well in better-watered areas, which are capable of supporting perennial grasses and where animal movements are more restrained. These schemes have had little success, however, in pastoral areas where animal grasses predominate and movements are extensive (Niger Integrated Livestock Project 1990). Fortunately, the animal grasses of the Sahel are relatively robust and tend to come back quickly once the rains return. This is particularly true if grazing pressure is reduced at the time of drought. Certainly this was the case in Niger following the 1984 drought, when rangeland resources after the summer of 1985 were far greater than the capacity of animals herds to utilize them. The experience of Niger, therefore, suggests that the long-term viability of the pastoral zone can be ensured only by increasing the alternatives available to herders in drought years so that they can reduce grazing pressure on the rangeland and allow it to recover as a valuable natural resource. This will also serve to lessen the trauma and suffering experienced by the herding population during drought.

Notes

The author gratefully acknowledges the important contributions made to this paper by Louise Cord, Louis Loutan, and Edgar Stem, each of whom lived in Niger during the 1984 drought and its aftermath and provided important insights into herder response to the drought and the effectiveness of government efforts to mitigate its impact.

1. The pastoral zone is defined here to include the area receiving on average between 100 and 400 millimeters of rainfall per year. This is somewhat broader than the area defined by Sollod (1990) as the "pastoral habitat," in that it includes more humid areas that are sometimes, but not regularly, put under cultivation, as well as drier areas that are grazed regularly during the rainy, but not the dry, season.

2. In similar ecological regions in wealthier countries, ranches are established that substitute capital and energy for high-cost labor, but production per unit of land area is generally no greater than in the Sahel. See de Vries and Djiteye (1982).

3. Sollod et al. (1987) is an important work that summarizes the major studies undertaken by the NILP team during and after the 1984 drought.

4. During the 1984–85 drought, 25 percent of the children of herding families in Niger were found to be malnourished (weight-to-height ratio less than 80 percent of national average), compared with the national prevalence of childhood malnutrition of 17 percent (Ministry of Public Health and Social Affairs, *Enquête Nationale sur la Morbidité et la Mortalité*, 1985, 32–33). An NILP survey at a food relief site in Kornaka, conducted in June 1985, found that 44 percent of the children between one and five years of age were malnourished (Niger Integrated Livestock Project 1985).

5. This study found that the number of tropical livestock units (TLUs) possessed by each family in the survey decreased on average from 13.2 in August 1984 to 3.2 at the end of the 1985 rainy season. The less successful herders had two and a half times the TLUs of the more successful herders in August 1984, but one-third fewer TLUs in February 1986. They also used higher-quality feed supplements less often than did the more successful herders.

6. Among the Twareg interviewed by Cord et al. (1986), the more successful herders had 54 percent more goat TLUs and 70 percent fewer cattle TLUs than did the less successful herders when the drought was over.

7. In addition, food deliveries were often too bulky to be handled conveniently by the nomads. Bimonthly receipts of food, for example, posed problems of transport and organization.

References

Cord, Louise J., Naissirou El Inguini, and Edgar Stem. 1986. "Successful Drought Strategies Among Twaregs of the Eduk-Kao Region." Niger Integrated Livestock Project, Tahoua, 10 July. Mimeo.

de Vries, F. W. T. Penning, and M. A. Djiteye. 1982. *La productivité des paturages sahéliens: Une étude des sols, des végétations et de l'exploitation de cette ressource naturelle*. Wageningen, Netherlands: Centre for Agricultural Publishing and Documentation.

Leonard, H. Jeffrey, ed. 1989. *Environment and the Poor: Development Strategies for a Common Agenda.* New Brunswick, N.J.: Transaction Books.

Loutan, Louis, and J. M. Lamotte. 1984. "Seasonal Variations in Nutrition Among a Group of Nomadic Pastoralists in Niger." *Lancet* 1 (April 28): 945–947.

Metzel, Jeffrey, and Peter Haymond. 1985. "Crisis Monitoring Report: May–June 1985." Niger Integrated Livestock Project, 7 July. Mimeo.

Metzel, Jeffrey, and Chip Stem. 1984. "A Draft Proposal for a Pastoral Center Drought Strategy." Niger Integrated Livestock Project, 10 October. Mimeo.

Ministry of Public Health and Social Affairs, Government of Niger. 1985. *Enquête nationale sur la morbidité et la mortalité.* Niamey.

Niger Integrated Livestock Project. 1985. "Situation nutritionnelle et recensement du site de Kornaka." Mimeo.

Niger Integrated Livestock Project. 1990. *Niger Integrated Livestock Project: Final Report.* Tufts University, 8 June. Mimeo.

Shaw, Peter. 1985. "Analyse financière de l'opération sauvetage des femelles du plan d'urgence." Niger Integrated Livestock Project, Tahoua, 22 November. Mimeo.

Sollod, Albert E. 1990. "Rainfall, Biomass, and the Pastoral Economy of Niger: Assessing the Impact of Drought." *Journal of Arid Environments* 18: 97–107.

Sollod, Albert E., Louise Cord, Abdou Nababa, Bagoudou Maidagi, and Yahaya Mani. 1987. *Livestock Development Strategy for the Drought-Prone Ecology of Niger.* Integrated Livestock Production Project, Niamey. Mimeo.

Starr, Martha. 1986. "Risk, Environmental Variability, and Drought-Induced Impoverishment." Boston University. Mimeo.

Stryker, J. Dirck. 1989. "Technology, Human Pressure, and Ecology in the Arid and Semi-Arid Tropics." In Leonard and contributors, 87–109.

4

Responses to Famine

Why They are Allowed to Happen

Peter Cutler

In this chapter, I attempt to go some way toward answering the vexing question of why famines happen, or rather, why they are allowed to happen. My personal starting point for this exploration is the failure of public institutions to respond sufficiently to the developing famines in parts of Ethiopia and Sudan in the early to mid-1980s. My interest continues because famines show no sign of abating and because the renewed calls for better information systems for famine early warning mostly miss the point. The response to famine is above all politically conditioned, and this reality has barely been explored in literature on famine.

It should be made clear at the outset that I consider it relatively straightforward for reasonably well-informed individuals to be able to discern the onset of famine conditions in famine-prone countries. By famine conditions I mean the loss of assets on a large scale by people historically vulnerable to mass destitution and associated starvation. Famine itself is usually manifested by mass migration as well as by elevated mortality from starvation and disease. The elements of famine risk are plain to see in massive distress sales of assets, grain price inflation, increase in demand for wage-earning opportunities, upsurges in petty trading, and so on.

I am not going to address the issue of socioeconomic vulnerability to famine, nor will I discuss the notion of food availability decline (FAD) versus loss of entitlements (Sen 1981). I will merely point out in passing that in the latter case, in my view, there is no dichotomy. Food availability decline is always an element in famine and is accompanied by social behavior augmenting the decline, even if FAD is not

72

measurable at the national or regional level. Thus, I go along with the argument already ably advanced by Devereux (1988) in response to Sen and his critics.

Disputes among professional observers concerning the phenomena accompanying famine are more likely to be over the precise social and geographical extent of deprivation, as well as about whether economic conditions will change sufficiently in the near future for mass starvation to be prevented. However, in such circumstances, few will disagree as to the need for action by public authorities to mitigate the distress.

The important question to consider here is: Why are sufficient steps to prevent famine not taken in the face of unambiguous evidence of need? This was the case in parts of Sudan and Ethiopia in late 1983 through early 1984, before the famines became public knowledge worldwide. It has also been the case more recently in southern Sudan, to take another pertinent example. I shall draw on these examples to illustrate my arguments.

The Conventional Model of Famine Early Warning

The implicit model underpinning efforts currently being made at improving famine early warning systems is that better information will allow better informed decisionmaking by policymakers and aid administrators. Underpinning this, in turn, is the common notion of the policy cycle. This is conventionally described as analysis of policy alternatives, choice of the best option, and implementation, evaluation, adjustment as necessary, and continuation of the policy chosen. We can find this policy cycle explicitly displayed in many textbooks on economic development.

According to the model, famine control would mean careful evaluation of available information, prioritization of cases (such as between countries, or regionally within countries), implementation of policy, its adjustment to meet changing conditions, and so on—all a rational, measurable process.

It has been pointed out cogently by Schaffer (1984) that the policy cycle is a myth. The agenda of choices is not dictated by objective technical criteria but by the biases of the people setting the agenda. Schaffer gives the dramatic example of the decision to drop atomic bombs on Japan in 1945. At no stage was the option of *not* dropping the bombs considered; the arguments were over *where* to drop them. Similarly, policy choices about famine control are dictated almost exclusively by political considerations. The political environment is not, of course, static and can change rapidly, as we shall see in considering the example of the response to the Ethiopian famine of 1983–85.

However, the ways in which famine relief aid is used and allocated will be dictated by the political priorities of the various actors involved and by their relative strengths.

Risk Avoidance Among Bureaucrats

A further aspect of the response to famine that needs to be explored is the role of bureaucracies among the different groups of actors involved. Well-informed individuals may be able to identify famine risk, but whether they can persuade key decisionmakers within aid institutions to act to prevent famine is another question. The groups of institutions concerned may be categorized under the headings of government, donors, intergovernmental organizations, and nongovernmental organizations.

Despite their different configurations, orientations, size, financial muscle, and political power, bureaucracies all have something in common, which is that their members generally practice risk avoidance. They do so because taking on extra risk does not usually lead to extra reward in large institutions with their rigid hierarchies, fixed salary scales, and benefit structures. Risk taking can prejudice your career if you are wrong. The idea of bureaucratic risk avoidance has again been advanced by Schaffer (1984) but may also be found in popular wisdom, where "passing the buck" is said to be an attribute of bureaucracies.

Schaffer has argued that bureaucrats practice risk avoidance by adopting a number of escape routes. Examples include resorting to mandates ("it's not our job to do that"); referring decisionmaking to a higher authority; or even more subtly, claiming that the efforts are already being made to combat the problem (famine), although resources are, regrettably, scarce. This implies that budgets are inescapably fixed, when in fact they may change. As we shall see later, budgets can expand if it becomes politically expedient. Escape routes can be invented to suit the situation, with procedural escapes being the most common, such as "we cannot act because the government has not declared an emergency," or "we must await the report of our fact-finding mission before action can be taken."

The Analytical Framework

Let us construct a basic analytical framework in order to make sense of the plethora of actors who are ostensibly involved in famine control. We can then consider their characteristics and from these deduce their likely attitudes in the event of looming famine. The actors may be categorized into four groups: the government of the famine-affected country; donor agencies representing the governments of rich countries that may be called upon to assist; the intergovernmental organizations (IGOs), such as the United Nations agencies and the European Community (EC); and the nongovernmental organizations (NGOs). Each group faces different sets of political constraints that affect its ability to prevent famine. We may start by considering the actions of the host government.

Priorities of the Host Government

The government of a country threatened by famine will respond to the threat with different degrees of enthusiasm, depending upon the political and strategic importance of the population at risk. Remote rural people rarely constitute a threat to the established order, so they are of little direct interest. For example, the Ethiopian state has traditionally ignored rural famine and has done so with impunity (Brietzke 1982; Pankhurst 1985).

Rural famine victims are likely to become a political issue only if their case is taken up by influential urban elites such as university students or the press. Thus, Emperor Haile Selassie found to his cost that rural famine could no longer be ignored in the manner of his forefathers; rather it became one of a number of tools used by his political enemies to dethrone him (Shepherd 1975; Brietzke 1982). By contrast, the governments of relatively democratic countries like India and Bangladesh are extremely sensitive to press reports of famine, which can be used as ammunition by the opposition parties to discredit the government's competence.

In other situations, where there is little or no free press, or where there is traditional disdain toward rural people on the part of the urban elites, then the fate of famine victims is likely to be ignored. Examples include the Beja in Sudan under Nimeiri's regime; the Dinka and other minority tribes in southern Sudan more recently; and the Karamojong in Uganda under Idi Amin. The lack of interest is compounded when the population enduring famine is considered an enemy. In such cases, neglect may be seen as deliberate, a successful display of government policy. The famine in southern Sudan is a most blatant case of this neglect, where even today victims who have escaped the war zone have been allowed to starve and die in record numbers virtually unaided.

The converse of neglect of remote rural people is the prioritization given to urban people. If famine threatens in the towns and cities, action will be taken quickly, for urban unrest can lead to overthrow of the government. What famine aid is available, however, will be allocated by government in accordance with its political and strategic priorities. In general, there will be a hierarchy, with urban populations in the most favored regions getting the most and rural populations in the least favored regions getting the least. This has been shown for Ethiopia, for example (Mitchell 1987; Cutler 1988), and for Darfur in Sudan (Keen 1988).

In this regard, we should beware of confusing what governments say they do with what they actually do. Some governments set up elaborate bureaucratic machinery to lobby for famine aid, using the condition of real victims as evidence. The aim is to gather in as many resources as possible, which will thereafter be allocated not on the grounds of need, but according to the government's own political priorities.

A good example of this resource-gathering behavior was the Mengistu government in Ethiopia, with its impressive Relief and Rehabilitation Commission (RRC), its famine early warning system, and its smooth public relations machinery. Other countries are beginning to follow suit by setting up similar organizations that can be used to capture resources, particularly foreign aid.

This contention is illustrated in Table 4.1. The right-hand column shows the distribution of population by province, according to the degree of need as assessed by the RRC in Ethiopia in mid-1985. As we would expect, the famine-torn provinces of Wollo, Tigray, and Eritrea figure prominently in the list. However, the level of aggregation is not very good, as all southern provinces get lumped together in one category, while a residual "other" refers to pockets of famine in the western provinces.

Table 4.1 Total Grain Consignments to the RRC:
April to August 1985

	% Grain	% Population Famine Affected
Wollo	24.5	32
South	36.5	30
Eritrea	21.5	11
Tigray	5.6	18
Other	11.9	9

The left-hand column indicates the amount of food aid distributed, at the height of famine relief operations, by the RRC in each region. We can readily see that food aid under the control of the RRC did not always go to famine-stricken populations in order of priority as assessed by that same agency. Notably, Wollo was considered by the RRC to be the worst-affected region, but ranked second as a recipient of food aid, outweighed by the southern provinces. We should note here that the famine barely affected the south, being confined to pockets of distress, so the RRC's estimate of numbers of southern victims may be exaggerated. Eritrea received a great deal more food aid than Tigray, despite having many fewer estimated victims. A Spearman rank-order coefficient shows a relatively weak correlation of 0.6 between order of need and order of food receipts.

The level of aggregation conceals further biases in food distribution at the regional level. It is clear from reports of fieldworkers and journalists at the time that food aid was allocated by the RRC in ways that supported the political objectives of government (Niggli 1985; Clay and Holcomb 1986; Mitchell 1987). In particular, food was used as an inducement to assist the policy of resettlement. Sometimes this policy was carried out by force; in other cases famine victims who volunteered for resettlement, and who were able-bodied, were given rations. Those who did not volunteer or who did volunteer but were considered old or unfit did not receive rations. Extremely marasmic elderly people and adolescents begging outside government food stores were a common sight even during the height of emergency feeding operations in northern Ethiopia in 1985.

We must, of course, be chary of always assuming that "the government" is in fact the individuals or parties having been elected to power, or even having seized it. If the government is made up of competing factions in an uneasy coalition, one faction may wield more influence than another. For famine control, it may be, for example, that the civilian government is willing to allow aid agencies to mop up the effects of war and starvation in some areas, whereas locally powerful "governments" (especially army officers) may have contrary ideas.

Central government is often powerless to enforce its decisions in remote regions, even if it has the desire to do so. It may sometimes go through the motions of allowing access to a famine area, knowing that it is unlikely that locally powerful groups will allow their enemies to receive aid. In such cases, even the central government's own famine relief officers may be prevented from doing their jobs, by threat or force if necessary. An egregious example concerns the looting of relief grain stores at Raga in Southern Kordofan, Sudan, in 1988 by the army and townspeople, during which operation the government's own relief officer was forced to flee the scene (Cutler and Keen 1989).

At this point it will be pointed out by critics of the approach adopted in this chapter that I am deliberately picking out worst-case examples of the primacy of the politics of resource allocation during famines. It is, of course, the war-torn African countries that currently have the worst famines and many of the worst examples of biased relief allocation. This is why naive optimists invariably turn to South Asian examples for inspiration as to how the process of famine early warning and response can be improved. Similarly, they point to African countries such as Botswana, Kenya, and Lesotho to show how successful famine control can be.

Unfortunately, such countries are not typical of famine-prone nations. They are peaceful, Western-aligned, and relatively prosperous. They have degrees of democracy and freedom of information unheard of in countries undergoing civil war. Yet, even in these excellent cases of famine management, one will find processes of biased resource allocation at work, each an accurate reflection of the prevailing balances of political power among ethnic groups and classes (see the excellent BRAC studies concerning the allocation of aid in Bangladesh, to take but one example). The outcomes just tend to be a lot less bloody.

Priorities of Donor Governments

Again we must be careful to differentiate between what donor governments say they do and what they actually do. One might be forgiven for getting the impression, according to the official version of the policy cycle, that information is received at the head office, carefully sifted, and objectively prioritized, for that is what donors say they do. The actual process is not like that at all. Information from "enemy" countries is pushed off the agenda and is barely considered. Information from allies is taken seriously. In the latter case, information about famine in some regions tends to be taken more seriously and acted upon than in others.

A most blatant example of this is U.S. support for famine victims in Darfur and Kordofan in 1984, as compared to the almost complete neglect of the Beja and the Ethiopian famine refugees in the eastern part of the country at the time. The latter two populations were far more accessible by road and were close to the seaport. Objectively the Beja and the refugees were in as much, if not more, need of famine aid in terms of death rates and levels of undernutrition. One is led to conclude that the Beja and displaced Ethiopians were considered of little political importance in comparison with the rebellious Darfurans and Kordofanis, whose provinces are uncomfortably close to Libya.

It should also be noted that if a friendly country takes steps to prevent famine, for example through purchasing food from abroad, then its sponsors will quickly sit up and take notice. Examples include Kenya and Bangladesh in 1984. These governments prioritized famine control among the rural poor and were rapidly supported by Western donors without having to elaborately justify their actions. An effective response to famine requires rapid host government action, even where donors are well disposed toward additional assistance. The host government has prime moral responsibility for famine control— that is, if one may continue to see famine as a moral issue in the face of political realities.

In cases when the government does not endeavor to control famine, the actions of donors become transparent. If little or no action is taken, then it is clear that the lives of famine victims are a great deal less important than existing trade and aid agreements. A case in point is Sudan, post-Nimeiri. Here the NGOs and IGOs struggled to deliver famine relief to displaced famine victims in the face of, at best, official indifference and, at worst, official obfuscation. Death rates in famine camps such as Abeyei and Meiram exceeding those recorded in the recent Ethiopian famine were the result (Cutler and Keen 1989).

Official pressure could have been brought to bear on the government to rectify this situation, in the form of threatened trade and aid sanctions. Instead, weakly worded memoranda were tabled requesting that Western NGOs be granted access to famine victims at the edge of the war zone. Given that most Western sponsors of the El Mahdi regime and its successor (Canada and the Netherlands being notable exceptions) failed to threaten or implement sanctions until Sudan's support for Iraq during the Gulf War was revealed, one must assume that the famine was officially condoned in the interests of maintaining Western influence on the government.

The Role of Intergovernmental Organizations

The IGOs, especially the UN agencies, are in a cleft stick. They are officially supposed to represent their member states, so the lead agency in a famine-affected country (usually the United Nations Development Programme, UNDP) is supposed to act according to the policies of that country's government. However, the agencies get the bulk of their funds from the rich countries. Consequently, they will tend to side with the paymasters, or at least do little to upset them. The penalties of doing so can be grave, as UNESCO (and, to a lesser extent, the Food and Agriculture Organization, FAO) have discovered. Head offices of UN agencies are particularly sensitive to these pressures and also are forced to reflect the views of their numerous client states.

One outcome of this process was FAO's insistence that twenty-four countries in Africa faced famine in 1983–84. Lobbying from African governments that were marginal cases ensured that they were placed on the list of affected countries and could claim a share of the potential spoils. Yet, no serious attempt was made by FAO to differentiate between degrees of severity of crisis among the twenty-four countries. Instead, donor agencies routinely received telexes making yet another famine appeal for cases both obvious and obscure.

In cases where the UN agency has representation in a country where there clearly is famine, yet the host government is doing little or nothing to respond, again it is in an uncomfortable position. If an emergency has not officially been declared, the Resident Representatives of the various UN agencies will find it extremely risky to cause a fuss. Expulsion may result, and there have been examples of this. UNICEF lost officials following the Ethiopian famine of 1973 and following lobbying and public exposure of famine by the Resident Representative for Sudan in 1988. We should further note that conscience-troubled individuals among the IGOs stand on their own. The rest of the UN system will not protect one of its members should he or she break ranks and risk expulsion.

The Role of the Nongovernmental Organizations

NGOs are in a contradictory position with regard to famine control. Often their staff are among the best informed of all the agency actors operating in a famine zone. Yet, they are the least likely to challenge the system or influence governments. This is because NGOs are highly vulnerable. Their activities are basically unessential to the host government; when one is expelled, others will generally be jostling to take its place.

NGOs tend to be competitive and fragmented, each jealously guarding its own information. Coordination among them tends to be poor and, at best, takes the form of agreements to stick to one's patch. It has been noted that famine relief operations resemble modern-day Berlin agreements, where African countries are carved up into agency spheres of influence (Independent Commission for International Humanitarian Issues 1985). Within these spheres, NGOs follow their own agendas and organize operations according to their own procedures. For example, it is often difficult to get agreement on standardized information-collection procedures or on such activities as measuring techniques and cutoff points for defining degrees of undernutrition with anthropometric data.

Although there may be cooperation and information sharing among NGOs, particularly at a regional level, there is little or no compulsion for them to follow agreed procedures. The host government often has little idea of what precisely these organizations are doing or whether their operations are effective. In some extreme cases, the government might not even be aware how many NGOs are operating in the country. One of the first tasks of the newly established Sudanese Relief and Rehabilitation Commission was to discover exactly how many NGOs were operating in Sudan.

As conduits of information about famine, individual NGOs may lobby government or donors, particularly their own government in the case of foreign NGOs. Again, coordination is usually limited to appeals for aid after the declared event, such as through the Disasters Emergency Committee in the United Kingdom. At least until recently —in 1990 there was a combined appeal to forestall famine in Ethiopia—it has been rare that collective lobbying takes place before famine becomes public knowledge.

A complicating factor is that some NGOs, especially those with a development orientation, may find it difficult to recognize the early symptoms of famine. In general, agencies suffer from tunnel vision; they know what is going on in their own operational areas but not nationally or regionally. Similarly, they tend to tackle famines in a piecemeal fashion, firefighting in their own project areas.

Since the famines of the 1980s, some NGOs have developed greater awareness of their potential role. Organizations such as Oxfam and Save the Children in the United Kingdom have invested heavily in regional information systems in famine-prone African countries. They have elevated themselves to a more powerful political position in the process, hoping to take on a greater international role in information brokering and consequent access to resources among agencies and governments. However, the information systems are expensive and are likely to be maintained only with recurrent injections of donor capital.

An Example of the Response to Famine: Ethiopia, 1983–85

Schaffer's idea of bureaucracies avoiding responsibility for effective action to combat famine is very useful in explaining how developing famines come to be ignored by the very institutions that ostensibly exist to prevent or, at least, mitigate them. However, if we are to explain how those same bureaucracies can become galvanized into extraordinary action, we must show how the concept of risk changes with changing circumstances.

An interesting example is the case of the 1983–85 Ethiopian famine, when it was initially risky for agency representatives to press for a response owing to resistance on behalf of their superiors in Europe and North America. Following the dramatic TV coverage of the famine, immense political pressure was put on those same organizations to respond. The risk profile had reversed; it had become risky *not* to be seen responding. Let us look at this case in a little more detail.

The Ethiopian famine was basically drought induced, with crop failures gradually becoming more severe and more widespread over a period lasting from approximately 1979 onward (English, Bennett, and Dick 1984; Cutler 1988). Crop failures were concentrated in northern regions inaccessible to the central government and, for the most part, were among populations politically and militarily opposed to the regime. Information about the famine was therefore partial, and an overall picture would have to be pieced together from both government and rebel sources. Despite this constraint, both sides were calling repeatedly for famine relief, especially from 1981 onward. These calls were endorsed by NGOs having access to the famine areas and at the international level by the Food and Agriculture Organization through the Global Information and Early Warning System.

In the meantime, there was tremendous reluctance among Western donors to support the famine relief efforts of the government, the rebels, or the NGOs. One of the more extreme examples of this was the response of the U.S. Agency for International Development (USAID), as documented by the General Accounting Office (GAO). This agency took five months to endorse the shipment of a paltry 838 metric tons of food aid to a U.S. NGO in 1982 and a further seven months to approve only half of a request for 16,000 metric tons in 1983 (U.S. General Accounting Office 1985; see also Chapter 5). Further examples have been documented for the European Community and other major food donors (Gill 1985). In the words of one EC official at the time, getting food aid for Ethiopian famine victims was extremely difficult because "it was always a question of how to present the problem" (Gill 1985, 79).

It is obvious from the lack of action on the part of donors that Ethiopia was to be given a minimum of famine relief assistance. What was forthcoming would only be in response to unambiguous "measurable" need, that is, distress migration of victims to famine camps. Such migration began in late 1982 and grew in fits and starts over 1983. By mid-1984 it had become massive and overwhelming in the northern provinces, with over one million people seeking relief. The response from the donors even at this time was extremely niggardly.

Various escape routes could be employed by agency officials to account for their lack of action. Most commonly, lack of concrete evidence could be cited, as access to the famine areas was very limited and no foreign agency was mandated to collect systematic information about the famine. Official government sources were ignored, largely on the grounds that the authorities could be said to be "crying wolf" year after year. One official was recorded as saying that if the figures were true "at least a million people would have died by now" (Cutler 1988, 362). The official was outspoken, but his words were an honest reflection of attitudes common at the time. It is also sad to reflect that the final death toll of the famine was considered by the UN eventually to have reached a million human beings.

The IGO view was strengthened by an Office of Special Relief Operations (OSRO) report, which in March 1984 argued that Ethiopia could handle only 125,000 metric tons of relief food annually, whereas 685,000 tons was actually estimated as being required at the time (Food and Agriculture Organization 1984). By accepting the apparent transport constraint, the OSRO report appeared to endorse the lower figure as a requirement. However, at the height of relief operations in 1985, up to 3,000 metric tons of food aid *a day* were brought into the country, and food aid requirements were then estimated at 1.5 million tons by FAO.

Many NGO employees were aware that the situation was deteriorating rapidly. This is clear from the minutes of the monthly meetings of the NGO coordination committee, the Christian Relief and Development Association, in Addis Ababa. However, the NGOs as a whole were fearful of appearing critical of government and donors and made no public statement about the famine until September 1984. This was very late in the day for effective action.

The Ethiopian famine became common knowledge in late October 1984, when television footage filmed by Michael Buerke and Mohammed Amin of the BBC was screened around the world. The Western public was outraged at what had occurred. Donations poured into charities operating in the famine areas, and questions about the slow response to the famine were put to political representatives of the people in democratic countries, where such questions could legitimately be asked. Suddenly, the risk profile changed dramatically for donors and IGOs and for those NGOs that did not already have operations in Ethiopia. There was now a risk that they would be blamed for inadequate action.

Their response was, for the most part, characteristic and clever. Long lists were produced detailing aid donations to Ethiopia past and present. Large grants were made by donors and IGOs to NGO subcontractors. Task forces were set up to assure the public that the famine was being prioritized. New funds were sought by agencies and voted by governments, although sometimes funds were simply transferred from less essential budgets. In the case of the UN system, completely new offices were set up to give the impression of concerted, effective action. One of these was the UN Office for Emergency Operations in Ethiopia (UNEOE).

If one reads accounts of the UNEOE, particularly that authored by Jansson, Harris, and Penrose (1987), one could be forgiven for believing that the UN oversaw the famine relief operation. This was not strictly true, as the UN did not have "the power of the purse" (Kent 1986). Western donor governments, mindful of their continued suspicions of the Ethiopian regime, poured as much aid as possible through the medium of their national NGOs, whose operations expanded dramatically as a result. Other resources were pushed through the IGOs. The Ethiopian government received only about one-third of the famine aid, which—as we have already seen—it promptly distributed according to its own priorities.

Meanwhile, UNEOE dispatched field monitors to try to identify the whereabouts of food shipments. Occasionally, when gross abuses or "mistakes" came to light, pressure from UNEOE would ensure that they were corrected. An example concerned the incineration of Ibnat relief camp and banishment of its occupants, which occurred in April 1985, carried out by an overzealous official who was later reprimanded for overstepping the mark. However, in other cases, such as regular distributions of relief food to the militia in Eritrea (which explains the relatively large allocations of food aid to government-held towns in this region, as illustrated in Table 4.1), a discrete diplomatic silence was maintained by UNEOE.

For many NGOs, the famine represented a bonanza of opportunity. Some entered the country for the first time and established relief and development projects. Others grew phenomenally and diversified from their normal development activities, setting up truck fleets and information systems. The latter became particularly popular, as the lack of early famine control was conveniently blamed by the donors on insufficient early warning. This bureaucratic escape route meant that funds were made available by donors immediately after the famine to boost information systems.

Unfortunately, as the famine came under control, the money supply dried up, and the NGOs and the IGOs began laying off staff. The recession in the famine industry, plus an understandable sensitivity on the part of agency staff, caused any shortfall in food production in the years of recovery to be viewed with alarm and to be held up as another potential famine. However, the famine gradually faded from the consciousness of the Western public, and the risk profile returned to its previous state, with the Ethiopian government being viewed with extreme suspicion by donors and with IGO staff unable to involve themselves in effective long-term development work.

Is Famine Control Improving?

Since the great African famines of the 1980s, a lot of work has been put into upgrading information systems, ostensibly to improve response to potential famine. There is no doubt that much of this effort is already paying dividends in terms of early warning, especially in Ethiopia, where timely warning was given of the threat of famine in the closing months of 1989.

Warning may have improved, coordination among agencies (notably NGOs) has certainly improved, and development efforts continue. Yet, famine control—the response to early warning—is still politically conditioned. We may take Sudan as a pertinent and current example. It is most depressing to witness all the sterling efforts being made in northern Sudan to predict and prevent famine, while a dreadful death toll has resulted from war and mass starvation in the south.

For much of the 1980s in Sudan it was politically difficult for humanitarian organizations, financed by Western powers, to persuade their sponsors to put pressure on an ally to find a peaceful solution to conflict and, at the very least, to allow access by humanitarian organizations to victims in or adjacent to the war zones. Existing trade and aid agreements, dictated by realpolitik, came first, as we might expect. Since the Gulf War, the situation has changed dramatically, with Western donors demonstrating extreme displeasure with the Islamic government in power. Nevertheless, the threat or even the reality of sanctions has had little effect on the government's foreign policy or on its treatment of famine victims.

It seems that if it is politically acceptable to both donor and host governments for organizations to labor to control famine, then progress can be made. If it is not, then professional relief and development workers are expected to acquiesce to conditions dictated by realpolitik. Unless professionals are willing systematically and consistently to challenge the status quo in such circumstances, and can at the same time gain the support of powerful actors able to influence or directly control the allocation of aid, famine will never wholly be eradicated.

Conclusion

The precise configuration of response to famine will depend upon the degree to which the government prioritizes famine control and upon relations between it and donor governments. To a lesser extent it also depends upon the government's ability to enforce its writ. The role of the IGOs and NGOs is secondary as a means of famine control. Famines happen because governments allow them to happen.

In general, the professional relief and development agencies will avoid the risks of challenging donors and the host government when famine breaks out among unpopular groups of victims. They utilize various easily identifiable escape routes in order to do this. A serious

political attack by a relief agency on donors and hosts can lead to
financial sanctions and even to expulsion of the agency or its representatives. Equally, IGOs and NGOs will reap rewards if the famine
becomes popularized and the donors and host government are forced
to act.

Without effective sponsors, famine victims become asset-stripped
and starve. Their best hope is to be born in a country with a reasonably free press, a concerned middle class, and a Western-oriented foreign policy.

References

Bangladesh Rural Advancement Committee (BRAC). 1979. *Who Gets What and
Why: Resource Association in a Bangladesh Village.* Dhaka: BRAC.
Brietzke, P. H. 1982. *Law, Development and the Ethiopian Revolution.* Lewisburg,
Penn.: Bucknell University Press.
Clay, Jason W., and B. K. Holcomb. 1986. *Politics and the Ethiopian Famine:
1984–1985.* Cambridge: Cultural Survival.
Cutler, Peter. 1988. "The Development of the 1983–85 Famine in Northern
Ethiopia." Ph.D. diss., London School of Hygiene and Tropical Medicine.
Cutler, Peter, and David Keen. 1989. "Evaluation of EC Emergency, Rehabilita-
tion and Food Aid to Sudan, 1985–88." Brighton, U.K.: Institute of Devel-
opment Studies, University of Sussex.
Devereux, Stephen. 1988. "Entitlements, Availability and Famine: A Revision-
ist View of Wollo, 1972–74." *Food Policy* 13, 3: 270–282.
English, J., J. Bennett, and B. Dick. 1984. "Tigray 1984: An Investigation."
Oxford: Oxfam.
Food and Agriculture Organization. 1984. "Ethiopia: Assessment of the Food
and Agriculture Situation." Rome: Office for Special Relief Operations.
Mimeo.
Gill, Peter. 1985. *A Year in the Death of Africa: Politics, Bureaucracy and the
Famine.* London: Paladin.
Independent Commission for International Humanitarian Issues. 1985.
Famine: A Man-Made Disaster? London: Pan.
Jansson K., M. Harris, and A. Penrose. 1987. *The Ethiopian Famine.* London:
Zed Books.
Keen, David. 1988. "The Distribution of Food Aid in Darfur." Oxford: Queen
Elizabeth House, University of Oxford, Mimeo.
Kent, Randolph. 1986. "The Aid Imbroglio." School of International Relations,
University of Southern California, Bedford College, London. Mimeo.
Mitchell, John. 1987. "The Famine Relief Operation in Wollo." London: Over-
seas Development Administration. Mimeo.
Niggli, Peter. 1985. "Ethiopia: Deportation and Forced Labor Camps." Cam-
bridge: Cultural Survival.
Pankhurst, Richard. 1985. *The History of Famine and Epidemics in Ethiopia Prior to
the Twentieth Century.* Addis Ababa: Relief and Rehabilitation Commission.

Schaffer, Bernard. 1984. "Towards Responsibility: Public Policy in Concept and Practice." In *Room for Manoeuvre*, edited by Edward J. Clay and Bernard B. Schaffer, 142–190. London: Heinemann.

Sen, Amartya. 1981. *Poverty and Famines: An Essay on Entitlement and Deprivation*. Oxford: Clarendon Press.

Shepherd, Jack. 1975. *The Politics of Starvation*. New York and Washington, D.C.: Carnegie Endowment for International Peace.

United States General Accounting Office. 1985. "The United States' Response to the Ethiopian Food Crisis." Report to the Honorable Byron L. Dorgan, U.S. House of Representatives, 8 April.

5

"Some Tragic Errors"

American Policy and the Ethiopian Famine,
1981–85

Jack Shepherd

Obviously, something went wrong. Literally hundreds upon hundreds
of thousands of people have died in the past two-year period. . . . For
whatever reasons, be it bureaucratic insensitivity at different points, be
it simply food projections that were off target or whatever the reasons,
the fact of the matter is, we made some tragic errors.
　　　　　　　—Representative Howard Wolpe of Michigan,
　　　　　　　　　　　　Chairman, Subcommittee on Africa,
　　　　　　　　　　　　House Foreign Affairs Committee
　　　　　　　　　　　　(House Committee 1985, 93–94, 102)

In December 1980, one month after Ronald Reagan's election to the
presidency, John Block, the Illinois farmer selected by the new president to be his secretary of agriculture, told reporters: "I believe food is
now the greatest weapon we have for keeping peace in the world."
Mr. Block envisioned the United States shipping its agricultural surpluses to hungry nations in return for "more stability in the world."

During the 1970s and 1980s, U.S. food aid became an increasingly
important instrument of U.S. foreign policy. Tremendous growth in
agricultural production in the United States came at a time of increasing hunger and malnutrition among many nations of the Third World,
especially those in Africa. In 1974, the Central Intelligence Agency
(CIA) (1974, 2) warned:

> The United States now provides nearly three-fourths of the world's net
> grain exports and its role is almost certain to grow over the next sev-
> eral decades. The world's increasing dependence on American sur-
> pluses portends an increase in U.S. power and influence, especially

vis-à-vis the food-deficit poor countries. Indeed, in times of shortage, the United States will face difficult choices about how to allocate its surpluses between affluent purchasers and the hungry world.

The CIA believed that the U.S. food surplus instrument would have an "enormous" impact on international relations. "It could give the U.S. a measure of power it had never had before—possibly an economic and political dominance greater than that of the immediate post World War II years" (Central Intelligence Agency 1974, 39). Moreover, the CIA analysis continued, any major food shortages might exacerbate a North-South confrontation, cause destabilization, and thereby enhance the power of food as an instrument of U.S. foreign policy. The CIA analysis continued (1974, 36–37):

> The elites of many LDC's tend to regard periodic famine as either natural or at least beyond their power to prevent, e.g. Bihar in 1967, Ethiopia and the Sahelian states in 1973. But the rural masses may become less docile in the future and if famine also threatens the cities and reduces the living standards of the middle classes, it could lead to social and political upheavals which cripple government authority. The beleaguered governments could become more difficult to deal with on international issues either because of a collapse in ability to meet commitments or through a greatly heightened nationalism and aggressiveness.

Implied in the CIA analysis was the possibility that food shortages could destabilize a fragile country and topple its ruler. The analysis was new and turned out to be timely. A month after this report was distributed to the Nixon administration, Emperor Haile Selassie was overthrown in Ethiopia—partly as a result of widespread popular unrest caused by a large-scale famine. The CIA analysis appeared to be correct: Food shortages could destabilize regimes. The perception— erroneous or not—that denying food aid might topple a government was not lost on Reagan administration officials ten years later.

By 1980, when Secretary Block was defining a foreign policy that would play a key role in the first Reagan administration, "the worst food crisis of this century" (Legum 1984, 25) was underway in Africa. By 1982, about 150 million people—perhaps one African in every three below the Sahara—needed emergency food aid. The United States had on hand the "instrument" that Secretary Block described. By the early years of the Reagan administration, the United States was growing and exporting more food than any other nation in the world. It dominated the world food supply. Two out of every five acres of U.S. farmland produced food for export; half of that food went to Third World markets (Schultz 1983). The United States was "the world's largest food donor"; U.S. silos stored half of the world's grain reserves (House Select Committee 1984; Congressional Research Service 1984a). This vast productive capacity, juxtaposed against Africa's desperate need, illustrated the awesome power of the U.S. food instrument available to President Reagan. The United States, by giving or withholding food aid—by feeding some people and not others—could control not only human lives but also governments.

Ethiopia offered an excellent, if tragic, opportunity for the Reagan administration to employ this food aid instrument. By 1983, more than five million Ethiopians were reportedly suffering from famine, and death from starvation was a daily occurrence in twelve of Ethiopia's fourteen provinces. Requests for food aid from Ethiopia exceeded 1.5 million metric tons. The House Select Committee on Hunger (1985, 2, 3, 5) said that in 1984 alone more than 300,000 Ethiopians starved to death. Ethiopia in 1981–84 also illustrates how food aid was used during the Cold War as an instrument of U.S. foreign policy. Ethiopia's Marxist government was the leading Soviet client in Africa; severe famine came to its people at the precise moment when the government of the world's leading food aid donor was in the hands of anti-Soviet, anti-Marxist ideologues.

The History of U.S. Food Aid

The history of U.S. food aid in the twentieth century contains two basic themes: the overwhelming use of U.S. food as a political instrument, and the persistent use of U.S. food aid as an anticommunist weapon. The two were often intertwined. Shortly after the Russian Revolution in 1917, U.S. food policy was linked to fighting communism. For example, President Woodrow Wilson informed the chairman of the House Appropriations Committee in 1918 (Hoover 1960, 362):

> Food relief is now the key to the whole European situation and to the solution of peace. Bolshevism is steadily advancing westward and has overwhelmed Poland, and is poisoning Germany. It cannot be stopped by force, but it can be stopped by food.

In May 1945, President Harry S Truman met with Secretary of War Henry Stimson to discuss the need to feed war-torn Europe. Truman (1955, 236) later wrote that Stimson

> observed that there was a strong probability of pestilence and famine throughout central Europe during the following winter. This, he felt, was likely to be followed by political revolution and communistic infiltration. Our defence against this situation would be the western

governments. . . . It was vital to keep these countries from being driven to revolution or communism by famine.

The first legislated method for dispensing U.S. food aid to other nations was the Agricultural Trade Development and Assistance Act (Public Law 83-480), passed in 1954. Commonly referred to as P.L. 480 or, later, as the Food for Peace Act, this legislation remains today the primary vehicle for selling or giving U.S. food aid to other nations.

During the first three decades of P.L. 480, U.S. presidents used food aid as a carrot and stick in a U.S. foreign policy predicated on confronting the Soviet Union and its satellite countries. P.L. 480 food was denied to countries that were already communist, such as Cuba or North Korea, or that nationalized U.S. property. The United States reduced levels of food aid as a signal to antigovernment insurgents to overthrow disfavored regimes—such as Diem in South Vietnam in 1963 and Allende in Chile in 1973; and it combined these policies with covert action (Truman 1955). "P.L. 480 permanently institutionalized U.S. food aid at a time when the Cold War shaped American foreign policy," writes Marc Cohen (1984, 141). "As a result, the U.S. government has provided food assistance to shore up favored regimes, and denied it to governments pursuing 'communistic' policies."

Under this policy, sub-Saharan Africa, with little to offer the superpowers, may have suffered more than any other continent. In 1975, despite widespread famine across the Sahel and Horn, sub-Saharan Africa received just 8.5 percent of all P.L. 480 assistance. Food shortages and starvation during 1981–84 caused that figure to rise to about 24 percent of all P.L. 480 relief aid by 1985, and then again fall sharply. At no time did sub-Saharan Africa receive more food aid than any other region except Central America between 1983 and 1986.

The Reagan Administration's Foreign Policy Orientation

When the Reagan administration took office in January 1981, it labeled its first term a "New Beginning" for conservative politics in the United States. These were men and women whose messianic vision saw foreign policy, and especially U.S.-Soviet relations, in simple terms: good versus evil, right versus wrong. The United States was infinitely virtuous, the Soviet Union infinitely wicked. The president called the Soviet Union "the evil empire" and "the focus of evil in the modern world" (Reagan 1985b and 1985c).

In a major policy shift, the Reagan administration advocated the support of insurgents seeking to overthrow communist regimes. Reagan officials believed that the Soviets had won new influence in at least nine countries during the previous decade: South Vietnam, Cambodia, and Laos in Southeast Asia; South Yemen in the Middle East; Afghanistan in South Asia; Nicaragua in Central America; and Angola, Mozambique, and Ethiopia in Africa. The president took office with an inviolate pledge: He would not lose "one inch of soil" to communism (Sewell, Feinberg, and Kallab 1985, 8). His policy instead would seek both a "containment" and a "rollback" of those communist gains.

In its first three budgets, the Reagan administration sought to trim P.L. 480 food aid program proposals while increasing military assistance to anticommunist countries. During its first year in office, the administration cut all P.L. 480 food aid allotments to Nicaragua, Poland, Mozambique, and Ethiopia despite increasing evidence of hunger in those countries. The suspension of food aid to Mozambique and Ethiopia even included P.L. 480 Title II emergency food aid requested as starvation spread among their people.

Next, administration officials highlighted a number of Marxist governments facing internal insurgencies. As Anthony Lake writes (1985, 141),

> Under Reagan there has been more emphasis on the removal of offending regimes, a higher tolerance or even encouragement of conflicts that impose costs on radical regimes and their people, a less activist diplomacy, more reliance on the threat of use of force, and less reliance on economic blandishments.

Previously, the United States had confined itself to helping noncommunist governments to defend themselves against Soviet-supported insurgencies. The new Reagan conservatives, however, sought an activist foreign policy that would directly support anticommunist insurgents seeking to overthrow pro-Soviet regimes. It was a new, innovative, and—to conservative Americans—highly attractive policy initiative. Most important, it was a policy that advocated action rather than reaction and that sought to reach beyond "containment" to "roll back" the tide of Soviet expansionism by supporting anti-Soviet insurgents.

During its first four years, officials of the Reagan administration put into place a new policy, later called the Reagan Doctrine. At its heart, the doctrine called for U.S. support for "revolutionary democracy" as a foreign policy; it sought to sponsor armed insurgencies against Soviet-backed governments in the Third World. President Reagan (1985a) called for active U.S. support of "freedom fighters" to turn back Soviet expansion along the edges of the empire. Reagan backed Islamic rebels in Afghanistan, revived the long-dormant opposition in the bush of Angola, and overtly and covertly funded guerrillas—

the "moral equivalent of our Founding Fathers" (Reagan 1985b)—opposing the Marxist government of Nicaragua. The president described his policy to Congress in these terms (Johnson 1986, 2):

> We must not break faith with those who are risking their lives on every continent, from Afghanistan to Nicaragua, to defy Soviet supported aggression and secure rights which have been ours from birth. . . . Support for freedom fighters is self-defense.

In his Saturday radio talks, President Reagan said that he supported freedom fighters anywhere because they were "fighting for an end to tyranny." He spoke of supporting "our brothers" fighting in revolutionary movements "in Afghanistan, in Ethiopia, Cambodia, Angola [and] Nicaragua." At the heart of Reagan's anticommunism was the idea that the United States would use its vast economic and political resources in support of anticommunist opposition everywhere in the world. And part of those U.S. resources, as John Block had made clear, was U.S. food aid.

Famine in Ethiopia

The first known famine in Ethiopia occurred in the ninth century, but detailed records of Ethiopian famines go back only to the sixteenth century. Amartya Sen (1981) reports that between 1540 and 1742 there were perhaps ten major Ethiopian famines.[1] Pankhurst (1961 and 1965) cites references to twenty-three major famines in Ethiopian chronicles between 1540 and 1800 and to an additional five in Tigray and Shoa provinces before the Great Famine of 1888–92. Pankhurst reports that Tigray suffered famine every five years between 1864 and 1929, and in 1913 and 1914 missionaries reported seeing "crowds of starving people and walking skeletons" in Tigray (Pankhurst 1965, 60).

The worst recorded famine in Ethiopia's history, "The Great Ethiopian Famine" of 1889–92, became "the benchmark" against which all subsequent environmental disasters were measured (McCann 1987, 30), perhaps because as many as one-third of the total Ethiopian population died. The Great Famine was so devastating that Ethiopians still call it *Kifu Ken* (evil days). Large numbers of people drifted around the highlands begging for food and searching in the forests for wild fruits and the roots of wild plants. Hungry peasants picked through animal dung for grain seeds or ground old cow hides into powder and made cake. A Lazarist missionary in Keren wrote in 1890: "Everywhere I meet walking skeletons and even horrible corpses, half eaten by hyenas, of starvelings who had collapsed from exhaustion" (Pankhurst 1965, 71).

The famine that occurred in Ethiopia between 1972 and 1974 might have been of little consequence—simply one in a chain of famines—except for two factors. First, about 200,000 Ethiopians are believed to have died from starvation or starvation-related causes during the two-year period. Second, the 1972–74 famine played a central and catalytic role in ending the 2,000-year-old Ethiopian empire—a role not lost on policymakers in the Reagan administration ten years later. The famine also put on the ground in Ethiopia private voluntary organizations (PVOs) whose workers were in place as famine conditions erupted again in the early 1980s. The two famines, 1972–74 and 1982–85, were not separate events.

The famine of 1972–74 contained several parallels to that of 1982–84 as well as to past Ethiopian famines. The reaction of the peasants was similar in 1972–74 and 1982–84; drought and war added to the failure of consecutive harvests, which in turn led to the eating of planting seeds and the final outward migration of peasants to the Addis-Asmara road in search of food. Also, both the Selassie and Mengistu governments denied to the Ethiopian people that starvation was taking place in the northern provinces—and did so to avoid embarrassment during a tenth anniversary celebration (the Organization of African Unity [OAU] in 1974 and, ten years later, the anniversary of the Marxist revolution and formation of the Workers Party).

On the U.S. side, Reagan officials appeared to have learned at least two major lessons from the 1972–74 famine. First, delay of food aid was seen as an acceptable policy, not as unconscionable. The international donors had established in 1972–73 a history of delay in getting food aid to Ethiopia (and other parts of Africa). In the early 1980s, despite warnings of widespread starvation, the donors reacted in much the same way; they complained of African states "crying wolf" or of "donor fatigue." The Reagan administration, by delaying food aid to Ethiopia, simply became part of this history and suffered no political or moral consequences from doing so.

Second, Reagan officials clearly believed that any delay of food aid could be politically catastrophic in Ethiopia. The administration's perception of the events of 1972–74 was that famine had destabilized Ethiopia and helped cause the coup against Haile Selassie. Famine might be used in 1981–84 to destabilize the Marxist government. To the administration, the history lesson was obvious: By coupling famine with delay of food aid, the donors might bring down a weakened government.

Of all the causes of Ethiopia's chronic famine, war may be the most significant. Civil war in the northern highlands added to Ethiopia's ecological degradation and diminished its agricultural output. The guerrilla war in Eritrea began in 1962, followed by war in Tigray in

1975; both wars concentrated in the populated central highlands, prime agricultural areas, and spilled over into surrounding provinces.

War blocked the principal port of Massawa, disrupted food shipments inland, and halted emergency feeding operations in the highlands. It combined with erosion and drought to destroy Ethiopia's ecology. "Erosion in many areas," Oxfam U.K. (1984, 16) reported, "is on a catastrophic scale." Long-term projects of soil and water conservation and reforestation were halted, reducing the prize for victory in this war to "an infertile wasteland" (Oxfam U.K. 1984, 15).

The Ethiopian government also used food aid as a weapon in its struggle against the Eritreans and Tigrayans: once in 1975, again in 1982, and for a third time in 1988. In 1982, when the Mengistu government tried to isolate and starve Ethiopians living in areas controlled by guerrilla forces in Eritrea or Tigray, the Eritrean Peoples Liberation Front (EPLF) set up the Eritrean Relief Association (ERA), and the Tigrean Peoples Liberation Front (TPLF) put together the Relief Society of Tigray (REST) to work with the international food aid donors. The guerrillas maintained that ERA and REST were separate, humanitarian organizations removed from the politics of their struggle. This nuance made them acceptable to the PVOs and church relief agencies.

The Reagan Response

By 1983, the extent and seriousness of the famine sweeping sub-Saharan Africa and the Horn were clear. The Food and Agriculture Organization (FAO) sent telegrams to twenty-seven nations, including the United States, warning them of "catastrophic food shortages" in sub-Saharan Africa; 120 million Africans in twenty-two countries needed four million tons of emergency food aid (Weinraub 1983; Kamm 1983). The Ethiopian government had itself made urgent appeals to the international donors and agencies for emergency food assistance; perhaps five million Ethiopians were affected by the famine, and the nation expected at least a 250,000-ton food shortfall in 1983 (Economist Intelligence Unit 1982; Steele 1983).[2] A U.S. government investigation of the administration's response to famine in Ethiopia stated: "The United States knew that a potentially serious food shortage situation existed in the northern provinces of Ethiopia in late 1982" (General Accounting Office 1985, i). A United Nations expert on Ethiopia said the country was "one of the most likely sites for the world's first super famine" (*Africa Research Bulletin* 1984b).

What was the Reagan administration response? Between 1981 and 1983, the administration sought to cut the P.L. 480 food aid program for sub-Saharan Africa by one-third, matched by an almost 300 percent increase in U.S. military aid to the same region (Wasserman 1983). The Reagan budget appropriations for Ethiopia remained level at 6,642 metric tons. For the fiscal year 1984 budget, planned in 1983, the administration sought to allocate *no emergency food aid* for Ethiopia despite that country's widespread hunger. It wished to cut its Title II allotment for Ethiopia to zero.

Nowhere is the Reagan policy more clear than in its treatment of Catholic Relief Services (CRS), the official relief and development agency of the American Roman Catholic community. From 1982 through 1984, the administration deliberately delayed its response to emergency food aid requests for Ethiopia by CRS. In 1982, CRS was the largest private voluntary organization on the ground in Ethiopia.[3] It had been operating P.L. 480 feeding programs in Ethiopia since 1975, mostly for preschool children and pregnant or lactating women. In the autumn of 1982, CRS workers submitted a written proposal to the U.S. Agency for International Development (USAID) for additional P.L. 480 Title II food aid for an emergency feeding program in Makelle, the capital of Tigray province. The request reached Washington in December 1982. CRS asked for 838 metric tons of P.L. 480 Title II food and the necessary ocean transportation fees; CRS would pay the inland transportation costs (General Accounting Office 1985, 13).

CRS thought 838 tons of food would feed some 5,000 families in Makelle for about nine months. The CRS request was supported by a cable from the U.S. Embassy in Addis Ababa. The cable described Makelle as "one of several areas of Ethiopia, which, in addition to the recurring problems of erosion and loss of soil fertility, is suffering from the effects of this year's drought, which is affecting an estimated one million people in the Tigray area alone." Displaced people, said the embassy cable, were "flocking to Makelle to temporary shelters" and CRS was concentrating in Makelle because it was one of the few places where food could be transported "with some degree of security by moving in convoys from Assab" (U.S. Embassy 1982, 1, 2).

The U.S. Embassy assured USAID that CRS had the experience and skill to handle such a program—a comment that, given CRS's record elsewhere in Africa, would appear unnecessary—and that it enjoyed a good working relationship with the Relief and Rehabilitation Commission (RRC) and other agencies in Makelle. The amount of food aid requested, said the embassy, was about one-tenth the amount of Title II food CRS handled yearly in Ethiopia. Further, CRS at the time was supervising seventeen food and nutrition centers throughout Ethiopia. Third, this request would allow CRS to assist those 5,000 families over the course of nine months "with a monthly family ration calculated to supply 90,000 calories," the amount determined to be an adequate supplement in such circumstances. The cable concluded (U.S. Embassy 1982, 2):

This will require 838 MT of Title II food, and we are confident that given the desperate plight of the townspeople of Makelle, CRS/NY will be able to fund the transportation and other minimal costs to bring to the people of Makelle this humanitarian assistance made possible by the people of the U.S.

Embassy supports this program.

Despite the urgency of the CRS request and the supporting cable from the U.S. Embassy in Addis Ababa, the Reagan administration took more than six months to approve the 838 metric tons of emergency food aid for Ethiopia. Moreover, when CRS requested an additional 4,500 metric tons in March 1983—reflecting the rapidly increasing famine in Tigray—the administration did not respond to that request for three months. Ken Hackett, sub-Saharan Africa regional director for CRS, detailed the requests and responses in an August 1983 letter to the author (Hackett 1983):

We have been agonizing since November, 1982, as to how to get the Administration to turn around on its position. Our November request to USAID for 838 MT for distribution in Tigrai did not receive a favorable response until May, 1983. By March, 1983, we had already increased the request by an additional 4500 MT. We received a favorable response (after Jay Ross' *Washington Post* article and a lot of Congressional pressure) in early July. At the same time we were able to convince the Administration to put back into the FY 1984 budget our expanded request for a regular food program of 11,000 MT.

The process was repeated in November 1983, when CRS again requested emergency P.L. 480 Title II food aid for Ethiopia—16,000 metric tons for its Makelle program and an expanded feeding operation reaching into the neighboring province of Eritrea. The jump from 838 to 4,500 to 16,000 metric tons reflected the rapid increase in the number of starving Ethiopians seeking food in the CRS camps in and around Makelle.

Before the CRS appeal of November 1983, two U.S. groups had visited Ethiopia to verify the starvation firsthand. In early August, a USAID team had spent two weeks in-country assessing Ethiopia's emergency food needs. The team concluded that at least 15,000 metric tons of food aid should be provided by the United States; this, it turned out, was half the projected food gap for Ethiopia in November and December 1983. Later that month, a delegation from the House Foreign Affairs Committee visited a feeding station in Gondar and met with PVO and Ethiopian officials. The delegation made "an urgent request" to State and USAID for increased emergency food aid and transportation assistance (General Accounting Office 1985, 16–17). In January 1984, USAID's Food for Peace office verbally informed CRS staff in Washington that the office was ready to recommend half of the request (8,000 metric tons) for approval. But the full CRS request was delayed until the first week of August 1984—about nine months after it had been received in Washington (General Accounting Office 1985).

The first CRS request had been delayed for almost six months. The second was delayed over a period of nine months. Whatever the reasons, the time lapse between receipt of the CRS appeals and approval by USAID "were considerably longer than the time required to process typical private voluntary organization food assistance requests" (General Accounting Office 1985, ii–iii). USAID officials later told a congressional investigation that "requests such as those submitted by CRS are normally approved within 2 or 3 weeks" (General Accounting Office 1985, i–ii, 11).

Why were the CRS requests delayed? The Reagan administration raised doubts about "the seriousness of the drought," the restrictions on movements of foreigners in Ethiopia that prevented verification of the hunger, and the fighting between government forces and guerrillas in the north "which created additional difficulties in delivering food to millions of hungry people" (General Accounting Office 1985, 14). But relief workers were already on the ground and fanned out across Ethiopia distributing food aid. The seriousness of the drought had been well documented by the press, the PVOs, and FAO. On 5 May 1983, the U.S. Embassy in Addis Ababa reported by cable to Washington that "drought and food shortage conditions in the north central region of Ethiopia constituted a disaster situation." (General Accounting Office 1985, 3). That same day, the chargé heading up the U.S. Embassy declared that a state of disaster existed in Ethiopia.

USAID was also troubled over whether or not CRS could account for and monitor all distributed U.S. food aid. This concern was exacerbated by two allegations of food diversions that were made public within a month of CRS's November 1983 request. But CRS was the largest and most experienced PVO operating in Africa at the time. If USAID thought CRS was reliable enough to handle the vast majority of U.S. food aid all over sub-Saharan Africa, why was CRS not reliable enough to handle it in Ethiopia?

The Reagan administration also delayed a major aid package for sub-Saharan Africa in early 1984 by linking it to its policy in Central America. The delay continued for almost seven months. House Speaker O'Neill said that the Reagan administration "showed its true colors" by stalling the move to feed hungry Africans. "Even when the situation in Africa had become terrible," he said (Sinclair 1984, A13),

> the administration held food aid legislation hostage to its murderous and illegal covert war in Nicaragua. If we did not give the Contras guns we could not give the Africans the food they need. It is a sad thing to say, but this administration has shown that it is ready to starve Africans so that it can kill Latin Americans.

Despite the failure of much of the 1984 harvest in Mozambique and the continuing famine in Ethiopia, neither country was budgeted for any Title II aid in 1984. The administration also wished to cut Title II aid for all of sub-Saharan Africa and reduced by $15 million its pledge to the World Food Programme for fiscal year 1985 (to begin 1 October 1984). Representative Howard Wolpe, who visited sub-Saharan Africa, including Ethiopia, several times in 1983 and 1984, called the Reagan administration's performance on the food aid supplemental "obscene." (Meszoly 1984, 3042). The *New York Times* (1984a, 24E), in an editorial, summed up 1984: "While Washington argued, millions in Ethiopia and other drought-ridden African countries remained hungry."

The Overt Policy

The Reagan administration's delayed response to famine in Ethiopia reflected its overt anti-Marxist ideology, coupled with internal decisionmaking procedures guaranteed to frustrate action and accountability. There were also at least four conventional political reasons why the Reagan administration responded as it did in 1982–84. These enabled the administration to waffle and delay. And lurking behind these was a second, covert policy.

Verification

Without a mission in Ethiopia, USAID depended on assessments by the U.S. Embassy, visiting USAID teams, the PVOs, and other agencies and donors. The United States, said a congressional investigation, was "sensitive and cautious about committing large amounts of food assistance to a Marxist governed country where detailed and accurate verification of real food needs could not be accomplished and where the possibility of food diversion existed" (General Accounting Office 1985, ii–iii). During 1982–84, various agencies inside the Reagan administration debated the validity of the food shortage claims by the Ethiopian government. These debates "directly impacted on the timeliness and amount of U.S. responses to the crisis" (General Accounting Office 1985, 6).

Diversion

During 1983 and 1984 the administration and other Western governments accused Mengistu of diverting donated food to the government's army or to the Soviet Union. The debate over food diversions in Ethiopia dominated congressional hearings in 1983, after the administration sought to cut off all food aid to that country. In 1984 a Congressional Research Service analysis stated (Congressional Research Service 1984b, 4):

> Various reports suggested that emergency food shipments were not reaching the target populations, but were being diverted by the Ethiopian government to pay for weapons from the Soviet Union. Also, subsequent reports accused the guerrillas of interfering in the relief effort. Reports by the U.S. Embassy in Ethiopia, the relief agencies, and the European Community (which conducted a special investigation) indicated that the diversions were not occurring.

There were, nonetheless, repeated accusations from the Reagan administration and in the media of food diversions in Ethiopia. At least three allegations occurred in 1983 alone. Only one involved U.S.-donated food, but all three caused delays in the Reagan administration's approval of P.L. 480 food to Ethiopia, especially the emergency requests by CRS in December 1982 and November 1983. USAID officials told a congressional investigation in 1985 (General Accounting Office 1985, 8) that the allegations "were treated with a high degree of caution, and there was an unwillingness within the U.S. government to approve any food assistance to Ethiopia until the alleged practices were examined and either dismissed or corrected."

Accusations of diversion gave the administration another sound reason not to act in Ethiopia. Moreover, checking each accusation greatly slowed the U.S. response to requests for emergency food aid for Ethiopia.

Was emergency food aid being diverted by the Mengistu government for its own use and benefit? Some diversion did indeed take place. Dawit Wolde Giorgis, appointed head of the Relief and Rehabilitation Commission (RRC) following the dismissal of Shimelis Adugna, served from 1983 through the height of the famine until the autumn of 1985, when he defected to England, later settling in the United States. Dawit said during an interview that the accusation that Shimelis Adugna had diverted emergency food aid to two Ethiopian government agencies and then covered up the fact from European Economic Community (EEC) auditors was true. Shimelis's only mistake, Dawit said, was putting everything in writing. He kept meticulous records of which agencies were to get diverted relief food and then, when he heard that the EEC inspectors were coming, Shimelis wrote instructions to his staff about how to get the inspectors off the trail. "Shimelis," said Dawit, with some humor, "had to destroy a paper path from Assab to the feeding camps. He was one day ahead of the inspectors."[4]

It is likely, Dawit said, that the RRC also diverted international food aid to the Somali Salvation Democratic Front, a pro-Ethiopian guerrilla force that operated along the Ethiopian-Somali border, "to keep that group operating." The RRC, Dawit said, also diverted emergency food aid to Sudanese guerrilla units, thought to be largely Christian, fighting in the south against the Moslem government of Jaafar el Nimeiri. Whether true or not, the accusation of diversions provided a convenient cover for delay. Even if true, such diversions were small and not enough to justify two years of delaying food aid or the deaths of hundreds of thousands of Ethiopians.

Distribution

Were all starving Ethiopians receiving emergency food aid? Surprisingly, no one disagreed on the answer. The Ethiopian government could not reach the majority of starving people, who had either fled across the border into Sudan or remained behind guerrilla lines in Tigray, Wollo, and Eritrea. A United Nations Disaster Relief Organization (UNDRO) report dated October 1983 (1983, 1) stated that "interagency mission confirms relief aid so far was necessary . . . however, the mission is alarmed by the small proportion of the needy people being reached."

That month, FAO in Rome reported (1983, 2) that of three million starving Ethiopians needing immediate emergency food aid, about one million "remain out of reach and continue to be severely affected by food shortages." In fact, the number of unreachable famine victims was probably higher. A 1984 congressional report found that perhaps as many as half of the known famine victims were located in the guerrilla-held areas and reachable only by the guerrilla relief agencies, REST and ERA (House Committee on Foreign Affairs 1984). REST, according to one relief worker (Carter 1985, 2-3), operated twenty-four camps in Tigray province and "a mill where wheat donated by the International Red Cross is ground into flour." The ERA set up forty-two relief camps in Eritrea for some 200,000 displaced and hungry people (Steele 1985).

Thus began the struggle for people's stomachs and with it, in theory at least, their political hearts and minds. Almost all overt emergency food that went to Ethiopia between 1982 and 1984 went into the government side. The Mengistu government continued soliciting international food aid for Ethiopians outside the areas it controlled. One relief worker told the *Christian Science Monitor* (1984, 3) that "the neediest people are not reachable through government channels."

By 1983, a strange process was unfolding. The bulk of emergency food aid coming into Ethiopia was going to the side of the battle lines on which the fewest hungry Ethiopians could be found. "Only 20 percent of those who needed food were in fact receiving it" (Oxfam-U.K. 1984, 3). The *New York Times* reported in August (1984, A6) that only one million of seven million starving Ethiopians were within reach of relief workers and emergency food aid on the government side. During testimony before the House Committee on Agriculture, when several members of Congress accused the Reagan administration of deliberately "holding off with a quick response" to the starvation in Ethiopia, Charles Gladson, assistant administrator in USAID's Food and Voluntary Assistance Office, explained the administration's position (House Committee on Agriculture 1983, 38): "There was a genuine concern . . . as to whether or not U.S. emergency food donations would reach those people in need in rural Ethiopia." This problem formed the foundation of the overt and covert Reagan administration food aid policies and provided an unusual political opportunity.

Marxism

The fourth concern of the Reagan administration focused on the fact that Ethiopia was the leading Marxist state and the Soviet Union's primary client in Africa. Ethiopia met the criteria for active intervention under the Reagan Doctrine: It was a significant outpost at the edge of the Soviet empire and a Soviet client struggling against indigenous guerrillas. This was aggravated by a nettlesome political burr: the celebration of the tenth anniversary of the Ethiopian revolution in September 1984, which followed twelve full months of preparation that drew off resources from fighting the famine. Dawit Wolde Giorgis called the celebration

> the most disgusting, unforgivable and irresponsible act. . . . By now thousands were dying every day and thousands had abandoned their homes, trekking the desert and mountaintops in search of food and shelter. More than 40,000 people had walked all the way from the northern part of Ethiopia and were at the gates of Addis. The RRC was instructed to stop them. The police were sent to make a human fence around Addis, to make sure none of these people would enter the city and spoil the show.[5]

In this respect, Mengistu was no different from Haile Selassie, who in 1973 had covered up a famine while Ethiopia was host to the tenth anniversary of the OAU. In 1984, the Mengistu government found the starvation "an ill-timed inconvenience" (Cohen 1987, 15). Roberta Cohen, an employee of the U.S. Embassy, wrote that the Mengistu government "deliberately hid the dimensions of starvation from its own public." The Mengistu government, she added, "considered famine contrary to the image of progress and accomplishment it wanted to portray on the occasion of the tenth anniversary of the revolution." The Marxist government sought to put a new face on the capital for the revolution's celebration. Cohen reported, "In Addis Ababa I witnessed bread lines moved from the main streets to less visible parts of the city, away from the view of foreign journalists and Communist guests from abroad who had come to participate in the festivities."

M. Peter McPherson, administrator of USAID, and other administration officials charged that Mengistu spent $100 million for new buildings, fresh paint, refurbishings, liquor, and food for the tenth anniversary (Meszoly 1984, 3043). Other Western reports placed the figure between $40 and $50 million (Harden 1984, A1). The Ethiopian government claimed that it spent about $1 million; Dawit Wolde Giorgis, after his defection, estimated the government's out-of-pocket costs at about $1.2 million.[6] The Ethiopians said that most of the costs were covered by contributions from friendly countries such as North Korea. Construction of a new 3,000-seat congress hall in Addis Ababa, for example, was paid for with $23.7 million from the Swedish International Development Agency (SIDA) and built by Finnish contractors (Smith 1984).

The administration also accused Mengistu of placing the anniversary celebration ahead of the emergency food aid operation by giving priority at its ports to ships carrying cement, paint, and other supplies for the revolution's celebration. McPherson accused the Ethiopian government of closing its ports to shipments of emergency food aid. Although the Mengistu government denied these charges, McPherson told the House Committee on Foreign Affairs (1985, 79) that

> it wasn't altogether popular in this [Reagan] Government to get food to Ethiopia, where the Government has a celebration costing millions of dollars . . . and where they gave priority in their ports to Soviet cement which delayed our getting food through the ports. It is not very popular in some quarters to give people in that country food.

That was certainly the case among policymakers inside the Reagan administration.

The Delay Mechanism

Political considerations have long been a dominant part of U.S. food policy, even in the case of famine. Many find that objectionable, especially when one disapproves of the policy. From a humanitarian perspective, does feeding starving people take precedence over politics? Should a country's sovereignty be violated to feed starving people, especially when that country denies them food?

In the case of the Reagan administration's actions in 1982–84, there are other troubling questions. How was the policy created? Did the covert nature of the policy, however admirable its intentions, create an atmosphere that gave all covert actions—support of anticommunist Contras, or even the release of U.S. hostages—noble stature?

To understand how the covert policy developed, we need to look briefly at how U.S. food aid policy was developed, who the policy-makers were, and how they exercised their power.

Before 1973, distributing U.S. food aid was a rather simple matter. The Department of Agriculture determined crop availability and set aside certain reserve amounts to maintain domestic food prices. The Department of State and USAID decided questions of foreign need and diplomatic advantage. "The farmers got price supports and the world's hungry got our food," write Gelb and Lake (1974–75, 176). The secretary of agriculture designated the food for exportation, and State and USAID did the dispensing. In 1973, this process began to change. Drought threatening to become famine across South Asia and Africa's Sahel was exacerbated by price increases in oil and food, fertilizer shortages, and continued population growth and poor harvests among impoverished Third World nations. A whole new set of bureaucrats worked their way into the P.L. 480 process: the Office of Management and Budget (OMB), the Council of Economic Advisors (CEA), the Council on International Economic Policy (CIEP), and the Department of the Treasury. OMB cornered the food aid budget process. Moreover, write Gelb and Lake, "State began to muscle aside its appendage, USAID, as food became a big bargaining chip that could be used in international negotiations." The bureaucratic structure started to grow, and by 1974—with famine looming in South Asia and emerging in Africa—it had its own assistant secretary–level food aid group under OMB with representatives from Agriculture, State, Treasury, and the National Security Council (NSC), which "coordinated allocations of P.L. 480 aid" (Gelb and Lake 1974–75, 178–179).

The doubling of agencies making decisions about P.L. 480 food aid strained bureaucratic skills. This manifested itself in the confused coordination of cables and memos, in the possible number of foul-ups and delays, in the number of senior officials who got involved, and in the vast range of interests to be reconciled. By 1981, the result was an intricate bureaucratic web that involved turf battles, policy concerns, and various foreign aid interests and objectives from such diverse agencies as State, Agriculture, OMB, NSC, and the CIA, which came aboard in the late 1970s.

During the first Reagan administration, all requests for P.L. 480 emergency aid were received and initially reviewed by USAID's Bureau for Food for Peace and Voluntary Assistance. When satisfied with "the appropriateness of the request," the bureau circulated it within USAID's geographic, policy, and service bureaus for review. "According to USAID officials," said a congressional investigation, "this review by USAID usually requires about two to three weeks from receipt of the request" (General Accounting Office 1985, 12). Gaining USAID's approval, the request for emergency food aid was passed along to the larger P.L. 480 Title II Working Group of the Food Aid Subcommittee of the interagency Development Coordinating Committee (DCC), which decided whether or not the food aid could be approved and released for shipment to the recipient country. The Working Group was chaired by USAID's Food for Peace director and consisted of representatives from USAID, State, Agriculture, and OMB; NSC was also present in the Working Group, either through OMB or with its own representative, depending on the country requesting food aid. The departments of Commerce and Treasury sent officials to these meetings—although this was rare—to express concerns from those agencies about the request under consideration (House Committee on Agriculture 1983). Under the Reagan administration, with its emphasis on realigning federal budget priorities, OMB assumed a lot more power and was no longer simply a budget office. Its representatives began shaping policy. Officials from the NSC and CIA also sat in on the Working Group, often at the request of OMB, to ensure that the president's policy directives were taken into account.

Throughout most of the first Reagan administration, there were no specific written guidelines or policy for the Working Group's operation with regard to the review and approval of emergency food aid requests. This meant that any faction, or agency, could play a significant role—and did. A congressional investigation (General Accounting Office 1985, 12–13) reported that between 1981 and 1984 the Working Group was "lax" in scheduling regular meetings and in keeping minutes of those meetings.

> Prior to the current [November 1984] African food crisis, the Working Group met infrequently to address emergency requests, with most of the communication between members concerning approval of requests being informally made via telephone.
>
> The documentation of the emergency approval process employed by the Working Group until the fall of 1984 was less than adequate since, other than the request approval cable, there is no documentation available to indicate (1) when the Working Group met, (2) what requests were considered, (3) what requests were disapproved and why, (4) what were the concerns of the individual members and how they were satisfied, and (5) what was the disposition of requests that were not approved.

This process was secretive and open to abuse. The world's largest food aid donor—the United States—during the worst famine of the century in sub-Saharan Africa relied on a Working Group made up of men and women from various executive branch agencies, each with its own agency interests, to hear requests for emergency food aid from other countries. The Working Group kept no written records of the requests for emergency food aid, nor any written records of meetings held to discuss those requests. Discussions, analyses, and decisions were all made by telephone. No written records existed—other than the U.S. Embassy cables requesting food aid—of when the Working Group met, the emergency requests considered, the discussion of those requests, an individual member's or agency's concerns or objections, or the disposition of each request. In fact, no vote was even taken. Once all concerns were voiced, final approval or disapproval was granted on the basis of consensus. Each representative had veto power over the decision, and the Working Group usually went along if someone objected. A standoff could be bucked upward on the bureaucratic chart to the DCC (General Accounting Office 1985), but no member of the Working Group remembered any appeal to the DCC. The process, with its lack of record keeping and its reliance on consensus, was open to control by Reagan appointees who could delay requests for emergency food aid solely for ideological reasons, and no one would know. This is precisely what happened.

By 1982, all major decisions regarding emergency food aid to Africa, and particularly Ethiopia and other Marxist states, were being made by NSC in the White House. The Reagan administration's foreign policy was formulated in a loose, some might say undirected, manner. Power flowed out of the Oval Office to top aides in the NSC, initially William Clark and then, in 1983, Robert McFarlane. There was enormous running room. So long as policy contained a strong anticommunist approach, NSC was left alone to create whatever policy it wished, or could. McFarlane, in explaining the origins of the Iran-Contra affair, for example, described the "policy vacuum" of 1981 created by the lack of a "thorough and concerted analysis" of administration objectives. This allowed the CIA to "make a pitch" and the words *covert* and *action* merged to create a policy of armed support for anticommunist rebels around the periphery of the Soviet empire (Rosenfeld 1987, A25). The covert U.S. policy toward Ethiopia originated in 1982 and was formulated in much the same way.

For almost twenty-four months, from late 1982 to late 1984, the NSC stalled or blocked the Working Group from sending emergency U.S. food aid to any Marxist nation in sub-Saharan Africa. "At top-secret sessions, the National Security Council was urged to head off the starvation with food shipments from America's overflowing bins." But the NSC resisted. According to columnist Jack Anderson, the NSC vetoed all decisions on aid to Ethiopia: "The NSC and its supporters insisted on using famine relief as a tool to extract political concessions from Ethiopia" (Anderson 1985, E18).

In 1984, Francis X. Carlin, then head of the CRS operation in Ethiopia, aid that NSC had "stonewalled" the Working Group over the 1982–83 and 1983–84 CRS requests for emergency food aid for Ethiopia, delaying the shipment of that relief food.[7] NSC continued to delay food aid to Ethiopia despite full knowledge of the extent of that nation's disaster. A secret White House report dated 5 May 1984 documented the severity of Ethiopia's famine and stated that "a disaster situation" existed in that country as early as 1983. But, the report continued, aid was "deliberately withheld" for political reasons (Vallely 1985, 12). The NSC staff on the Working Group took the position that the Ethiopian Marxists should get help from their Soviet backers or make strategic concessions before receiving U.S. emergency food aid. Some members of the Working Group agreed and wanted U.S. emergency P.L. 480 aid to Ethiopia made conditional "on restraints on their anti-U.S. propaganda. We wanted Mengistu to tell his people that the emergency relief food came from the Free World."[8] To the majority of the Working Group who disagreed, however, the NSC staffers "repeatedly quoted intelligence reports that detailed Mengistu's indifference to his starving people. They read reports to us about Mengistu withholding money from the RRC, diverting food aid to his army or the Soviets, or not employing Ethiopian army vehicles to help move the food inland from the ports to the camps."[9] The NSC/CIA continued blocking action by the Working Group until late October 1984.

Covert Policy and Mechanism

The Reagan administration put into place two policies, one overt and the other covert. The overt policy, as we have seen, was based on "containment"—deliberately cutting and delaying food aid to the Mengistu government despite reliable and factual accounts of famine spreading among the people of Wollo, Tigray, and Eritrea provinces. The public reasons for the administration's policy of cuts and delays—verification, diversion, distribution, and Marxism—formed the basis for the overt policy toward Ethiopia.

Two of those concerns—distribution and Marxism—also formed the basis for the administration's covert policy in Ethiopia. That policy was designed to "roll back" the Soviet intrusion in the Horn by supplying U.S. food aid and other material through the "back door" in Sudan to insurgents fighting against the Ethiopian government. By delaying food to the government side while supplying food and other material to Eritrea and Tigray, the Reagan administration sought to destabilize or even bring down the Marxist Ethiopian government.

As mentioned, one of the central foreign policy goals pursued by the Reagan administration was the removal of pro-Soviet regimes wherever they might be found. It supported "freedom fighters" in Nicaragua, Afghanistan, and Angola and directly attacked regimes in Grenada and Libya. Reagan officials were more willing than previous administrations to use "economic, diplomatic and paramilitary instruments of coercion against regimes considered too close to the Soviet Union" (Sewell, Feinberg, and Kallab 1985, 4).

By 1982, "covert paramilitary action assumed a prominence in Washington that it had not enjoyed since the Vietnam war" (Sewell, Feinberg, and Kallab 1985, 5). Indeed, the Heritage Foundation, which played a major role in shaping administration policy during its first term, called for the United States to "employ paramilitary assets to weaken those communist and non-communist regimes that may already be facing the early stages of insurgency within their borders and which threaten U.S. interests." Among the African countries ripe for paramilitary support, said the Heritage Foundation report, were Angola, Libya, and Ethiopia (Heritage Foundation 1984, 353–355). The Reagan administration in 1981 put together a foreign policy that placed "more emphasis on the removal of offending regimes" and even encouraged "conflicts that impose costs on radical regimes and their people" (Heritage Foundation 1984, 141). This was the case whether that radical regime was in Managua or Addis Ababa.

In Ethiopia, the fact that famine put most of the starving people behind rebel lines created a unique foreign policy opportunity. The United States could employ food aid as an instrument of the Reagan administration's anticommunist doctrine. The Mengistu government soon found itself caught between East and West, between ideological affinity and sources of food. Shimelis Adugna, the RRC commissioner until late 1983, said that "the Communist states that supported the overthrow of Emperor Haile Selassie in 1974 have given next to nothing in the way of assistance." On the other hand, he was "certain that Western governments would have responded more generously if Ethiopia were not a socialist state" (Steele 1983, 2).

With delay—or "containment"—in place, the Reagan administration put together the action or "rollback" mechanism. This was a covert paramilitary action undertaken to aid anti-Mengistu insurgents.

That policy actually began in 1981, when President Reagan signed a presidential "finding"—an authorization that gets its legality from the National Security Act—directing the CIA to fund a "nonlethal" campaign in support of "democratic resistance" to the Mengistu government in Ethiopia. One initial difficulty for the administration's strategists was identifying a resistance group that had a reasonable chance of success but was neither Marxist nor secessionist. At first, the EPLF and the TPLF were unacceptable, primarily because of their own Marxist ideologies and, in the case of the EPLF, secessionist demands.

The administration wanted some organization that would take power, not secede. After a brief search, Reagan policymakers discovered an obscure group called the Ethiopian People's Democratic Alliance (EPDA), and the CIA started pumping $500,000 a year to them, with the president's approval, for a propaganda campaign to undermine the Mengistu regime. The small propaganda campaign included audio and video tapes of anti-Mengistu speeches by leading exiles in the United States, which were shipped into Ethiopia by diplomatic pouch and distributed to dissident "cells." But the EPDA was based in London, far from the actual fighting and starvation.

By the autumn of 1983, pursuing the Reagan administration's advocacy for covert support of "freedom fighters," the CIA geared up for direct "resistance tactics" against Mengistu. "Senior Administration officials" started planning "for covert paramilitary training of armed guerrillas committed to overthrowing the current Ethiopian regime" (Tyler and Ottaway 1986, A1). That meant a change in focus to work with the EPLF and TPLF.

There were at least five reasons why the Reagan administration would make this shift in policy and overlook the Marxist and secessionist characteristics of the TPLF and the EPLF.[10]

First, the guerrillas were established opponents of the pro-Soviet Mengistu government and were fighting against that regime; they were "the enemy of our enemy" (Senate Subcommittee 1985, 45).

Second, guerrilla factions were more or less united against the Mengistu regime, and both the EPLF and TPLF had been successful in the field against the Ethiopian army.[11]

Third, the EPLF and the TPLF controlled most of the ground in the famine area and most of the starving people.

Fourth, in 1983–84 Mengistu was spending $487,000 a day on his army—the third largest in Africa behind Egypt and South Africa—and 46 percent of his $600 million national budget on defense.[12] Supporting the guerrillas would continue that drain on a weakened government.

Fifth, representations on behalf of the United States by Saudi Arabia gave rise to hopes that some moderate, pro-Western element might eventually emerge among the guerrillas.

Finally, there was no one else to deal with. The administration took what they got. While not perfect, in some ways the Ethiopian guerrillas were the "freedom fighters" that the Reagan Doctrine wished for: They needed U.S. support; they could absorb large-scale covert U.S. aid through a cooperative U.S. ally (Sudan); and they had the perfect humanitarian cover of feeding huge numbers of starving people under their control. Ethiopia, therefore, became an excellent testing ground for using U.S. food aid as an instrument of U.S. foreign policy—of winning hearts and minds through stomachs.

The instrument for covert action was put into place in the spring of 1983. While the administration was delaying food aid to the Ethiopian government through the "front door," a second, covert group was formed to coordinate operations behind guerrilla lines in Eritrea and Tigray provinces. In April 1983, at the direction of the White House, the NSC along with USAID and State established the Interagency Group on Ethiopia and the Sudan (IGETSU).[13] The plan was to ship P.L. 480 emergency food aid through the "back door" into Eritrea and Tigray by way of Port Sudan in Sudan. According to a senior IGETSU official, the agency's primary concern was "a balanced food aid program which would provide relief to those in need, regardless of location" in the guerrilla areas (General Accounting Office 1985, 7–8).

U.S. officials said that there was no direct contact between the Reagan administration and the guerrillas, and that the United States used as its primary conduits into Eritrea and Tigray a variety of PVOs, most notably the Lutheran World Federation/World Service, based in New York City, and Mercy Corps International in Seattle, Washington. "To put it mildly," a West European diplomat told the *Christian Science Monitor*, "cross-border relief is an extremely sensitive issue" (Girardet 1985, 1).

An incredible process got underway. At the same time that the administration was preparing to cut Ethiopia's P.L. 480 emergency food aid for fiscal year 1984 to zero and Reagan officials were delaying the CRS emergency food requests for Makelle—the capital of Tigray in government hands—other administration officials on IGETSU began rapidly expanding the "back door" relief pipeline from Port Sudan into Eritrea and Tigray on the guerrilla side.[14] In contrast to the overt process, IGETSU's members "quickly reached" a consensus "that assistance had to be provided to the hungry people in northern Ethiopia." They immediately approved $1.5 million for the cross-border operation (General Accounting Office 1985, 8).

As IGETSU geared up, U.S. food aid flows across the Sudan border increased from 1,000 tons a month to 3,000 tons a month. Within eight months in 1983, the Reagan administration moved 17,000 tons through the "back door" pipeline (Senate Subcommittee 1984). By mid-1984, the flow had reached 10,000 tons a month (*New York Times* 1985). The administration approved another $3.5 million for the purchase of grain by PVOs in the insurgent-held areas. Relief groups estimated that up to 15,000 tons of grain were available for purchase from merchants in western Tigray alone (Putka 1984). This part of the program touched off heated debate within NSC, where some policymakers wanted to send the money directly to support the guerrillas.

The Reagan administration, however, was careful not to aid the guerrilla organizations directly. In addition to Lutheran World Relief and Mercy Corps International, USAID sought to have CARE in New York take over the logistics of moving all U.S. emergency food aid from Port Sudan to the Ethiopian border, where it was turned over to the PVOs and the guerrillas (Steele 1985). Although some food aid was flown into Khartoum and trucked across the border,[15] most came by ship to Port Sudan. U.S. chargé Korn describes the operation (Korn 1986, 136):

> AID dealt only with the Western private voluntary agencies, who in turn handled all necessary arrangements with REST and ERA. This mechanism did not offer absolute assurance against American relief food falling into the hands of rebel soldiers, just as the United States could not be absolutely certain that food it gave to the RRC would not be diverted to improper use.
>
> [The Reagan administration, however, never raised the issue of food diversion on the guerrilla side.]
>
> Bringing food across from Sudan was only a partial solution to the problem of famine in northern Ethiopia. There were no roads, only tracks, and trucks had to travel exclusively at night to avoid detection and attack by Ethiopian aircraft. Still, . . . it was the only way to get help to people in the large rebel-controlled enclaves.

Coordination of the cross-border feeding operation was done by the Emergency Relief Desk in Khartoum, a consortium of eight church groups. This was complicated since several PVOs worked both sides of the fighting inside Ethiopia. Lutheran World Relief and Mercy Corp International, joined by World Vision, CRS, the Evangelical Church of Eritrea, and the International Committee for the Red Cross (ICRC), all operated in parts of Tigray and Eritrea. The ICRC had "extensive activities in the provinces of Tigray and Eritrea," said Bradford Morse, director of the United Nations' relief operations in Africa, "and they [had] many, many feeding stations there" (MacNeil/Lehrer 1985, 6).

Working both sides was risky business since the Ethiopian government, whose leaders were suspicious of relief workers, could shut down operations on their side quickly. The associate executive secretary of the Mennonite Central Committee commented on a decision to allocate funds to ERA for food purchases inside Eritrea: "It is not an easy choice. Potentially we are risking the wrath of the Ethiopian government" (*Christian Science Monitor* 1984, 1).[16]

Most of the emergency food aid went across the border in unmarked bags carried by the ICRC or Lutheran World Relief. The "back door" was actually a system of roads, one an all-weather track from Port Sudan to Kasala, where it joined a paved road that crossed the border to Teseney. The Sudanese sometimes closed the border at Kasala to keep out Ethiopian refugees. That forced operations to another, more rugged route in eastern Sudan which followed the seasonal secondary road along the coast and crossed at Karora, then twisted down along the northern highlands to Nakfa. The ERA frequently used this road to supply food and medicine to twenty-three settlement camps in the EPLF base area (Steele 1985; *Africa Confidential* 1985).

Large amounts of food aid were continuously sent by truck from Port Sudan into Eritrea and Tigray over the rugged mountain roads. This underscored the Reagan administration's commitment to the operation. The administration approved funds in 1983 for at least eighty-six trucks for the "back door" IGETSU operation (Ottaway 1985). (By contrast, the administration refused funds for trucks on the Mengistu side because U.S. officials thought they might be used for military purposes. No such fear was raised concerning trucks for the IGETSU operation.) By 1985, U.S. and relief officials in Khartoum said that at least 200,000 tons of emergency P.L. 480 food and 225 trucks were in the pipeline for delivery in Eritrea and Tigray to feed as many as three million people (*Los Angeles Times* 1985). At one point, there was a back-up at Port Sudan of about 25,000 tons of grain (House Select Committee on Hunger 1985).[17]

The movement of U.S. emergency food aid to Port Sudan and from there into Eritrea and Tigray provinces was swift and much larger than the response that went to the Ethiopian government's side in 1983–84. And when the United States stepped up its aid to the Mengistu government after October 1984, it also increased emergency U.S. food aid to the guerrilla side. Between October 1984 and March 1985, for example, 115,000 tons of emergency U.S. food aid went into Eritrea and Tigray through the "back door" of Port Sudan (Ottaway 1985).

The IGETSU operation appears to have had at least three objectives, which fell into a progression: to get food aid to the majority of Ethiopians suffering from the famine; to keep Mengistu from exporting his revolution to guerrilla movements in neighboring states, especially Sudan; and to support and sustain insurgents who were imposing political and economic costs on this Marxist regime and might weaken it. The operation quickly became a poorly kept secret. In 1983, news reports circulated in the United States that the Reagan administration was using the "back door" to funnel not only emergency food aid into Eritrea and Tigray, but arms as well. In October 1983, *Newsweek* reported (1983, 38) that the CIA was shipping "secret aid to friendly forces in Chad, Ethiopia, Angola and the Sudan. . . . Training arms and financial assistance are also given to military forces in Ethiopia, Angola and the Sudan."[18] Two weeks later, Steve Coats, director of issues for Bread for the World, testified before the House of Representatives (House Committee on Agriculture 1983, 83) that "the CIA is supplying arms to rebels in Ethiopia." No independent confirmation could be made of this report. But, as we shall see, the

CIA's major role in formulating U.S. food aid policy in the NSC, plus the principal thrust of the Reagan Doctrine to oppose Marxist regimes by supporting insurgents against them, could lead to the conclusion that the IGETSU operation might mix guns with food.

It is also likely that the government of Jaafar el Nimeiri in Sudan played a major role in providing sanctuary and weapons to the guerrillas. For one thing, that government was itself under attack. Insurgents fighting in southern Sudan against Nimeiri's government took refuge in Ethiopia. Moveover, a Reagan administration deputy assistant secretary of defense told a House subcommittee in March 1984 that Libya was providing money, arms, and training for the dissidents in southern Sudan and that Ethiopia was trying to destabilize Sudan by providing supplies and sanctuary (House Subcommittee on Africa 1984).[19] For its part, the Nimeiri government sheltered Eritrean and Tigrayan guerrillas, funnelled light arms and ammunition to the Ethiopian guerrillas, and provided protection for them. Princeton Lyman, then deputy assistant secretary of state for African affairs, testified that the Ethiopian guerrillas moved easily across the Sudan border "to take safe haven or when they are retreating," which made it difficult for Mengistu's army to trap or defeat them. Journalists reported that the 1985 Ethiopian spring offensive against the guerrillas was aimed at severing the pipeline "that brings in military supplies from Sudan to the region" and at halting relief convoys "that have been secretly ferrying food from Sudan to at least 160,000 starving people" (Iyer 1985, 37). Given the terms of the Reagan Doctrine, the threats to Sudan from Ethiopian- and Libyan-supported rebels, and the role and needs of the EPLF and TPLF, a likely scenario is that the United States, through IGETSU, supplied food and trucks while helping Nimeiri's Sudan supply arms. It is also likely, as we shall see, that Saudi Arabia played a central role in getting arms to the EPLF and TPLF through the "back door."

Finally, if the Reagan administration's intention was only to feed hungry Ethiopians, why did it delay food aid going to the government side while quietly setting up and then rapidly supplying a food aid operation through the "back door" to the rebel side? If "a hungry child knows no politics," as Peter McPherson maintained, then U.S. food aid should have been quickly distributed to hungry children wherever they were found in Ethiopia. The role of the NSC, coupled with the covert nature of IGETSU, indicate another intention: that by delaying and cutting food aid to the government side while undertaking a large-scale "back door" operation, the Reagan administration wished to use food aid as an instrument of its foreign policy in Ethiopia.

How successful was IGETSU and the "back door" operation? At the very least it prevented the Mengistu government from using starvation as a weapon against the guerrillas and those Ethiopians in guerrilla-held areas. During 1982–84, Mengistu tried to use starvation to shape domestic policy. In late 1984, Chris Carter, a relief worker with Grassroots International, told a U.S. television program (MacNeil/Lehrer 1985, 2-3): "I believe. . .that the Ethiopian government intends to starve out the population that it has been unsuccessful in crushing militarily. . . ." Dawit Wolde Giorgis added that "there was a tacit understanding" among Ethiopia's "hardline elements," including Mengistu, "to let nature take its toll and deprive these areas of much needed assistance. It was believed that by denying the population food and other assistance, the guerrillas would perish, the people [would be] punished and the area depopulated."[20]

During a meeting between David Korn, the U.S. chargé in Addis Ababa, and Tibebu Bekele, the Ethiopian foreign minister, on 24 December 1984, Korn openly discussed the U.S. "back door" operation. "Tibebu blurted out with more candor than he probably intended," writes Korn, "that 'food is a major element in our strategy against the secessionists.'" Indeed it was. The Ethiopian army had tried to cut off food supplies to the rebels.[21] At the least, IGETSU was responsible for blunting Mengistu's attempt to starve his own people into submission. IGETSU kept food aid flowing into Eritrea and Tigray and negated the government's starvation policy.

After Korn's discussion with Tibebu, the Reagan administration made the "back door" operation more overt and in measured steps increased its pressure on the Mengistu government. In March 1985, Vice President George Bush toured the refugee centers across the Ethiopian border in Sudan. In Khartoum, Bush, Chester Crocker, and Peter McPherson met with President Nimeiri to discuss stepping up the cross-border operation. Later, U.S. and Sudanese officials came up with three plans, whose details underscore the enthusiasm of the Reagan and Nimeiri governments for the "back door" program.

The first plan called for adding 800,000 tons of emergency food aid—a vast amount—and 500 trucks to the cross-border operation. The second plan sought budgeting from the U.S. Congress to fund a paved two-lane highway more than 350 miles from the Sudan-Ethiopian border to Tigray—a "deep penetration" of the guerrilla-held provinces. This was tantamount to challenging the Mengistu government to bomb a relief road. "The Sudanese," said one senior U.S. official, "were even more gung-ho on this one than we were." The third plan involved a more modest provision of 240 trucks for the existing "back door" operation (Vallely 1985, 12).[22] Plans were to have been completed during President Nimeiri's visit to Washington in April. But Bush buckled under to the Ethiopians,[23] and on 6 April 1985 Sudan's Nimeiri was overthrown by a coup. The new military regime, headed by General Abdul-Rahman Suwar Dahab, sought to improve relations with Ethiopia, causing U.S. officials to worry that the Sudanese would scuttle the "back door" operation.

The coup temporarily slowed U.S. operations. Later in 1985, the administration was able to send in 150 ten-ton trucks, half to ERA and half to REST, for the cross-border operation. About 55,000 tons of food, stockpiled at Port Sudan, flowed across the border, according to the World Food Programme in Khartoum. The goal in late 1985 was to move 15,000 tons of food a month, "although this was dependent on the cooperation of the Sudanese authorities." There was conjecture that Sudan, following the coup, would crack down on the TPLF and EPLF and the Ethiopian refugees in exchange for Mengistu's lessening support for the Sudan People's Liberation Army of John Garang.

The Reagan policy toward Ethiopia, put into place by the NSC and the Working Group, drew its strength from history and the support of allies. The Reverend Charles Elliott, in 1982–84 director of Christian Aid in Great Britain and a professor of development policy at the University of Wales, had "an intimate knowledge of official attitudes" inside the British and U.S. administrations (Lean 1984, 1). Reverend Elliott believes that policymakers in both the Thatcher and Reagan administrations knew well the events of 1972–74 in Ethiopia. "They [British and U.S. officials] thought that if there was a major catastrophe, it would probably change the regime again," he said in October 1984. "They took the view that, if there was another famine, it would serve the Ethiopian Government right, that they had it coming to them" (Lean 1984, 1).

The administration found another old ally in the Arab world. Saudi Arabia had a vested interest in getting the Soviets out of the Horn and stabilizing the region; it especially wanted the Soviet navy out of the Dahlak Islands off Ethiopia and, if possible, out of the Red Sea. The Saudis, who had served as successful U.S. proxies elsewhere,[24] aided the Reagan administration's covert operation with financial and diplomatic support. The administration turned to the Saudis, with their knowledge of the various rebel factions, for assistance in organizing and financing the anti-Mengistu guerrillas (Roberts, Engelberg, and Garth 1987). The Saudis were thought to be principal arms suppliers to the guerrillas. They also pressed the guerrilla factions to unite against Mengistu and won tenuous peace agreements between the TPLF and the EPLF and the large number of guerrilla organizations struggling against the central Ethiopian government (*Africa Research Bulletin* 1984a). This debt was repaid, in part, during the Gulf War of 1990–91, when U. S. troops halted the Iraqi advance across Kuwait into Saudi Arabia.

Policy Shift

In late October 1984, the Reagan administration suddenly changed its food aid policy that had been in place for three years. The catalyst for this dramatic shift was the BBC-TV news film taken during late October in Ethiopia. The film, broadcast on 24 October in Great Britain and the United States, showed about 102,000 starving people crowded into tents and tin shelters at a government relief camp in Korem. Public reaction demanded that something be done to help. For at least three reasons, the Reagan administration moved large amounts of food aid quickly into Ethiopia.[25]

Election Year

The BBC film shown on U.S. television triggered a deep and surprising public response. Updates appeared on U.S. television almost nightly after 24 October. The presidential election was coming on 6 November, and although President Reagan held a comfortable margin in the polls, the image of Harry Truman's victory over Thomas Dewey in 1948 has long haunted the Republican Party. It is difficult with the passage of time to recall the enormous and unprecedented public outcry over the famine and the generosity of the response that followed the television news films from Ethiopia. To ignore that awakening might have cost President Reagan a significant share of the electorate, although probably not the election itself.

Agricultural Surpluses

The United States had harvested a record wheat crop in 1982, the fourth largest wheat crop in history in 1983, and the second largest wheat crop in history in 1984 (King 1985). By the beginning of 1985, the Department of Agriculture reported holding in government warehouses more than twenty-four million metric tons of edible commodities acquired during the previous four years as payment on price support loans to farmers. The 1984 harvest also left about 4.5 million tons of wheat and 2.6 million tons of corn in farmers' storage bins. In all, the United States held two-thirds of the world's grain stocks. In fiscal year 1985 (starting 1 October 1984) the Reagan administration would pay $19 billion to U.S. farmers in subsidies and other nonproduction payouts (House Committee on Foreign Affairs 1985; King 1985b; Echikson 1985). Together, these were additional incentives to dispose of accumulated U.S. agricultural resources.

Mother Teresa

No other single event had the impact of a letter from Mother Teresa to Ronald Reagan. In October 1984, Mother Teresa knew that President Reagan was in a reelection campaign and that her Sisters of Charity feeding Ethiopians at Latchi and elsewhere needed emergency food aid quickly. Perhaps it was simply fortuitous timing, but just nineteen days before the election, Mother Teresa sent a hand-written letter to the president asking him to help her Sisters of Charity feed the starving Ethiopians. "I know you will help me to send food as soon as possible to our poor. I will pray for you—this is the only way I can show my gratitude. Please do something for our people" (Teresa, Mother 1984). Copies of Mother Teresa's letter circulated quietly in the executive branch. The letter had a significant impact on the hardliners in the Working Group. "After that letter they knew there were going to be exceptions" to the president's anti-Marxist policy. "It was a signal to the agencies and the Working Group that the White House was caving in. The NSC was caving in."[26]

And cave in they did. The policy shift had immediate and dramatic results. By October 1984, the United States had earmarked just 16,380 metric tons of emergency P.L. 480 food for Ethiopia. Within a month following the BBC film, that amount jumped to 45,000 metric tons and then to 130,000 metric tons. By the end of 1984, the U.S. pledge reached more than 216,000 metric tons and four months later, 500,000 metric tons—more than thirty times the amount at the beginning of the fiscal year. When it wished to move swiftly, the Reagan administration could do so. On 28 November, for example, President Reagan ordered the rerouting to Ethiopia of 80,000 tons of soy-fortified bulgur and corn-soy-milk aboard the SS *Sam Houston,* a freighter already underway to India (Meszoly 1984).

After the autumn of 1984, the levels of emergency food aid sent by the United States to sub-Saharan Africa, while appearing large by comparison to earlier Reagan administration years, were small when compared to the total agricultural stockpile. In neither fiscal year 1985 nor 1986 did U.S. emergency food aid exceed 10 percent of the stockpiled commodities. As a perceived policy, however, increased food aid to Africa was a no-lose situation for the administration; it pleased Congress, farmers, and humanitarians. Presumably, it also pleased Africans.

Representative Wolpe, in a television interview on 18 November 1984, said:

> The tragedy that we are facing really could have been avoided. . . . To suggest that somehow we've been surprised isn't really quite accurate. We knew two years ago the dimensions of the tragedy that we were facing. Not only the United States but [also] the entire world was very, very slow to respond (Meszoly 1984, 3042).

Conclusions

Officials of the first Reagan administration put in play a policy of delaying, denying, and cutting food aid to Ethiopia. This was done as part of a larger global policy of blunting the expansion of the Soviet Union and its Marxist ideology. Despite evidence of food shortages and starvation, U.S. food aid was denied to Poland, Mozambique, Angola, and Ethiopia. In addition, a covert policy was undertaken in Ethiopia, in which U.S. food aid and other material were supplied through the "back door" of Port Sudan to guerrillas in Eritrea and Tigray. The policy had both political and humanitarian implications. It could be seen as supporting insurgents seeking to overthrow the Soviet Union's largest client state in Africa, as destabilizing the Marxist government of Ethiopia, and as getting urgently needed food aid into those regions where the majority of Ethiopia's starving people were located.

Was the Reagan policy successful? Put another way, did the ends justify the means? In 1990, the Soviet Union, itself breaking apart, withdrew all aid to Ethiopia. In 1991, the Eritrian and Tigrayan guerrillas reached Addis Ababa and overthrew the Mengistu government; Mengistu himself fled to Zimbabwe. As of this writing, a new coalition government had held national elections and was struggling to keep Ethiopia together. It is unlikely that U.S. food aid through the IGETSU operation destabilized the Marxist Ethiopian government or defeated Mengistu. It may have indeed supported the guerrillas, but without Soviet economic and military support, Mengistu was finished. Rather than Reagan, it was Gorbachev who brought about the end to Marxism in Ethiopia.

The Reagan administration pursued a covert foreign policy that viewed Ethiopia as a political opportunity. It did so without the benefit of open debate in which the lack of any humanitarian concerns in that policy might have been exposed and examined. Its officials created a "we-know-best" arrogance at the NSC and other agencies that resulted not only in covert operations in Ethiopia, but also in the Iran-Contra scandal and the Iraqi-Russian food-for-arms affair that extended into the Bush administration.

Worst, for two years Reagan officials delayed responding to requests from Ethiopia for emergency food aid , favoring their covert political foreign policy opportunity over the plight of starving people. But when covert operations are seen as an acceptable foreign policy choice, "some tragic errors" result. Reagan officials placed these political choices above the lives of, in Representative Wolpe's words, "hundreds of thousands" of Ethiopian peasants, who had no choices of their own.

Notes

1. Pankhurst cites eleven "major famines" between 1540 and 1752: in 1540, 1543, 1623, 1650, 1678, 1700, 1702, 1747, 1748 and 1752 (Pankhurst 1961, 347).
2. U.S. satellite projections put the shortfall at two million tons.

3. By 1984, CRS had an annual budget of $430 million with operations in seventy Third World nations. In sub-Saharan Africa, the agency operated in twenty nations and accounted for more than 90 percent of the P.L. 480 aid for that part of the continent (Senate Subcommittee on Foreign Relations of the Committee on Foreign Relations 1984, 65, 69).

4. Dawit Wolde Giorgis, interview with the author, Norwich, Vermont, 20-22 November 1986.

5. Dawit Wolde Giorgis, comments to the author before the Face-to-Face dinner, The Carnegie Endowment for International Peace, Washington, D.C., 23 June 1986.

6. Dawit Wolde Giorgis, interview with the author, Washington, D.C., 24 June 1986.

7. Francis X. Carlin, interview with the author, Washington, D.C., 18 July 1985.

8. Source within USAID, interview with the author, Washington, D.C., 5 May 1985.

9. Source within OMB, interview with the author, Washington, D.C., 10 April 1985.

10. The TPLF was especially troubling to the Reagan administration. It claimed to be truly Marxist and said that the Mengistu government was merely paying lip service to Marxism. The struggle between them was basically ideological. The TPLF's primary attraction for the administration was the desire of some of its members for "self-determination" under which the province would govern itself free from Addis Ababa. The EPLF, however demanded complete independence from Ethiopia.

11. All during the famine the Mengistu government refused to abandon its annual spring offensives and persisted in attacking guerrilla positions in Tigray and Eritea. The fighting included battles for control of an EPLF 5,000-hectare irrigated farm at Ali Ghidir—in an obvious effort to hurt the guerrillas' food supplies. The guerrillas also attacked relief camps on the government side. In 1983, twelve relief workers were taken prisoner by the TPLF in Korem and held for about two months before being released unharmed. The TPLF claimed that the workers had been shown conditions among the starving people in Tigray province (*Africa Research Bulletin* 1983).

12. The International Institute of Strategic Studies reported that Mengistu's armed forces were among the largest in sub-Saharan Africa: three mechanized divisions, twenty-one infantry divisions, 100 combat aircraft, and Soviet and Cuban advisers (Cowell 1984).

13. IGETSU was withheld from most members of congress and the U.S. public until December 1984. It was first mentioned publicly by then Vice President George Bush in March 1985. Twice during public testimony in 1984, Peter McPherson told joint hearings before the House Committee on Foreign Affairs and the Select Committee on Hunger that he would discuss the U.S. "back door" operations only in closed session. "In a closed hearing," McPherson told the joint hearings, "I would be prepared to detail some of what we are doing in the guerrilla controlled areas" (House Committee on Foreign Affairs and the Select Committee on Hunger 1984,8). And later McPherson added: "I would like to talk in closed session about how food is getting into the guerrilla areas instead of talking in this open session, if I might, Congressman" (1984, 29).

Earlier in the year, however, Julia Chang Bloch, head of the Food for Peace program at USAID, made the following slip to the Senate Subcommittee on

Foreign Relations (1984, 52): "We are now working with international organizations as well as private voluntary organizations to see how we can reach behind the government lines. It is not an easy problem."

14. The General Accounting Office said that the IGETSU cross-border operation "directly impacted on the time to approve the two CRS requests for emergency food assistance" on the government side (General Accounting Office 1985, 8).

15. Dawit Wolde Giorgis, interview with the author, Washington, D.C., 26 June 1986.

16. CRS was the principal PVO on the government side while several other agencies worked from inside Sudan to distribute food in the guerrilla areas. This was a politically contentious role, and some relief workers considered CRS "a tool" of the Mengistu government (Askin 1985, 9).

17. Representative Ted Weiss (D-New York) said that CRS alone was trying to feed 900,000 people in Tigray and another 100,000 Tigrayans in Wollo (House Committee on Foreign Affairs 1985, 53).

18. *Newsweek* also pointed out (1983, 38) that the Reagan administration's budget for intelligence operations had increased 17 percent a year since 1981, faster even than the defense budget.

19. Noel C. Koch, deputy assistant secretary of defense for international security affairs, testified that Ethiopia was supporting guerrilla efforts in southern Sudan aimed at toppling the Nimeiri government. Representative Don Bonker (D-Washington) asked Koch: "Do we have documented proof that Mengistu is assisting in a very heavy way to bring down the Government of Sudan?" "Yes sir," replied Koch, "we have that evidence" (House Subcommittee on Africa 1984, 36).

20. Dawit Wolde Giorgis, interview with the author, Washington, D.C., 24 June 1986.

21. The guerrillas also tried to use food against the government. In September 1983, eighteen U.S. religious and relief agency leaders called on the secretary general of the United Nations to seek a cease-fire in the Ethiopian highlands to facilitate the distribution of food aid. The guerrilla fronts, no political novices, picked up the idea and championed the offer of "a free passage of food." The EPLF invited donors to contribute to ERA, and the TPLF promised free passage to all relief aid through its territory; it even offered to remove its land mines from the roads (Russell 1984, 28). The call for a food passage and a cease-fire was repeated by the guerrillas in 1984 (*Wall Street Journal* 1984).

22. After Vice President Bush's visit to Khartoum, the administration said that it would channel 90,000 tons of grain through the PVOs into Eritea and Tigray (Calabrese 1985).

23. Vice President Bush went from Khartoum to the African Famine Conference in Geneva, where he was to give the keynote address. Before his speech, however, Bush held a secret meeting with Goshu Wolde, Ethiopia's foreign minister, Chester Crocker, assistant secretary of state for Africa, and Dawit Wolde Giorgis. The Ethiopians expected Bush to make a hard-hitting speech about food being deliberately withheld by the Mengistu government from the majority of starving Ethiopians. Instead, the vice president toned down the speech and simply pointed out that the United States pledged to continue to help starving Ethiopians in the guerrilla areas and would not stand by "as famine took its toll in northern Ethiopia." This was the first

public mention of the "back door" operation (Calabrese 1985, 28). The Ethiopians were delighted by the emasculated address of the vice president. Goshe Wolde told a press conference after Bush's speech that "food is being distributed" in the north and there are "virtually no starving civilians there" (*Economist* 1985, 57; Momoh 1985, 504).

24. Through the Nixon, Ford, Carter, and Reagan administrations, Saudi Arabia has also assisted U.S. foreign policy operations in Afghanistan, Nicaragua, Pakistan, Somalia, Sudan, Yemen, and Zaire (Ungar 1985). In Afghanistan, the Saudi Arabian government matched the United States in a jointly run fund to purchase "hundreds" of Stinger missiles for the Islamic guerrillas "even though Congress would not permit such sophisticated weapons to be sold to the Saudis themselves." Several wealthy Saudi princes also contributed cash to the guerrillas (Pear 1988, A1).

25. On 10 October, a USAID assessment team made a dramatic eyewitness report by cable of the starvation to the secretary of state with copies to U.S. embassies in Africa and Western Europe. The assessment team drove along the main road from Addis Ababa to Korem in Wollo province. "USAID officer drove both ways," said the cable, "and on return was stopped seven times by starving children (5–12 years old) lying in the road refusing to move until small pieces of bread were scattered on roadsides [which] they scattered to pick it [sic] up."

The team reported finding 200,000 people living in the Korem shelter. These included more than 7,000 "severely malnourished children and adults requiring care [who were] drawn selectively from shelter population." The death rate was about seventy children a day. Some people had walked to the shelter from villages up to 100 miles away. New people came into the shelter at the rate of about 100 a day. They lived "under plastic sheets and straw huts they build themselves."

"Korem represents only the visible tip of the iceberg," the assessment team reported. At Harbu, in Wollo, another 205,000 people quietly waited for food aid. The RRC coordinator in Wollo told the team that the number of people needing help had climbed from 1.3 million to more than two million in September. Twenty percent were children under the age of six. "Present operations are not touching that order of magnitude, and with best intentions, it is unlikely that massive deaths in Welo [Wollo] can be avoided over the next three months."

There is no evidence that this cable, despite its dramatic reporting, received any more attention than the previous assessment team cables sent to State and USAID in 1983–84 (USAID cable 1984).

26. John Swenson, interview with the author, Washington, D.C., 17 May 1985.

References

Africa Confidential. 1985. "Ethiopia: Eritrean Update," 11 December, 7.

Africa Research Bulletin. 1983. "Ethiopia: USAID Workers Kidnapped." 1–30 April: 6804.

Africa Research Bulletin. 1984a. "Ethiopia: Eritrean Guerrilla Congress." 1–30 June: 7280.

Africa Research Bulletin. 1984b. "Africa's Drought—Countdown to Disaster." 15 October–14 November: 7480.

Anderson, Jack. 1985. "NSC Resisted Giving Aid to Ethiopia." *Washington Post,* 16 January, E18.

Askin, Steve. 1985. "War in Eritrea Compounds Famine Misery." *Africa News,* 18 November, 9.

Calabrese, Michael. 1985. "Ethiopian Aid Undercuts an Independence Effort." *Wall Street Journal,* 9 May, 28.

Carter, Chris. 1985. Grassroots International. Quoted on "The MacNeil/Lehrer Newshour," 28 January. Transcript 2436.

Central Intelligence Agency. 1974. *Potential Implications of Trends in World Population, Food Production, and Climate* (August). Photocopy.

Christian Science Monitor. 1984. "Politics Hinders Food Aid to Starving People in Ethiopia," 20 July, 1.

Cohen, Marc J. 1984. "U.S. Food Aid to South-east Asia, 1975–1983." *Food Policy* 9 (May): 139–155.

Cohen, Roberta. 1987. "Censorship Costs Lives." *Index on Censorship* (May): 15.

Congressional Research Service. 1984a. *Feeding the World's Population: Developments in the Decade Following the World Food Conference* (October).

Congressional Research Service. 1984b. *U.S. Assistance to Ethiopia: Foreign Aid Facts Updated 12/27/84* (27 December).

Cowell, Alan. 1984. "African Famine Battle: Aid Has Been a Villain." *New York Times,* 29 November, A1.

Echikson, William. 1985. "US-Europe Food Battle Escalates." *Christian Science Monitor* 12 June, 9.

Economist Intelligence Unit. 1982. *Uganda, Ethiopia, Somalia, Djibouti, Fourth Quarter.* London.

Economist. 1985. "Famine in Africa: Here Is the Food, Now Get It There" (16 March): 57.

Gelb, Leslie H., and Anthony Lake. 1974–75. "Washington Dateline: Less Food, More Politics." *Foreign Policy* 17 (Winter).

General Accounting Office. 1985. *The United States' Response to the Ethiopian Food Crisis.* Report to the Honorable Byron L. Dorgan, House of Representatives, GAO/NSAID-85-26, 8 April.

Girardet, Edward. 1985. "Politics Blocks Aid Vital to Ethiopia." *Christian Science Monitor,* 2 May.

Hackett, Kenneth. 1983. Letter to the author, 31 August.

Hackett, Kenneth. 1984. Prepared statement before the Senate Subcommittee on Foreign Relations, *Hunger in Africa,* 98th Cong., 2d sess., 1 March.

Harden, Blaine. 1984. "Ethiopia Scolds Aid Donors." *Washington Post,* 12 December, A1.

Heritage Foundation. 1984. *Mandate for Leadership II: Continuing the Conservative Revolution.* Washington, D.C.: Heritage Foundation.

Hoover, Herbert. 1960. *Famine in Forty-five Nations: Organization Behind the Front, 1914–1923.* Vol. 2, *An American Epic.* Chicago: Henry Regnery.

House Committee on Agriculture. 1983. *Review [of] the World Hunger Problem (Secretary John R. Block),* 98th Cong., 1st sess., 25 October.

House Committee on Foreign Affairs. 1984. *The Impact of U.S. Foreign Policy on Seven African Countries: Report of a Congressional Study Mission to Ethiopia, Zaire, Zimbabwe, Ivory Coast, Algeria and Morocco and a Staff Mission to Tunisia, August 24–27, 1983,* 98th Cong., 2d sess., 9 March.

House Committee on Foreign Affairs. 1985. *African Famine Situation,* 99th Cong., 1st sess., 30 January and 19 February.

House Committee on Foreign Affairs and the Select Committee on Hunger. 1984. *World Food and Population Issues/Emergency Assistance to Africa,* 98th Cong., 2d sess., 2 August and 13 September.

House Select Committee on Hunger. 1984. *Effective Uses of Agricultural Abundance for Hunger Relief,* 98th Cong., 2d sess., 20 September.

House Select Committee on Hunger. 1985. "Situation Report 7," 27 June.

House Subcommittee on Africa of the Committee on Foreign Affairs. 1984. *Sudan: Problems and Prospects,* 98th Cong., 2d sess., 28 March.

International News Column. 1984. *Wall Street Journal,* 31 October, 1.

Iyer, Pico. 1985. "Ethiopia: The Politics of Famine." *Time,* 20 May, 37.

Johnson, Robert H. 1986. "'Rollback' Revisited—A Reagan Doctrine for Insurgent Wars?" *Policy Focus* (January).

Kamm, Henry. 1983. "22 African Nations Said to Face a Catastrophic Shortage of Food." *New York Times,* 19 October.

King, Seth S. 1985a. "Another Bumper Wheat Crop Is Forecast for US." *New York Times,* 11 June, D3.

King, Seth S. 1985b. "U.S. Food for Africa Is Called Costly." *New York Times,* 1 February, A10.

Korn, David. 1986. *Ethiopia, the United States and the Soviet Union.* Carbondale: Southern Illinois University Press.

Lake, Anthony. 1985. "Wrestling with Third World Radical Regimes: Theory and Practice." In *U.S. Foreign Policy and the Third World: Agenda 1985 86,* edited by John W. Sewell, Richard E. Feinberg, and Valeriana Kallab, 119–145. New Brunswick, N.J.: Transaction Books.

Lean, Geoffrey. 1984. "Charity Chief Says West Held Back Food to Topple Ethiopia: 'Britain and U.S. Blocked Famine Aid.'" *Observer,* 28 October, 1.

Legum, Colin. 1984. "Ethiopia Dramatizes Africa's Food Crisis." *New African,* December.

Los Angeles Times. 1985. "U.S. Cancels Aid for Ethiopia's Rebel Areas," 1 July, 9.

MacNeil/Lehrer Newshour. 1985. "Politics of Famine," 28 January. Transcript.

McCann, James. 1987. *From Poverty to Famine in Northeast Ethiopia: A Rural History 1900–1935.* Philadelphia: University of Pennsylvania Press.

Meszoly, Robin. 1984. "Foreign Policy: African Drought Poses Major Aid Challenge." *Congressional Quarterly* (1 December): 3039–3040.

Momoh, Eddie. 1985. "Drought: The Mounting Emergency." *West Africa* (18 March): 504.

Newsweek. 1983. "National Affairs: America's Secret Warriors," 10 October, 38.

New York Times. 1985. "Feeding Ethiopia Without Illusions," 19 January, 20.

New York Times. 1983. "Requiem for a Grain Embargo," 31 July, A21.

New York Times. 1984. "Responses to Famine," 4 November, 24E.

New York Times. 1984b. "Drought Is Said to Threaten Lives of 7 Million in Ethiopia," 21 August, A6.

Ottaway, David B. 1985. "U.S. Helps Ethiopia Rebel Area." *Washington Post,* 14 April, 13.

Oxfam U.K. 1984. "Behind the Weather: Lessons to Be Learned. Drought and Famine in Ethiopia," 13 July. Photocopy.

Pankhurst, Richard K. P. 1961. *An Introduction to the Economic History of Ethiopia: From Early Times to 1800.* London: Lalibela House.

Pankhurst, Richard K. P. 1965. "Some Factors Depressing the Standard of Living of Peasants in Traditional Ethiopia." Paper presented to the Faculty of Arts, University College, Addis Ababa. Mimeo.

Pear, Robert. 1988. "Arming Afghan Guerrillas: A Huge Effort Led by U.S." *New York Times,* 18 April, A1.

Putka, Gary. 1984. "U.S. to Increase Secret Food Aid for Ethiopians." *Wall Street Journal,* 17 December, 39.

Reagan, Ronald. 1985a. Nationally televised news conference, 21 February.

Reagan, Ronald. 1985b. Speech before the Conservative Political Action Conference, Washington D.C., 1 March.

Reagan, Ronald. 1985c. Speech before the National Association of Evangelicals, Orlando, Florida, 8 March.

Roberts, Steven V., Stephen Engelberg, and Jeff Garth. 1987. "Prop for U.S. Policy: Secret Saudi Funds." *New York Times,* 21 June, A1.

Rosenfeld, Stephen S. 1987. "Cowboys From the Start." *Washington Post,* 15 May, A25.

Russell, Eric. 1984. "Eritrea: The Forgotten Drought." *New African,* December, 28.

Schultz, George. 1983. "Foreign Aid and U.S. National Interests." Speech to the Southern Center for International Affairs, Atlanta, Georgia, 24 February.

Sen, Amartya. 1981. *Poverty and Famines: An Essay on Entitlement and Deprivation.* Oxford: Clarendon Press.

Senate Subcommittee of the Committee on Appropriations. 1985. *U.S. Policy Toward Anti-Communist Insurgencies,* 99th Cong., 1st sess., 8 May.

Senate Subcommittee on Foreign Relations of the Committee on Foreign Relations. 1984. *Hunger in Africa,* 98th Cong., 2d sess., 1 March.

Sewell, John W., Richard E. Feinberg, and Valeriana Kallab. 1985. *U.S. Foreign Policy and the Third World: Agenda 1985–86.* New Brunswick, N.J.: Transaction Books.

Sinclair, Ward. 1984. "U.S. Aid to Ethiopia Stirs Controversy: Reagan's Response to Drought at Issue." *Washington Post,* 31 October.

Smith, Gayle E. 1987. *Africa News,* 30 November, 6.

Smith, Gayle E. 1984. "The International Response to the Human Crisis in the Horn of Africa." Paper presented to the Conference on the Horn of Africa, Blackburn Center, Howard University, Washington, D.C., 25 August.

"Statement of Food Aid Needs by Charles E. Hanrahan, Specialist in Agricultural Policy, Congressional Research Service." 1985. Before the House Select Committee on Hunger, 25 July, 4.

Steele, Ian. 1983. "Ethiopia, in Grips of Severe Drought, Has 'Critical' Need of Food, Supplies." *Baltimore Sun,* 2 May.

Steele, Jonathan. 1985. "Guerrilla Dispute Halts Food Aid." *London Guardian,* 12 September.

Teresa, Mother. 1984. Letter to Ronald Reagan, 19 October, San Francisco.

Truman, Harry S. 1955. *Memoirs: Years of Decisions.* New York: Doubleday.

Tyler, Patrick, and David B. Ottaway. 1986. "Ethiopian Security Police Seized, Tortured CIA Agent." *Washington Post,* 25 April, A1.

Ungar, Sanford J. 1985. *Africa: The People and Politics of an Emerging Continent.* New York: Simon and Schuster.

United Nations Disaster Relief Organization. 1983. *Situation Report 11*, Geneva, 10 October.

United Nations Food and Agriculture Organization. 1983. "International Alert on Emergency Food Supply Situation of Selected African Countries." Situation 82–83 Outlook 83–84, Rome, 19 October.

U.S. Embassy, Addis Ababa. 1982. Diplomatic cable to Secretary of State, Washington, Department of State, 22 December. Photocopy.

U.S. Embassy, Addis Ababa. 1984. USAID cable to Secretary of State/Embassies in Brussels, Canberra, Djibouti, Khartoum, Mogadishu, Nairobi, Ottawa, Rome, Geneva. "Subject: Assessment Team Visit to Welo Region." 10 October. Photocopy.

Vallely, Paul. 1985. "Famine: Russia and US on Collusion Course." *London Times*, 4 June, 12.

Wall Street Journal. 1984. "World News Reports/Topics," 31 October, 1.

Wasserman, Gary. 1983. "The Foreign Aid Dilemma." *Washington Quarterly*, 6, 1: 96–106.

Weinraub, Bernard. 1983. "Famine in Africa Is Called Worst in a Decade." *New York Times*, 7 June, A1.

Willis, David K. 1984. "Ethiopia: Hunger Over War." *Christian Science Monitor*, 30 October, 1.

Part III

Famine Relief and Development

Introduction

Even if American policy toward Ethiopia had been more genuinely humanitarian (see Chapter 5), it is often impossible to provide effective relief to people trapped in areas of relentless conflict. But when famine occurs in the absence of armed struggle, relief becomes probable and development in the context of relief becomes possible. To link development to relief, and relief to development, is a relatively new idea—one that poses challenges and opportunities for governments and donor agencies alike. Part III is an examination of this linkage.

Chapter 6 focuses on developmental approaches to relief with the intent of reducing vulnerability to drought and famine. Written by Mary B. Anderson and Peter J. Woodrow, Chapter 6 is based on the International Relief/Development Project at Harvard University's Graduate School of Education. This project studied more than forty relief projects in Asia, Africa, and Latin America that successfully combined relief with broader social and economic development in times of disaster. The arguments concerning famine management advanced in Chapter 6 reflect both the innovative conceptual framework employed by Anderson and Woodrow and the lessons derived from their analysis of different relief projects.

Chapter 7, by Joel R. Charny, overseas director of Oxfam America, is the first of two chapters in this book written by a practitioner responsible for managing a program (the second being Chapter 10 by Ulrich). While Oxfam's preferred approach to famine is developmental, its experience reveals how difficult it is to stay developmental when societies are in crisis, when political pressures intrude, and when surges of donor support dispose to rapid, highly visible action to meet people's most basic needs. The combination of more money to spend and more critical needs to satisfy encourages program initiatives very much larger than the small-scale development projects that Oxfam America normally supports. Many things can go wrong—and go wrong they did, in various ways and to different degrees, in Cambodia, Ethiopia, and Negros Island. Only when responding to the flooding that devastated Bangladesh in 1988 was Oxfam America able to hold to its disaster response policy and help prevent famine while strengthening the capacity of local communities to minimize future flood damage.

Chapter 8, by Hussein M. Adam, examines ten indigenous private voluntary organizations in the Sahel and their responses to the region's propensity to drought. These organizations were all born in the 1970s, in the context of famine, or in the 1980s, at a time of renewed stress. While their agendas vary enormously, not one of them considers itself a relief agency. Adam refers to them collectively as VDOs (voluntary development organizations). The VDOs in the Sahel are caught in the dual dilemma of striving for self-reliance while being painfully dependent on international donors, and of promoting development among people who have been marginalized and on lands that have been degraded by past development. Adam shows the promise of Sahelian VDOs in spite of these dilemmas. To the extent that they serve as an instrument of popular if not yet democratic accountability, VDOs in the Sahel represent a form of development in their own right. They just may be the best agents of famine detection and response available in a vast region subject to repeated stress.

6

Reducing Vulnerability to Drought and Famine

Developmental Approaches to Relief

Mary B. Anderson and Peter J. Woodrow

There are many approaches to famine. Efforts are made to provide "early warning" of impending famine. "Disaster management" courses cover the management of drought and famine responses. Studies are conducted on the "coping mechanisms" of famine-prone peoples. A large international apparatus has been created to provide food aid to famine victims efficiently and effectively. These all represent a growing worldwide concern with, and response to, the human tragedy of hunger. But each approach is partial and, in and of itself, inadequate. The real goal—ultimately the only valid approach to famine—is to prevent it.

Drought, which is often the ostensible cause of famine, cannot be entirely prevented, though much can be done to restore ecological balance through reforestation and land reclamation that will result in more effective water retention and conservation. Similarly, widespread crop failure may not be entirely preventable though, again, changing certain human misbehaviors that cause land deterioration can greatly reduce the incidence of such failures.

On the other hand, famine, the widespread morbidity and mortality that result from lack of food, can be prevented. Famine in today's world results from human misuse of natural resources and from ill-designed human systems for producing, marketing, and distributing food rather than from overall production shortages, climatic failures, or fixed resource constraints. Famine in the late twentieth century can be overcome through human action. Some argue that the development of systems for the rapid distribution of food from areas of surplus to areas of deficit constitutes the best method for preventing

large-scale hunger. Others argue that local self-sufficiency in food production through regenerative agricultural practices provides the best
potential solution (Rodale International 1988). This paper will examine approaches to famine response and prevention that are not limited
to a choice between these two positions but, in some sense, respond to
both. We shall discuss the impact of global food distribution efforts on
the local capacities of famine victims and shall offer criteria for planning famine relief so that it promotes systemic, long-term development of victim capacities for producing and storing sufficient food to
prevent famines.

Through a recent collaborative research project, we have found
that it is possible for international famine assistance either to promote
the capacities of people who suffer from famine so that they are better
able to handle future food crises, or to leave those it purports to help
worse off and even more vulnerable to subsequent disasters. The first
part of this chapter briefly describes the project out of which the findings emerged, and presents the salient lessons learned about the relationships between disasters and development. The relevance of these
lessons to famine response is also discussed. To illustrate alternative
strategies for promoting development in the midst of crisis, in the second part of the chapter famine response programs are presented and
analyzed for their impact on capacities and vulnerabilities.

Lessons Learned Through the
International Relief/Development Project

In 1986, a number of nongovernmental organizations (NGOs) and government bilateral and multilateral donor agencies joined together in a
collaborative project to examine their experiences providing relief at
times of disaster. The purpose of the International Relief/Develop-
ment Project (IRDP), located at Harvard University's Graduate School
of Education, was to explore the linkages between relief and development and to extract lessons from past experience that would help
agencies provide relief in future disasters in ways that both met
immediate needs and intrinsically supported basic development. The
IRDP studied forty relief projects which were undertaken in response
to a range of disaster types, including refugee emergencies, earthquakes, floods, typhoons, volcanic eruptions, and famines. (The general lessons learned from the International Relief/Development
Project and a selection of the forty project case histories are presented
in Anderson and Woodrow 1989.) While the project did not focus
exclusively on famine, it did study a number of relief efforts in famine
situations, and the general lessons learned have direct relevance to

famine prevention. We turn now to a summary of these lessons and a discussion of their relevance to famine situations.

Lesson 1

Not all crises become disasters. A disaster is a crisis situation that outstrips the capacity of a society to cope with it (Krimgold 1976). Societies can develop both economic and social systems so that they do not require outside assistance to handle a crisis; that is, they do not experience "disasters" because they can cope with whatever crises they face without excessive loss of life and property.

Relevance to famine. Examples abound of societies which, when faced with food shortages, are nonetheless able to prevent starvation among the people in the area of the shortages. Sometimes they do so by redistributing food within their own economies; sometimes they purchase food internationally; sometimes they provide food directly to those who suffer shortages; sometimes they make monetary payments to those in need who then make the necessary purchases. Drought conditions and resultant crop failures in the midwest of the United States in 1988 and 1989 did not result in massive hunger and migration in search of food. Overall the society had a sufficiently diversified economy and sufficient access to stores of food to prevent famine.

Similarly, drought and food shortages in parts of the Soviet Union in the 1980s were handled through purchases of additional grains on the international market. In spite of severe droughts in 1984–87 in the states of Gujarat and Rajasthan, India prevented famine through its employment guarantee programs, providing paid employment for all workers who would otherwise have faced starvation (Ressler 1989). Each of these societies has developed sufficient resources and social systems for preventing famine within its borders.

Lesson 2

In areas where disasters occur, not everyone suffers equally, and some people do not suffer at all. Vulnerability is the concept that best explains *who* suffers from any given disaster.

Through an examination of over thirty situations in which relief assistance had been given to people in a disaster situation, the International Relief/Development Project developed a framework for understanding the vulnerabilities that comprise the basic causes of disasters as well as for analyzing the best ways to provide relief assistance. This framework is represented by the matrix in Figure 6.1, which shows that vulnerabilities can be divided into three interrelated categories: the material/physical realm; the social/organizational realm; and the

Figure 6.1 Capacities and Vulnerabilites Analysis

	Vulnerabilities	*Capacities*
Physical/Material *What productive resources, hazards, and skills exist?*		
Social/Organizational *What are the relations and organizations among people?*		
Motivational/Attitudinal *How does the community view its ability to create change?*		

motivational/attitudinal realm. (The matrix in Figure 6.1 also includes a column for "Capacities" which is discussed below. See also Anderson and Woodrow 1989.)

Poverty is the most obvious physical vulnerability. Poor people often live in economically precarious areas and have few resources for preventing or recovering from crises. They live on marginal lands where soil fertility is low; their houses are constructed of less durable materials; their children are malnourished; they have low educational attainment and, therefore, few employment options; they do not buy insurance policies.

Other physical characteristics also make some individuals more vulnerable than others. In general, women are more vulnerable to disasters than men in that they usually have fewer resources, including income and employment options, and have more limited mobility because of social strictures. As managers of food distribution, women tend first to cut down their own food consumption in times of shortage in order to preserve more for other family members, thus putting themselves at risk before their families.

In addition to physical or material vulnerabilities, there are also vulnerabilities in two other realms—the social/organizational and the motivational/attitudinal—which make groups, and individuals, susceptible to disasters. Where societies are divided along class, caste, or racial lines, they tend to be more vulnerable to crises than societies which are cohesive, neighborly, and in which there is a high degree of mutual caretaking. Groups and individuals who are excluded from decisionmaking and other social power structures tend to be more vulnerable than those who share or hold power. Societies or groups in which the prevalent mood is one of discouragement and powerlessness are more vulnerable than those in which people feel a sense of efficacy and share some motivation for effecting change.

Relevance to famine. In modern times, there has never been a drought-induced famine so pervasive that the children of the rich have died of hunger. (The situation may be different in a war-induced famine.) Droughts, and the famines they sometimes bring, are usually localized, both geographically (Independent Commission 1985) and in terms of the groups of people who are affected. Even in areas of extreme food shortage, not everyone goes hungry. Some individuals and groups have resources for coping (Downing 1990); they have greater wealth with which to buy food; they have family members in other areas with whom they can go and live or who can send remittances; or they have the ability (knowledge, wealth) to organize an early exodus from a famine-prone area.

Conversely, even when a larger society copes effectively with food shortages to prevent famine, some groups and individuals still suffer. Although the drought in the United States in the summer of 1988 did not result in widespread hunger, it did have a negative, and even "disastrous," impact on certain individuals and segments of society. Because of failed crops, farmers lost their farms and had to migrate to find new occupations, if they were fortunate enough to find alternatives. Food prices rose causing hardship for families whose household budgets were strained.

Famine, however, is the occurrence of large-scale hunger causing major portions of populations to migrate in search of food. Famine occurs where entire groups of people are vulnerable, economically and/or socially.

Recent famine in the Horn of Africa vividly illustrates the several areas of vulnerability. Because of increased pressures on the land in the form of growing human and animal populations, the carrying capacity of the land has deteriorated in recent decades. Deforestation and soil erosion have lowered agricultural productivity. The introduction in some areas of large-scale cropping patterns involving the use of fertilizers and irrigation, the improvement in health conditions of animals that have resulted in larger herds, and the drilling of boreholes to supply water for increasing numbers of humans and animals have all contributed to lowering the water table. When severe drought occurs, traditional coping mechanisms are no longer adequate to sustain family survival. People are materially more vulnerable now than in the past.

Conditions of war also leave people politically and socially vulnerable to food shortages. War forces people to move to inappropriate lands. War destroys crops and tools; and, in too many cases, food has become one more weapon in the arsenals of governments or other forces which attempt to maintain or gain positions of power. People who experience repeated loss of their crops and the uncertainties imposed by conflict also may lose any sense of political or social power.

Although they may mean well, outsiders who "impose" relief assistance on "victims" (Harrell-Bond 1986) and who themselves assume all decisionmaking and organizing power for meeting the crisis may increase the vulnerabilities of those who suffer, leaving them further victimized by the aid itself.

Lesson 3

Disaster "victims" have important capacities which are not destroyed in a disaster. Outside aid to these victims must be provided in ways that recognize and support these capacities if it is to have a positive long-term effect. When relief assistance is given without recognition of these capacities, it can undermine and weaken them, leaving those whom it is intended to help even worse off than they were before.

Capacities can also be understood best by looking at them in the three categories discussed above for vulnerabilities and shown on the matrix in Figure 6.1. No matter how poor people are or how much they have lost through a disaster, they still have some material capacities. Even if they have lost all material possessions, they have their own abilities to work and the skills and knowledge with which to produce. In addition, societies have social/organizational capacities, including such things as leadership, governance and decisionmaking systems, and clan and family ties and loyalties. Societies also have attitudinal/motivational capacities. They have shared belief systems, religious or ideological. An older woman from a village which had suffered repeated volcano and typhoon disasters in the Philippines said that they have "fighting spirit."

When disaster strikes, outside aid is offered out of a sense of concern for the victims and a genuine desire to help. The impacts of disasters are, in the first instance, physical. Houses fall down, crops are destroyed, people are injured or sick. Outside assistance, thus, focuses on the obvious and urgent physical needs which people face. If crops have failed or been destroyed, food is sent. If illness or injury has occurred, medical care and medicines are sent. If homes are destroyed, tents or other construction materials are provided, as are household goods, clothing, blankets, etc.

However, by focusing on meeting immediate physical needs of disaster victims, those who wish to be helpful can (and often do) ignore both the material things that people already have or can procure locally as well as their social/cultural/motivational strengths. Aid agencies and their donors identify the swift meeting of physical needs as the goal, and their overwhelming concern becomes logistical efficiency. Where can we get the best contributions of drugs, tents, food? Which planes can be chartered to fly these items in to the needy people? How can we monitor all donations to ensure that these gifts truly reach the neediest? How can we staff our effort to ensure that we are fully accountable to our donors for the use of their gifts?

By allowing these concerns to become paramount, relief organizations usurp all control and decisionmaking power from the victims. People who need *things* are robbed even of their social power as others take charge of meeting immediate physical needs.

Relevance to famine. A television crew filmed the following events in a major feeding camp in Ethiopia in the winter of 1984-85. The trucks carrying donated grain pulled into the camp, and soldiers and relief workers began to unload the sacks. Some grains fell from a corner of a sack as it was carried to its storage place. An old woman—a famine "victim"—stooped in the dust to recover the fallen grains. One of the relief workers saw her and asked what she was doing. She explained that she was gathering up the grain that would otherwise be lost. She was told to stop. "But," she protested, "if I do not do this, who will?" The answer, "No one. But it is not your job. Please, go, sit down and wait; we will feed you."

Lesson 4

A distinction should be made between needs and vulnerabilities. Needs arise at times of disaster, and relief assistance must focus on meeting them in a timely manner. Underlying the disaster—the basic causes of the disaster—are long-term vulnerabilities. There are many different programming options for meeting needs, some of which address vulnerabilities.

Relevance to famine. Hunger and starvation are caused by food shortages, but these shortages often result from much deeper causes than a seasonal crop failure. Soil erosion, lowering water tables, desertification, and deforestation have occurred over time and thus require larger and longer efforts to reverse. Relief assistance must, in the first instance, provide food to hungry people. The food should, and can, be provided in ways that promote future ecological rebuilding. (We shall discuss below a project which provided food to people suffering current shortages in return for their work in land reclamation.)

Lesson 5

The long-term developmental impacts of relief aid are determined by *how* the aid is given more than by what is given. Agencies providing assistance should do both a "capacities assessment" and a "needs assessment" as they begin their work. It is impossible to understand needs with any accuracy without also assessing the ability of the people themselves to meet their needs through the capacities they have. To fail to do this is to risk swamping a society with unnecessary goods while, at the same time, weakening existing social structures needed for long-term development.

Relevance to famine. Even in feeding camps, food can be provided to people in ways that utilize their own distribution systems. It is even better to distribute needed food to people who remain on their land and in their homes, so that they can undertake land improvements in fallow seasons and are in a position to plant crops as soon as conditions allow. Below we shall discuss a project that used the idle labor of famine "victims" to construct roads that allowed the delivery of food to their homes and, thus, avoided establishment of feeding camps. Other examples exist where free food distribution has disrupted local markets so that farmers' incentives to grow food and their ability to make a profit have been undermined.

Lesson 6

An intervention's impact on capacities and vulnerabilities varies according to its duration and scale. All relief efforts, no matter how brief or small, can recognize and build on capacities; addressing vulnerabilities often takes more time, more resources, and a larger-scale effort.

It is always possible for those who provide relief to recognize that those whom they help have resources and capacities even though they have suffered from a disaster. Having recognized such capacities, relief workers can rely on these local abilities and encourage them. However, even though relief workers may recognize deep-seated problems that constitute the vulnerabilities of a group they are helping, there may be very little that the relief effort can do to address, or reduce, these in the immediate term. Because vulnerabilities are basic and have often become endemic over time, it also takes time, and longer-term efforts, to change them.

Relevance to famine. In a feeding center, where masses of hungry people have assembled to seek free food as a last resort, relief workers can organize the processes through which food is provided to rely on the existing family or other social structures of those in the camp. Women, the basic managers of food, can be relied on to arrange food preparation and distribution. Both men and women can take part in camp decisions and planning about living arrangements, health care, public health activities, the setting of priorities, etc. However, because famine often arises from basic deterioration in land quality and disruptions of water supplies, both circumstances that require solutions on a large scale and over time, immediate feeding programs can do very little to address these issues. This difference, between relying on and promoting capacities and reducing basic vulnerabilities, will be further illustrated below in case examples.

Implications of IRDP Findings
for Famine Prevention or Response Programs

Relief program planners should consider three important sets of information: (1) the immediate needs that result from a crisis situation; (2) the capacities of those whom the disaster has struck; and (3) the long-term, underlying circumstances and trends, described above as vulnerabilities. The challenge is to use these three sets of information to design a program that meets immediate needs in such a way that, at the very least, does not damage the capacities of the society and, at best, promotes capacities and reduces vulnerabilities. Analyzing needs, capacities, and vulnerabilities is *necessary* for the design of emergency programming so that it has a positive developmental impact; but is not *sufficient*. Program planners still must make judgments about probable outcomes in each context. The power of the framework suggested above is that it provides a way to gather and organize confusing and/or contradictory information in a systematic and thorough way to develop an effective program strategy. By program strategy we mean a staged approach that links the provision of immediate assistance to desired long-term outcomes in a logical sequence of activities. The "logic" of a program strategy arises from the specific contextual realities of local needs, capacities, and vulnerabilities. The lessons presented in Figure 6.1 point to identifiable and clear strategic directions.

Program or project strategies may begin in one cell or another of the Capacities and Vulnerabilities Analysis matrix presented in Figure 6.1. For instance, a feeding program for people in drought areas could begin by relying on the people to decide on distribution priorities and to design the food assistance program themselves through their own leadership and decisionmaking structures. Such a strategy would start in the social/organizational capacities realm. On the other hand, a program which started with physical/material capacities would not emphasize the participation of people in decisions, but might well employ their labor and other skills for transport, delivery, and monitoring of aid.

Some of the classic models of famine response provide telling negative examples of program strategies. In a feeding camp situation, the "victims" are often assumed to be completely helpless, without skills, energy, or motivation to assist in the process of running the camp or in the process of distributing food. After some time, this assessment becomes self-fulfilling and results in a dependency syndrome.

The IRDP examined the experience of over thirty nongovernmental organizations in more than forty relief projects in Africa, Asia, and Latin America. The projects were chosen because they had, in some way, managed to link relief efforts with social and economic development. Each of the projects also illustrates a particular strategy for meeting urgent needs while promoting development. We turn now to a discussion of some of these illustrations of strategic program and project options.

A Physical/Material Approach: Increasing Capacities

A project in Ethiopia undertaken by Save the Children Federation (SCF/USA) is a good example of a major famine relief effort which relied on local physical and social capacities and built on them. (For a full project description, see Anderson and Woodrow 1989, 135–155.) In late 1984, SCF was asked to provide relief to a large district, Yifat na Timuga, in north central Ethiopia where people were beginning to leave their homes and gather at roadsides and towns, seeking food. SCF decided that a primary objective was to avoid the disruptive and dehumanizing feeding camps so common to famine relief programs. Accordingly, they developed a strategy of encouraging people to stay in their homes or return to them, and promised to bring food as close to their villages as possible.

Many highland communities in Ethiopia are virtually inaccessible by truck. Often the only way to reach them from the main roads is by several days' journey by pack animal over dirt tracks. SCF staff consulted with the local peasants associations about how to increase access to the scattered communities in the district so that food could reach remote areas. The peasant associations mobilized men and women who were idled by the drought to work on road construction. Working in teams of two hundred, under the guidance of an Ethiopian engineer hired by SCF, they built stone roads on the existing animal tracks so that trucks carrying relief grain could use them. During the first year of the food relief project, 450 kilometers of roads were built in this way.

SCF also hired young high school graduates to work in teams to survey the villages in the district. These teams of rural rehabilitation aides (RRAs) traveled by foot from village to village, and house to house, interviewing family members, measuring levels of malnutrition, and teaching a simple method of oral rehydration therapy (ORT) to mothers. On designated days, villagers gathered at specified points near their villages to receive the grain shipments distributed by the RRAs. At the same time, immunizations were provided by Ministry of Health workers and additional public health lessons were transmitted by the RRA teams.

Some villages remained inaccessible. Additional community capacities had to be harnessed to deliver food to these areas. Many people in the district still had donkeys, even after the less hardy (and more edible!) sheep and cattle had died. Donkey trains were organized by villagers to deliver grain to the most remote areas, a much less expensive solution than the dramatic air drops used elsewhere in Ethiopia during the same period.

The strategy of this project was mainly to utilize existing community capacities (labor, animal tracks, educated youth, pack animals) and to promote additional or increased capacities (roads, mothers' knowledge of ORT, skills of RRAs). Some aspects of the program began to deal with longer-term issues. After the first year, the program began to expand work on village-based public health and medical care, to promote reforestation and erosion control, and to introduce improvements in agricultural practices.

An Environmental Approach: Reducing Vulnerabilities

Not far from the SCF project, the Ethiopian Red Cross, with support from the Red Cross Societies of Japan, Sweden, and the Federal Republic of Germany, embarked on a multisectoral strategy to address the profound environmental problems in two districts of Wollo Province. (For a full project description, see Anderson and Woodrow 1989, 111–133.) The Disaster Prevention Project (DPP) was concerned with the long-term issues of soil degradation, agricultural practices, water conservation, uses of vegetation, and diversification of income. This ambitious effort came as the third of three overlapping phases in an extended project that began with food distribution, followed by agricultural rehabilitation, including provision of seeds, tools, oxen and fertilizer. Rather than waiting until the food crisis had passed to set the DPP in motion, the Ethiopian Red Cross decided to work on long-term issues even during the crisis. Many of the benefits from this effort will not be realized for years.

The Red Cross recognized that the area would continue to require regular provision of relief if the farmers could not grow sufficient food—a difficult prospect even in "good" years. The DPP placed strong emphasis on training local farmers in agriculture and soil conservation techniques. It employed people (through food-for-work) on terracing projects, irrigation works, construction of roads, establishment of tree nurseries, and planting of trees. Later project phases included development of fish cultivation in local lakes, a vital source of protein during drought periods. At a more fundamental level, the DPP sought to change the attitudes of local people toward their environment by introducing practical ways to maintain and preserve it.

The project strategy concentrated in the physical/material area but, unlike the SCF program described above, was oriented toward reducing vulnerabilities rather than increasing capacities.

Assisting Peoples in Transition: Creating New Social Capacities

Another possible program strategy is to start in the social/organizational realm. The American Friends Service Committee (AFSC), in cooperation with the Government of Mali, worked with a group of nomads whose livelihoods had been devastated in the drought of the early 1970s. (For a full project description, see Anderson and Woodrow 1989, 279–299.) The thrust of this project was to establish an entirely new social enterprise: a nomad village called Tin Aicha. Although nomads traditionally move constantly to pursue their pastoral livelihoods, more than a hundred nomad families volunteered to experiment with a new way of life. Doing this required that they adapt old social structures or develop new ones, change their orientation toward their own labor, and reorient their relationship with the Malian government.

Through the project, each family received land on the shores of Lake Faguibine, near Goundam. The nomads learned agricultural techniques and these, mixed with modest livestock herding, provided family income through diversified economic activities. They also developed the administrative and decisionmaking apparatus of a "normal" Malian town, adapting their traditional governance structures to the village form.

The government provided an agricultural extension worker, teachers for a school, a nurse for a clinic, and established a cooperative store. Eventually, buildings were constructed for all these enterprises, and the men were trained in construction skills while the women learned to fire bricks. AFSC provided development workers to work with community leaders in exploring new coping strategies responsive to the circumstances brought on by repeated drought. Sometimes these staff provided necessary "grease" to the government wheels. In addition, AFSC funded community projects, such as the construction of the buildings, and facilitated training programs for social workers, health aides, and for villagers in well digging and the building trades.

The village of Tin Aicha developed steadily through the late 1970s. When the drought of the early 1980s arrived, the new social structures and economic survival strategies of the village were tested. Many Tin Aicha families left the area temporarily, seeking employment elsewhere as farm or construction laborers, or moving south with their animals to find pasturage. The school in Tin Aicha, which had by then been expanded to nine grades, continued throughout the drought period. Many people said that this was the most important stabilizing base for the community.

The nomads of northern Mali continue to struggle with the future viability of their traditional lifestyle, now threatened by chronic drought and encroaching sedentary farming. The village of Tin Aicha represents an early and quite successful experiment at mixing pastoral and agricultural activities in the nexus of a new social entity.

Building Motivational Capacity

Under the leadership of a charismatic sheikh, a community in drought-prone Somalia established a stable and virtually "drought-proof" community. (For a full project description, see Farah and Harris 1987.) The project is unusual in that it started in the motivational/attitudinal area. The sheikh provided strong inspiration and a set of principles which guided the community. All community strategies to improve agricultural and livestock practices were motivated by shared beliefs and a strong sense of community belonging and responsibility. Over twenty years of community history, the group expanded to three sites, multiplied its membership many times, and diversified its sources of income. In a country where many people live on the margin and suffer from periodic drought, the Sheikh Bananey Cooperative stands out as a viable enterprise.

A motivational/attitudinal approach would be difficult and, in many cases, inappropriate for an outside group to pursue. Nonetheless, the Sheikh Bananey Cooperative received considerable financial and material assistance from foreign organizations but always on its own terms. The Cooperative established its own priorities; assistance from the outside was permitted only if it fit the Cooperative's criteria.

Layers and Levels of Relief/Development Programming

India has developed successful strategies for preventing famine through its widely respected Famine Codes. In the states of Rajasthan and Gujarat, where the IRDP visited drought relief projects, efforts were underway at several levels, representing somewhat different, but complementary, strategies. (For a full project description, see Anderson 1988.)

First, the national and state governments have established overall policies and guidelines for the implementation of relief activities. These include clear indicators in terms of failed crops that cause relief measures to be taken at local administrative levels. Funds are provided to guarantee employment in public works projects for those in need so that no one starves. National government workers monitor the progress of activities at the state and local level. One official in the disaster response hierarchy noted that India was running out of appropriate drought-relief public works projects. He suggested that people should receive relief payments to support schooling or skills training as an alternative to the public works approach. Payments for work or for training are concentrated on building capacities; the public works approach adds physical infrastructure capacity while the education/training approach builds human resources.

Second, at the village level and encouraged by community development NGOs, local leaders in Gujarat and Rajasthan identified projects for community action to benefit the whole community. Land that had become wasteland through overuse and erosion was reclaimed through labor-intensive efforts. Communities organized themselves so that women and men from families in need were employed digging water catchment basins and holes to plant trees. If the rains would come in time, the resulting community forests would eventually provide sorely needed fuel wood, fruit, and other products as well as reduce erosion and runoff. Another community/NGO program approach was the establishment of cattle feeding camps during the worst periods of drought. When individual families could no longer feed their cattle, they put them into these camps, supplied by fodder brought in from other areas. Through joint action and with government funding, some local stocks of cattle could be maintained, making it easier for families to recover when the drought ended.

These community activities focused on physical/material strategies aimed at reducing vulnerabilities in the short and long term. Because they were community-based joint actions, they depended on and strengthened social/organizational abilities as well.

Third, at the household level, drought-relief projects provided aid to individual families to increase their own productive capacity or reduce their farm's vulnerability to future droughts. Distressed farmers received direct payments to undertake improvements on their own land: deepening wells, building terracing or other erosion-retarding structures, planting trees or other beneficial vegetation. These funds were sufficient to provide food for the family while its members worked at home on basic improvements that they did not have time to undertake in normal growing seasons.

Activities at these levels—national/state, community, and household—represent different aspects of an overall strategy of drought response and famine prevention. Some efforts assist families to survive the worst effects of the drought. Others, over time, reduce vulnerability to drought and increase community and family capacities to cope.

Other Places, Other Strategies

Each set of crisis circumstances suggests its own strategies for promoting development while meeting immediate needs. Most of the discussion above has focused on responses to or prevention of famines resulting from weather and ecological deterioration. Conflict and war also exacerbate and at times cause massive crop failure and hunger. Logically, a development strategy for responding to famine during a war would be one that focused on reducing the underlying causes of the conflict: long-term social/organizational vulnerabilities. In addition, motivational issues are often linked to issues of justice and oppression that underlie conflict. Strategies for famine response/prevention must deal with political as well as economic, social, and psychological issues to be fully effective.

For the outsider (whether from the next village, from the capital city, or from another continent), the primary emphasis in all strategies for development in times of crisis must be to support existing capabilities. This casts anyone who provides relief assistance as an "ally" for development rather than as a manager of donated food. Survival is paramount, but as the examples above illustrate, developmental work does not have to await the passing of a crisis. Crises are intimately linked to the essential development situation of communities. Strategies for meeting crises must address fundamental development, which, in a basic sense, may be defined as "the process through which vulnerabilities are reduced and capacities increased" (Anderson and Woodrow 1989, 12).

Note

This chapter is reprinted here, with permission, from the British journal *Disasters* 15 (March 1991): 43–54.

References

Anderson, Mary B. 1988. "Projects Supported by Oxfam America in Rajasthan and Gujarat States, India." International Relief/Development Project Case History 28. Available from Disaster Management Center, University of Wisconsin.

Anderson, Mary B., and Peter J. Woodrow. 1989. *Rising from the Ashes: Development Strategies in Times of Disaster*. Boulder: Westview Press.

Downing, Thomas E. 1990. "Monitoring and Responding to Famine: Lessons from the 1984–85 Food Crisis in Kenya." *Disasters* 14, 3: 204–229.

Farah, Mohammed Hassan, and Christopher M. Harris. 1987. "Case Study of the Sheikh Bananey Cooperative." International Relief/Development Project Case History 15. Available from Disaster Management Center, University of Wisconsin.

Harrell-Bond, Barbara. 1986. *Imposing Aid: Emergency Assistance to Refugees*. Oxford: Oxford University Press.

Independent Commission on International Humanitarian Issues. 1985. *Famine: A Man-Made Disaster?* London: Pan Books.

Krimgold, Frederick. 1976. *Overview of the Priority Area Natural Disaster*. New York: United Nations.

Ressler, Everett M. 1989. "Drought in India: Lessons Learned." *UNDRO News* (May/June).

Rodale International. 1988. "Regenerative Agriculture in the Third World: Building on Capacity Not on Need." *International Ag-Sieve* 1, 1.

7

Coping with Crisis

Oxfam America's Disaster Responses

Joel R. Charny

This chapter modifies and expands upon a talk given by Christine Okali, then Africa regional director of Oxfam America, to the Workshop on Famine and Famine Policy of Tufts University on 28 January 1988. Okali's seminar, entitled "Responding to Crisis: Creative Adaptation by a Development Agency," analyzed Oxfam America's response to the 1984–85 famine in the Sahelian belt of Africa and from it drew lessons concerning the broader issues facing development agencies when they attempt to respond to famine on a massive scale.

In this chapter I draw on Okali's analysis and that of other former colleagues who helped shape Oxfam America's response to famine in Africa. My own direct experience in large-scale famine response, however, has involved work related to Asian programs: in Cambodia during the famine in 1979–80 and more recently helping to shape the agency's involvements in the Philippines and Bangladesh in responding to the food shortages affecting displaced sugar workers on the island of Negros in 1985–86 and to the unprecedented flooding in Bangladesh in 1988. Thus, while I will discuss the African crisis of 1984–85, I can analyze the agency's experience in Asia with more authority. I will examine Oxfam America's experience in coping with famine response based on my ten-year experience with the organization. An account of Oxfam America's particular policies and experiences will, I hope, have broad relevance to those analyzing what constitutes famine and how best to prevent or respond to its occurrence.

As William Shawcross points out in his book on the Cambodian relief effort, *Quality of Mercy: Cambodia, Holocaust, and Modern Conscience*

(Shawcross 1984), honest reflection and self-evaluation are not exactly hallmarks of the voluntary agency community. According to their own public relations pieces it seems that the agencies always do well, regardless of the grave mistakes in judgment that journalists and other independent investigators continually uncover. Without making any claim that I can transcend this tendency to present one's work in the best possible light, I will try to present as forthright a picture as possible of the dilemmas facing a small development agency such as Oxfam America as it mounts relief efforts in response to massive human suffering. The analysis presented here is my own and is not necessarily shared by my colleagues at Oxfam America.

Principles of Oxfam America and Disaster Response

Oxfam America is a small, Boston-based development and relief agency, founded in 1970 as an independent offshoot of the British Oxfam (now known officially as Oxfam United Kingdom and Ireland). The name *Oxfam* derives from the cable address of the Oxford Committee for Famine Relief, founded in Oxford, England, in 1942 to respond to a famine in Nazi-occupied Greece. Oxfam America's initial undertaking was to provide relief during the famine in Bangladesh triggered by the war for independence from Pakistan. Thus, the establishment of the two sister institutions, though founded three decades apart, was in each case bound up in the response to famine.

In its first decade of existence, Oxfam America was tiny by U.S. private voluntary organization (PVO) standards. By 1978, total income for a small portfolio of development projects amounted to $500,000. These funds were generated entirely from private contributions. To maintain its independence, Oxfam America has had a policy of neither soliciting nor accepting government funds. By seizing the moment and following Oxfam U.K.'s lead into Cambodia in 1979, however, the agency was able to increase its income tenfold to $5.5 million in 1980. After stabilizing a little below this level for several years, the Ethiopian famine crisis led to another huge increase in income from $5.2 million in the last noncrisis year of 1983 to $16.7 million at the height of public concern in 1985. Agency income subsequently fell off and has stabilized at about $10.5 million. It should be obvious, even from this brief history, how Oxfam America's growth has been directly correlated to famines that grip the donor public in the United States, leading to sudden surges of income.

The paradox is that Oxfam America identifies itself first and foremost as an international agency that funds self-help development projects in poor countries. Disaster relief is an essential component of the agency's mission, but development is the priority. Staff involved in the overseas program devote the majority of their time to identifying and supporting long-term development initiatives. The development of country and regional programs ideally reflects a partnership between Oxfam America staff and the staff of local organizations. Oxfam America brings to bear its own analysis of the primary issues or obstacles to development and empowerment in a given setting, but this analysis is informed by that of local grassroots leaders and development experts from the governmental and nongovernmental sectors. Once program goals are established, Oxfam America functions as a foundation, supporting local organizations that have effective projects in line with the agency's strategy in a particular context. The close partnership with local institutions is one of the prime underpinnings of Oxfam America's work overseas.

A corollary of the importance of partnership is that Oxfam America is not an operational agency. It does not operate its own projects overseas. When wells need to be dug or future union leaders trained, Oxfam America funds local institutions to perform these tasks, rather than sending expatriate staff or hiring local people itself. The closest the agency comes to an operational presence is when it helps local organizations identify experts to provide technical support to a particular project or group of projects. Sometimes these resource people are consultants to Oxfam America rather than staff of a local organization. But these experts are still expected to play a support role within a program identified and carried out by Oxfam America's partner institutions.

Another important characteristic of the agency in the context of a discussion of famine relief is that, as noted above, Oxfam America does not accept government funding as a matter of policy. The agency cannot be a channel for P.L. 480 foodstuffs in a disaster setting. In practice, this policy, coupled with the avoidance of an operational role, has meant that Oxfam America has developed very little direct experience with large-scale distributions of food or other commodities.

The Cambodian relief effort in 1979–80 involved not only unprecedented levels of income and program operations for the agency, but also Oxfam America's first significant efforts to develop a presence in the media in the United States. The involvement in Cambodia generated the first attempts within Oxfam America to try to resolve the potential contradictions and pitfalls for a small development agency trying to alleviate large-scale famine. While staff were enthusiastic about the effort in Cambodia from the beginning, there was concern on the part of the board of directors that the agency would lose its unique development-oriented approach to overseas work. Board members at this time had joined the agency largely out of a commitment to small-scale development work in partnership with local communities. Because there was immense need in Cambodia, which demanded a response, the program ultimately received board support. At the same time the program seemed to many on Oxfam America's board to jar the agency from its fundamental mission. There were too many troubling anomalies about the Cambodia program. Its scale dwarfed previous Oxfam programs. The agency was supporting a team of expatriates in Phnom Penh. Where was the local community involvement? To the extent that there was local participation it was by government officials, not the peasants who were the intended beneficiaries of much of the agency's funding. An aggressive public relations effort was necessary to raise funds, but was Oxfam America compromising its principles by portraying Cambodians as abject victims? And what about the issues of monitoring and accountability in a politically conflicted situation in which Oxfam America, by functioning only inside the country (and not along the Thai-Cambodian border), seemed to be taking sides?

To their credit, staff and board engaged in an extended dialogue on these issues in 1980 and into 1981. The result was a sound disaster response policy which is still in effect. It bears close examination because it shows how staff and board dealt, within a policy framework, with the difficult task of resolving the tensions between long-term work and disaster relief.

The policy first defined terms and stated the principles that should guide Oxfam America's response to a disaster. (See Appendix for the complete text.) In keeping with the agency's experience during the Cambodian relief effort, the statement defines disaster response broadly to include grants, fund raising, public communications, education, and advocacy. The statement then affirms Oxfam America's main goals as promoting understanding of and support for equitable, self-reliant development among the world's poorest people, providing grants to meet development and emergency needs, and educating and advocating for equitable, self-reliant development *and* self-help recovery from disasters by the very poor [emphasis in original]. Appropriate disaster responses "are essential to meeting Oxfam America's main goals." Provision of relief aid, such as food, may sometimes be necessary, but Oxfam America's "primary commitment of funds and other resources will be to help people to help themselves." Development "is the primary goal of Oxfam America in any disaster situation."

The policy then establishes guidelines for disaster response. Important themes run through these guidelines. Perhaps most significant is the statement that any disaster project "should enhance the capacities of people to help themselves and restore their own productive capacities." Further, the project "should strengthen indigenous organization and participation for responding to the disaster and for continuing in reconstruction and development." The guidelines challenge the agency "to make a distinctive contribution" in its disaster response.

Thus, the thinking within Oxfam America, even in this early 1980s policy statement, drawing important lessons from the recent involvement in Cambodia which revolutionized the agency, was very much to respond to disasters with development goals and principles in mind. In the actual projects overseas the emphasis should be on building local capacity to reconstruct and develop.

The policy statement underscores this theme by stating specifically that responsibility for the development of the disaster response should lie with staff already responsible for development projects in the geographic area where the disaster occurs. In other words, there should be no special disasters unit or disasters officer with global responsibilities for the agency's disaster programs.

Regarding the political context, so critical in situations of manmade disaster, the guidelines merely state that "political conditions within the disaster area should permit Oxfam America to serve its basic goals through a disaster response." This statement offers wide latitude for interpretation in any concrete situation. The cases discussed below will demonstrate precisely how difficult it is for agencies to serve their basic goals when political conflict is the primary cause of disaster.

Domestically, the disaster response should provide opportunities to educate the American public concerning self-reliant development. Regarding fund raising and communications work, the disaster response should mean a net increase in funds available so as not to take funds away from ongoing development programming. There was evidently much discussion of communications and fund-raising strategies by the Oxfam board. On the one hand, images of self-reliance, dignity, and self-help capacity are to be the norm, with reconstruction and development aspects of the response emphasized. Yet a note is then inserted that states, "This need not preclude the use of simple advertising which appeals straightforwardly for compassionate responses." There is tension in most overseas development and relief agencies between program and fund-raising staff over the images that compel the American public—more and more hardened to images of suffering—to give needed funds. The tension is unresolvable, except on a case-by-case basis.

Oxfam America's 1981 disaster response policy, therefore, is noteworthy for the following:

- Its emphasis on the primacy of reconstruction and development work within a disaster response

- Its insistence that this reconstruction and development work be oriented toward funding through indigenous institutions and the creation of local capacity
- Its view of a disaster response as a broad-based initiative, involving not only overseas grant making, but also domestic education and advocacy, all pointing toward furthering the long-term development goals of the agency

Disaster Responses: Achievements and Problems

The policy framework just described suggests that Oxfam America will have certain strengths and weaknesses as it approaches its response to famine. The achievements and problems of disaster response in Oxfam America's history relate directly to the advantages and limitations of the agency as reflected in its internal policies and structures.

The following strengths in responding to famine grow out of the agency's policy framework.

The imperative to build long-term development work into any famine response makes it more likely that root causes of famine will be addressed. Since famine derives from a long-term lack of resources on the part of the very poor, there are clearly developmental reasons that lead the crisis to develop the way that it does and to affect most severely the populations that it does. If the response is sound, attempts to address root causes as part of a famine response will make it more likely that famine can be prevented in the future.

Free of the pressure to provide food aid, and guided by the imperative of building local capacity, the agency has greater flexibility to respond in appropriate ways to famine. The aid effort is more likely to be driven by what local people need than by imperatives to deliver food or other materials the agency has access to through its headquarters operation.

The agency is better able to ignore U.S. government pressure to respond a certain way in a disaster setting because neither the specific disaster response nor the long-term viability of the agency depends on the receipt of government assistance.

These strengths are matched by several significant weaknesses that limit the effectiveness of Oxfam America's famine responses:

The emphasis on development means that the agency is less effective than it could be in dealing with recurring disasters. The lack of a disasters unit, or similar structure, means that staff with development expertise get thrown into disaster responses without adequate preparation. While they are better able to identify possible long-term initiatives within the disaster response, they tend to repeat basic mistakes of previous disaster response efforts. And there is no unit at headquarters to provide guidance and to institutionalize lessons learned from previous relief operations.

The refusal to become operational, coupled with the need to disburse large sums of money rapidly to satisfy donors, means that Oxfam America is forced to fund projects of other expatriate nongovernmental organizations (NGOs) that have accepted an operational role. This is especially true in countries that lack solid local structures able to mount large-scale relief programs on their own. Thus, while stating that the agency is not operational, Oxfam America staff simply pass the funds and the responsibility to other agencies that are willing to implement large-scale relief programs directly. Oxfam America still accepts responsibility for monitoring and evaluating these programs, but another layer of bureaucracy is placed between the agency and its intended beneficiaries. This tends to complicate issues of evaluation and accountability.

These main strengths and weaknesses, and additional ones related especially to the political context of famine relief, will emerge again in the following discussion of Oxfam America's specific relief responses.

Cambodia

The 1979 famine in Cambodia was man-made, the final consequence of a decade of destruction inflicted upon Cambodian society, first during the civil war from 1970 to 1975, then during the brutal rule of the Khmer Rouge from 1975 to late 1978, and finally in the immediate aftermath of the Vietnamese invasion of the country, which ended Khmer Rouge rule in 1979. These events inflicted tremendous stress upon the people of Cambodia, resulting in perhaps 1.5–2 million deaths and reducing the survivors to at best a meager level of subsistence in a ruined landscape.

Oxfam America followed the lead of Oxfam U.K. and responded to the famine with relief and reconstruction supplies shipped from outside Cambodia for distribution by the country's government, the People's Republic of Kampuchea (PRK). In an agreement that then Director General Brian Walker reached with the government in October 1979, Oxfam U.K. would mount a major aid program through government channels and would not fund programs that would benefit Khmer Rouge remnants who were fleeing to the Thai-Cambodian border. Oxfam U.K. was the first and only aid organization that agreed to an important condition laid down by the government that in order to work inside the country, agencies must agree not to work across the border as well. Most other major aid organizations working inside the country, including the leaders of the multilateral Joint Mission, UNICEF, and the International Committee of the Red Cross, mounted programs on both sides of the political conflict, which continued to engulf Cambodia throughout the relief period.

By accepting the PRK government conditions, Oxfam U.K. and the supporters of the Consortium program that was established under its umbrella violated a fundamental humanitarian principle of providing aid to all sides in a situation of civil strife. At the time the agreement was reached, however, far from being widely criticized, Oxfam U.K.'s decision was praised as a bold, plucky attempt by a small, nonbureaucratic agency to overcome political obstacles so as to reach famine victims. In retrospect, the decision to work exclusively inside Cambodia was justified by the relative lack of assistance to the interior (due largely to the anti-Vietnamese politics of the major donors to the relief effort), and by the opportunities to engage in reconstruction assistance—which was more in keeping with the strengths of the development agencies supporting the Consortium—as opposed to providing relief in camp settings at the border.

Oxfam America joined the Oxfam Consortium relief program, contributing about $4.2 million over a fifteen-month period from October 1979 to December 1980. The Consortium brought together twenty-seven agencies from Europe, Australia, and the United States and raised more than $40 million for Cambodian relief and reconstruction.

From the very first shipments of goods into Cambodia by barge from Singapore in October 1979, Oxfam Consortium staff moved beyond basic relief needs to more fundamental reconstruction assistance. Early shipments included not only food and medicines but agricultural supplies (at this stage primarily hand tools and vegetable seeds), twine and spare parts for the fishnet factory in Phnom Penh, and chemicals for the Phnom Penh water works. The focus on industries that produce basic goods for consumers and agricultural producers was probably the Consortium program's most significant contribution to the relief and rehabilitation effort. The Consortium especially contributed to the rehabilitation of several textile factories in Phnom Penh that produced badly needed traditionally patterned colored cloth for a population that had been forced to wear only black during the Khmer Rouge period.

Oxfam America earmarked the majority of its contributions for purchases of agricultural inputs for the 1980 rainy season rice crop which, depending on how early the rains begin, is planted in April, May, and June and harvested in November and December. The rationale for the focus on this sector was obvious: Cambodia had been food self-sufficient in the 1960s and enough rice land was available to feed the current population. The primary obstacles appeared to be the lack of agricultural inputs, not only rice seeds and fertilizers, but also irrigation pumps to ensure that the crops would be watered through to maturity in drought-prone areas, and plow tips and hoe heads for agricultural implements. Draft animals were in terribly short supply, but to its credit the Consortium did not get involved in the import of tractors. The success or failure of the effort to support rainy season rice production in 1980 would determine whether acute food short-ages would persist.

In March 1980, out of concern that not enough agricultural assis-tance was reaching the peasantry in time for the impending rainy sea-son planting, Oxfam America also became involved in probably the most innovative aspect of the entire Cambodian relief program, the effort to supply peasants coming for food to the Thai-Cambodian bor-der with basic agricultural supplies to take back with them for plant-ing in the interior. An Oxfam America consultant, John Dennis, who knew rice production well from his work in Thailand, helped to con-ceptualize the program, choosing local rice varieties and other basic inputs that made up the "subsistence agriculture package." The agri-cultural assistance was linked to a vaccination program for draft animals and to ox cart repair so that all the basic production and trans-port needs of Cambodian peasants could be met in the course of one round-trip to the border.

Oxfam America's involvement with the cross-border program ended when Vietnamese troops struck at the key distribution point at Nong Chan in June 1980. The government in Phnom Penh saw the entire border operation, with some justification, as an attempt to destabilize the country by drawing peasants away from their villages at the key planting time and then, under cover of cross-border supply efforts, by infiltrating antigovernment forces into the country. The Vietnamese strike at the border coincided with efforts by Oxfam U.K. to get Oxfam America to cease its involvement at the border on the grounds that cross-border assistance violated the Consortium's agree-ment of October 1979 with the PRK to work only through government channels. Oxfam America staff were bitterly divided: To maintain the border operation would run the risk of being drummed out of the Consortium, but to bow to Oxfam U.K. pressure would end what many saw as the agency's one "distinctive contribution" to the people of Cambodia. The Vietnamese strike at Nong Chan gave those who favored recommitting to the Consortium the opening they needed to argue that the border operation was in jeopardy and that it was best to continue working inside the country. And that was the decision that Oxfam America's board and staff came to at the end of June 1980.

As noted above, Oxfam America developed its disaster response policy in early 1981 to distill lessons learned from the involvement in the Cambodian relief effort. Clearly, the operation in Cambodia had weak points, which the disasters policy sought to address.

The Cambodia response supported by Oxfam America had a strong reconstruction component. The Consortium left the provision of food and medicines to the World Food Programme and other multilateral agencies and focused the bulk of its assistance on the reconstruction of agriculture, industry, transport, and health. In this sense, Oxfam America's Cambodia program was well within the policy later set by the board.

Where the Consortium program fell short was in the appropriateness of the materials supplied, especially viewed from the long-term perspective embodied in the disaster response policy. This was particularly a problem in the agriculture sector. Oxfam America spent thousands of dollars on imported modern rice seed varieties of limited utility to the Cambodian peasantry, who had little experience with modern varieties and whose land was unirrigated. The small diesel-powered irrigation pumps supplied to make up for the lack of irrigation systems quickly broke down due to ignorance of basic maintenance procedures and the lack of spare parts and an effective distribution system for the parts that were available. It was only several years later that Oxfam U.K. initiated a training program for Khmer mechanics in one province, a program that has been instrumental in improving utilization rates for the pumps supplied during the relief effort. During the famine period, the Consortium's focus on the 1980 cropping season was so intense that basic development principles were cast aside in favor of a crash effort to raise production immediately.

This approach—importing materials from outside the country—ignored the capacity of the peasantry to recover using available resources. This was especially true in Cambodia in 1980, where the famine was entirely man-made and where local food resources could be exploited as soon as there was a minimum of social and political stability. Once it was established that a foraging trip for fruit, wild food sources, or fish would not risk one's life, the survivors could begin to rely on the natural reserves of the Cambodian food system. Part of the reason agencies came to this understanding so late in the emergency period derived from their staffs' isolation in Phnom Penh from the peasants in the countryside. Certainly more resources could have been directed to building peasant capacity to support themselves on the land short of importing large quantities of modern rice varieties, chemical fertilizers, and so on. But even in retrospect it is difficult to see how these programs could have been developed without day-to-day contact with peasants. The great strength of the cross-border agricultural supply effort was precisely that the components of the subsistence agricultural packages were determined *after* detailed interviews with peasants arriving in droves at the border.

Not all the blame for failing to build local capacity lies with Oxfam America and the other aid agencies. The government was intensely interested in building capacity, as decimated as the country was after the civil war and the years of Khmer Rouge rule. But the government's primary objective was to build capacity within an ideological framework of allegiance to socialism and to Vietnam. At this early stage, even when agencies expressed an interest in training, the government generally rebuffed them, asserting that training needs were being adequately served by Vietnamese advisers, experts from the Soviet bloc, and through education abroad in socialist countries. To the extent that support for training was provided by the agencies, it tended to be through informal service of a limited number of technical experts working side-by-side with their Khmer counterparts. For the Consortium program this was the case in the transport area, for example.

In addition to the lessons embodied in the disaster response policy, Oxfam America learned the following as the result of its involvement in the Cambodia relief effort:

- Maintaining the principle of providing assistance to both sides in a political conflict is vital, even in the face of pressure to choose a single side.
- Governments and forces resisting governments place their security needs above the needs of the populations under their control and will put intense pressure on humanitarian agencies to conform to a narrowly defined political security agenda of the government or resistance movement.
- In the context of civil war, reconstruction assistance is preferable to food assistance, which is more easily diverted to soldiers and other unintended beneficiaries.
- Local resources and needs should be carefully assessed before agencies make commitments to import large quantities of material assistance. Purchases should be made locally whenever possible.

Horn of Africa

The famine crisis in the Horn of Africa resulted from a period of drought that extended across the Sahel belt and was exacerbated by war between the Ethiopian government and secessionist movements in Eritrea and Tigray. While Oxfam America became concerned about drought and its consequences in 1983 and attempted to alert its donors to the crisis in the summer of 1984, mass starvation in the Horn, especially in Ethiopia, did not become widely known until the BBC aired dramatic footage of children dying in a feeding camp in October 1984. This footage, picked up immediately by NBC in the

United States, provoked an outpouring of worldwide concern and led to the mounting of a relief effort that dwarfed what had been provided to Cambodia. Oxfam America's overall income nearly tripled to $16.7 million, and the agency spent $4.5 million on emergency programs in the Horn of Africa in 1984–85.

From inside an agency like Oxfam America, the media's power to affect public perceptions never felt more immense, nor had such immediate consequences. One day Oxfam America staff were preparing for a year of austerity and concentrating on a reduced number of development projects, even in drought-affected areas of Africa, because appeals for emergency assistance had failed to rouse the donors. The next day staff were dealing with an avalanche of funding from donors demanding that programs be mounted immediately to save the starving. Even more dramatically than in the case of Cambodia, staff had to develop relief programs almost overnight, without a network of staff on the ground in the region.

At the outset, staff did attempt to analyze the crisis in the Horn based on the lessons learned from the involvement in Cambodian relief. While there were more differences than similarities, the overriding constant was the existence of war and political conflict that would determine the character of the entire famine response. As in Cambodia, there were sides. On one side there was the Ethiopian government, a Marxist government with which the United States had frigid relations; and on the other, there were secessionist movements, also Marxist, in two provinces of northern Ethiopia: Eritrea and Tigray. The drought was most severe in these two provinces. This provided ideal conditions for the conflicting parties to use the famine for political advantage. The government could attempt to use the famine to weaken the secessionist movements by denying food to the people under their control and by moving populations that could be reached to government-controlled feeding centers and then permanently out of the famine zone through forced resettlement programs. The secessionist movements—the Eritrean People's Liberation Front (EPLF) and the Tigray People's Liberation Front (TPLF)—could try to prevent the movement of people under their control to the government-controlled feeding centers and attempt to use the famine crisis to discredit the Ethiopian government and build international support for their little-known causes.

Relief agencies immediately faced the question of which side would provide the most effective channel to reach starving people; at the same time, they had to negotiate their way through a political minefield, since each decision had political as well as humanitarian consequences. It was to be expected that both sides would use relief supplies to further their political and strategic aims in the conflict.

The famine in the Horn of Africa, however, differed in fundamental ways from that in Cambodia. While there were legitimate disagreements as to whether natural factors or Ethiopian government policies were the primary cause of the drought and resulting food crisis, it was undeniable that parts of northern Ethiopia had not seen rain in three years. The environment for growing food had been subject to intense stress in recent years. This meant that the famine victims depended far more on international food deliveries to stave off starvation than the population of Cambodia, which had survived by foraging for food. Opportunities for reconstruction, therefore, were not as readily available. Further, the task in the Horn was not societal reconstruction, as in Cambodia, but getting food to a potential seven million famine victims and providing them with the means to feed themselves in the future. In this sense, the relief effort in Ethiopia was narrower than in Cambodia. Finally, governmental and nongovernmental organizations with high professional standards and extensive experience existed on both sides of the conflict to serve as channels and implementors of relief and rehabilitation projects. These included the Ethiopian government's Relief and Rehabilitation Commission (RRC), an Ethiopian NGO consortium, Christian Relief and Development Association (CRDA), the Eritrean Relief Association (ERA), the humanitarian arm of the EPLF, and the Relief Society of Tigray (REST), the humanitarian arm of the TPLF.

Oxfam America's relief response in the Horn of Africa was in several respects a step forward from that in Cambodia. In responding to famine in the Horn, the agency did mount significant relief and rehabilitation programs on both sides of the political conflict. In the United States, tremendous pressure was brought to bear on the agency to choose one side or the other. In the region, ironically, the protagonists to the conflict accepted Oxfam America's assistance on its own terms, without conditions. The pressure to work exclusively on the Ethiopian government side came primarily from members of Oxfam America's board of directors. They supported the position of the Organization of African Unity (OAU), which has held the colonial boundaries of Africa to be inviolate after independence even though these boundaries divide traditional tribal groupings and contain different conflicting ethnic groups. The potential for ethnically based separatist struggles exists throughout Africa. Therefore, to prevent the political disintegration of the continent, the OAU opposes any support for separatist movements such as those in northern Ethiopia. If such support had to be granted to prevent starvation, it should be limited to emergency food supplies and it should receive little or no mention in Oxfam America's communications about its famine response. On the other hand, the U.S. partisans of the causes of the EPLF and the TPLF, including several former and then current staff members, mounted an intense lobbying campaign to get the agency to abandon its program in government-controlled areas on human rights grounds; they claimed that the Ethiopian government was using a policy of coercion and forced starvation to break the resistance to their control of Eritrea and Tigray.

Oxfam America's response in the Horn improved on that in Cambodia through better planning of its assistance in the area of agricultural rehabilitation, especially in its work with ERA and REST. In conjunction with the trained staff of these two organizations, and with the help of agricultural experts from the region, Oxfam America was able to identify appropriate seed varieties available on the local market, purchasing seed either in the affected regions themselves, in Sudan, or occasionally in Kenya. Although access to rural areas was difficult due to the war, Oxfam America staff were able to support an agricultural rehabilitation strategy through planting of appropriate food crops chosen by local peasants. On the Ethiopian government side, Oxfam America—working in conjunction with the International Livestock Center for Africa (ILCA)—was able to support the development and farm-level extension of innovative agricultural technologies, including the single-ox plow, which promised to make a significant long-term contribution to peasant-level food production under difficult environmental conditions in Ethiopia. To date this work has had a practical application primarily in areas outside the zone most severely affected by the drought. Direct agricultural assistance in drought-affected areas included oxen, seeds, and hand tools.

There were at least two significant problems with Oxfam America's response to famine in the Horn. First, Oxfam America allowed itself to be entangled by what Mary Anderson and Peter Woodrow, in their recent book on disaster response, *Rising from the Ashes* (Anderson and Woodrow 1989), call "the myth of speed." Oxfam America tried to respond as rapidly as possible, with unprecedented amounts of resources, to a long-term crisis that had suddenly burst into popular consciousness. In so doing, the agency skewed its use of funds too much in the direction of basic relief assistance. Oxfam America funded feeding programs of other operational agencies in camp settings where long-term work was virtually impossible because the peasants were off the land. The imperative, one imposed on the agency by the donor public and by the press, was always to "get the money out the door." The agency tried with all the best intentions to provide financial support to effective projects, but in the short term the available options tended to be high-visibility emergency projects, which are not Oxfam America's strength.

The second problem is related to Oxfam America's position as a humanitarian organization working in the midst of intense political conflict. As described above, the agency resisted intense pressure and worked on both sides of the war in the Horn. In this sense, it passed the minimal test of humanitarian effectiveness. On the other hand, the agency was largely silent in the face of Ethiopian government policies that staff knew firsthand were counterinsurgency measures detrimental to the famine victims. The most significant of these measures was forced resettlement, the movement of large numbers of people, ostensively for their own long-term benefit, from drought-affected northern provinces to provinces in the south. Although the southern provinces were undeniably more fertile, the forced movement off the land appeared to be primarily a military strategy aimed at depopulating areas where the secessionist movements were strong. Meanwhile, throughout the country the government was implementing a policy of villagization, or the grouping of homesteads widely scattered in traditional settlement patterns into small villages with houses close together. Again, the program had an ostensive developmental rationale—to provide better government services to the population—but this appeared less important than enhancing the government's political control over the peasantry.

Oxfam America did not fund resettlement and, as a matter of policy, has chosen not to work in areas where villagization programs are underway. But the agency, to avoid antagonizing the Ethiopian government and thereby ensure its continued ability to work in the country, took no strong public stand against resettlement. An agency that did so, Médecins sans Frontières (Doctors without Borders, a French NGO that supplies emergency medical assistance), was expelled from the country without their protest having had any discernible impact on the pace of resettlement of people from contested areas of Ethiopia. Can Oxfam America afford to compromise its humanitarian principles or look the other way based on the obligation to preserve its programs to help people in need? Are its programs large enough and effective enough to justify compromising with government policies that have a far greater impact on poor people? Alternatively, could the Oxfams working in Ethiopia have had any greater impact than the seemingly futile posturing of Médecins sans Frontières?

While there is room for legitimate disagreement on these issues, the agency should have been a stronger voice against Ethiopian government policy, even if it meant being expelled. In the arena of international public opinion, agencies such as Oxfam have more leverage than they dare to use.

Negros Island, Philippines

Since Spanish times, Negros Island has been the Philippines' primary producer of sugar cane. Negros Occidental, the larger and more populated of the island's two provinces, has been planted almost exclusively with sugar cane since the Philippines took up the Cuban portion of the U.S. sugar quota in the early 1960s. Production of sugar cane was organized feudally, with workers totally dependent on the plantation owners for wages, food, and social services. When the international price of sugar collapsed in the early 1980s—a problem exacerbated in the Philippines by the vertical control of the industry granted to corrupt and wasteful cronies of President Ferdinand Marcos—the plantation welfare system also collapsed, leaving the workers without means to support their families.

Although the situation on Negros in 1985–86 was serious, famine is probably not the appropriate term to describe the situation. Very few adults were dying from hunger. They were able to forage for food or to pick up casual employment to stave off hunger. Many migrated to other parts of the Philippines. Thousands of children, however, were suffering from acute malnutrition. The crisis was described as a famine in the Philippines press partially to discredit Marcos, who was then being challenged by Corazon Aquino, and partially because the Filipino elite had joined the worldwide response to the Ethiopian famine, while ignoring a hunger crisis in their own backyard. Marcos tried to deny that there was a problem on Negros, and his government balked at making an agreement with the United Nations Children's Fund (UNICEF) to begin large-scale supplementary feeding on the island. When Marcos was toppled in the "people power" revolution of February 1986, pictures of emaciated children on Negros, juxtaposed with the greedy excess of the ruling family, made the point that the revolution was just. Aquino's government moved immediately to cooperate with UNICEF to devise a response to the Negros crisis. For the international donors to the Negros relief effort, fighting famine on the island was an immediate, visible way to show support for Aquino's fledgling government.

The food crisis on Negros was entirely man-made, deriving from the exploitation inherent in feudally organized plantation agriculture. The New People's Army (NPA), the armed wing of the Communist Party of the Philippines, had made significant advances on Negros in the early 1980s, fueled by the poverty of the sugar workers and the breakdown of the plantation welfare system. Owners had ceased planting in more isolated, upland parts of Negros not only for economic reasons but also because of NPA activity. While the sugar workers could grow some food crops on abandoned plantation land, they lacked the resources needed to support themselves as peasants on the land. Moreover, upland soils tended to be rocky and infertile compared to lowland areas, and irrigation was generally unavailable. Thus, while the food crisis on Negros was affecting the families of all sugar workers, it was probably most devastating for former workers using abandoned plantation plots with marginal soils, that is, the areas more likely to be under the influence or control of the NPA.

The relief effort on Negros was implemented in the midst of a low-intensity guerrilla war. The issue facing the agencies responding to the crisis was how to respond to the food needs of the displaced sugar workers throughout the island, including areas which—although beyond the reach of the government due to security factors—held the greatest number of potential victims of malnourishment and starvation.

Oxfam America had already been supporting one alternative proposed by the largest labor union on the island, the National Federation of Sugar Workers (NFSW). The union had organized a farm lot campaign, an attempt to convince plantation owners who were leaving sugar land fallow to allow workers to plant food crops on it for their families. No title would be granted to the workers, and the land could be confiscated at any time for return to sugar production or the production of other industrial crops. In this sense it was a desperate, stopgap measure on the part of the union to try to help its members meet their immediate food needs. In spite of the limited nature of the program, the majority of plantation owners resisted it, to the point that groups of hired toughs circulated on Negros destroying the workers' farm lots. Nonetheless, the program was a rare example of sugar workers trying to meet their food needs through their own organized efforts.

The dilemma for Oxfam America was that NFSW was above all a trade union and had only limited capacity for project implementation. Oxfam America's initial grant for the farm lot campaign was only $20,000. It would be several years before NFSW's ability to provide adequate technical support to the agricultural production of the sugar workers caught up with the union's capacity to generate funds for the farm lot campaign. NFSW was not even seeking support for emergency feeding programs, even though it had the capacity to reach workers on some of the more isolated plantations. Thus, Oxfam America had to find other channels if it wished to deal directly with the hunger crisis.

After commissioning a report from two local resource people who analyzed the options for responding to the food problems on Negros, Oxfam America decided to provide a large one-time grant to UNICEF for its emergency feeding program. Four factors compelled Oxfam America to choose a foreign, multilateral agency rather than a local NGO or other indigenous structure. First, UNICEF had an international reputation for effective work with child and maternal programs, although it prefers to work on long-term development projects rather than relief. Second, UNICEF's program emphasized direct wet feeding in centers developed with the participation of mothers and their malnourished children, rather than distributing dry food to adults who might consume it themselves or give it, whether voluntarily or at gunpoint, to soldiers. Third, UNICEF had set an objective of building a broad coalition of local organizations to work on the program under the UNICEF umbrella. These organizations would include outreach structures of the Catholic church able to reach people in need in the conflict zones. Finally, UNICEF emphasized its ability to set up a careful, ongoing monitoring system for the program. A major weakness of local organizations that might have mounted independent feeding programs was their ability and even willingness to satisfy Oxfam America's reporting and monitoring requirements.

Oxfam America's grant to UNICEF was $300,000, minimal funding compared to Cambodia or Ethiopia, but the largest grant the agency had made to date in the Philippines and larger even than some initial government contributors to the UNICEF program. The grant supported supplementary feeding of 85,000 children for ten weeks. It included an additional $5,000 to commission an independent evaluation of the project upon completion of the funding period.

The UNICEF feeding program succeeded in arresting the decline in the nutritional status of children brought to the feeding centers. In some cases, significant improvements in nutritional status were registered. The wet feeding method, as anticipated, meant that children were the primary beneficiaries of the program. There were virtually no instances of the sale or diversion of relief food. The program purchased the food in the Philippines, as it should have in a country so well endowed with food resources. The feeding program also generated local employment through the establishment of enterprises to produce and package Nutri-Paks (special processed high-nutrient foods) for use in the feeding centers.

In the context of political and social conflict on Negros, however, the program had several flaws. UNICEF had the best of intentions in seeking to establish a broad-based coalition of implementing agencies. In practice, however, the bulk of the feeding programs were conducted in relatively accessible areas through government agencies and nongovernmental organizations set up by the plantation owners. Isolated areas where malnutrition was more severe according to UNICEF's own initial surveys were proportionally ignored in the implementation of the feeding program. The program implementors, dominated by the local elite, had no interest in placing resources in the hands of alternative institutions that were mobilizing people to challenge the feudal structures that had disempowered the workers and had created the hunger crisis on the island. Thus, by working primarily through government structures and planter organizations, the program had the consequence of reinforcing the feudal system of elite "dole-outs" (to use the Filipino phrase). Worker-controlled organizations and the Basic Christian Communities of the Church, which involve substantial worker participation, participated only negligibly in the UNICEF feeding effort.

This criticism does not even address the issue of reconstruction and development assistance, which is supposed to be at the heart of any Oxfam America disaster response. The UNICEF program included maternal health education and community garden programs, but these were not supported by Oxfam America. In financial terms they were relatively minor components of what was primarily a supplementary feeding program. Using local food resources, the feeding program proved unsustainable by UNICEF and, in a significant setback to the original design of the program, was taken over by CARE in 1987 using imported food supplied by the U.S. Agency for International Development (USAID).

In retrospect, Oxfam America should not have supported the UNICEF feeding program at the level that it did. The emotions of the moment, fueled by photos of skeletal children, the excesses of the Marcos family, and enthusiasm for the political changes promised by Aquino, led staff to recommend a larger contribution than was necessary. The availability of funds for emergency programs was another factor that led the agency to respond with such a sizable grant. Since UNICEF had little difficulty generating funds for the feeding program, Oxfam America's resources would have been more wisely husbanded for programs addressing the root causes of the hunger crisis on Negros. Had these programs not been immediately available, more staff time and effort could have been devoted to financing efforts to create the capacity among the sugar workers and their supporting organizations to implement such programs.

Bangladesh

During the 1988 monsoon season, all three major rivers in Bangladesh —the Brahmaputra, the Ganga, and the Meghna—crested at the same time, leading to unprecedented levels of flooding in this flood-prone deltaic country. An estimated thirty-five million people lost their homes, livestock, food stores, and crops. While famine conditions did not develop, the 1988 floods were an immense natural disaster affecting far greater numbers of people than either the disaster in Cambodia or in the Horn of Africa. Most of those affected were peasants with marginal landholdings who had few assets even before the floods struck.

Oxfam America recognized the magnitude of the disaster immediately. Since its inception, the agency has funded work in Bangladesh, and it felt an obligation to respond to the crisis. Lacking a field presence in the country, the agency relied on the Oxfam U.K. field office in

Dhaka to provide information and an immediate response to the flood disaster. Staff were also in touch with leaders of one of Bangladesh's leading NGOs, Comilla Proshika, whose leaders happened to be in Boston when the flooding peaked. They carried back small quantities of badly needed water purification tablets and promised to keep in touch regarding emergency and rehabilitation programs that Proshika would be planning.

For the immediate emergency response, Oxfam America funded the work of Oxfam U.K., which had mobilized hundreds of Bangladeshi volunteers to organize the purchase of locally available food supplies and the preparation and distribution of *chapatis*, lentils, and rice. Through local NGOs, Oxfam America funded the provision of emergency food and water purification tablets.

Once the waters began to recede, efforts had to be made to get crops planted for the winter cropping season. This crop would be crucial for providing poor peasants with some food buffer against hunger early in 1989. Working through the impressive network of local NGOs in Bangladesh, including the Bangladesh Rural Advancement Committee (BRAC), a long-time partner, Oxfam America supported the supply of seeds for crop production, including wheat, rice, and a variety of vegetables. The local agencies provided the agricultural inputs on a loan basis, either interest free or at modest rates. Repayment would be made into village-level revolving funds which local groups had managed before the flood disaster. Oxfam America directed as much of its assistance as possible to women, who play a central role in village-level food production.

Another important rehabilitation program was cash for work. The floods severely damaged Bangladesh's road and communications network, causing bottlenecks in the distribution of food to isolated rural areas. Thus, both food distribution and food-for-work programs were slow in starting. Monawar Sultana, a Boston-based Bangladeshi staff member of Oxfam America, conducted interviews in October, about six weeks after the floods peaked, which showed rural people were desperate for cash employment. Local NGOs, with funds provided by Oxfam and other donors, were able to mobilize villagers for reconstruction projects, especially road, dike, and housing repair, with payment in cash which then circulated in the local economy. Sultana's follow-up interviews in July and August 1989 indicate that the cash-for-work programs were among the most valued interventions in the immediate aftermath of the flood disaster.

As of the summer of 1989, Oxfam America was pursuing longer-term flood prevention and rehabilitation programs through local organizations in Bangladesh. The goal is to develop concrete initiatives that will enhance the capacity of local people to live with floods and minimize their damage. The anticipated foci include better housing designs, the construction of emergency shelters, and reforestation.

The response to the 1988 flood disaster in Bangladesh, alone among the disaster responses analyzed in this chapter, followed Oxfam America's disaster response policy to the letter. What enabled Oxfam America to act on its principles in this case were the capacity of local Bangladeshi NGOs and the absence of war and political conflict. The agency's extensive experience in the country was another positive factor. Staff with excellent knowledge of the country, working closely with Oxfam U.K. and the staff of local NGOs, moved quickly to develop an effective, development-oriented response to the crisis. Oxfam America staff must recognize the underpinnings of the agency's response in Bangladesh and be more cautious in the future about the types of intervention the agency undertakes in situations less conducive to an effective response by a small development-funding agency such as Oxfam America.

Conclusion

Oxfam America's principles of development compel the agency to concentrate on empowerment in its overseas programs. But disasters affecting the poor of Asia, Africa, Latin America, and the Caribbean occur with depressing frequency. The human suffering caused by these disasters is equally compelling, and Oxfam America accepts the challenge of responding to famine and lesser disasters even if the agency's strengths lie in long-term development.

Oxfam America's disaster response policy is sound. The primary objective of all funding in a disaster situation should be the rapid rehabilitation of local capacity working in partnership with indigenous institutions. Assistance toward this primary objective is more likely to be appropriate to local conditions and to be controlled by the disaster victims themselves.

As the cases discussed in this chapter indicate, however, Oxfam America did not always follow its own policy guidelines. Three primary factors have caused this agency disfunction in its disaster responses: political conflict, lack of indigenous organizations, and the imperative—at once self-imposed and imposed by the donor public—of rapidly spending donations on emergency relief. Oxfam America, and other agencies, need to face these issues directly if future disaster responses are to adhere more closely to the principles of the disaster response policy.

Political conflict. In future disasters in which political conflict plays a determining role, Oxfam America should apply more rigorously the standard of its disaster response policy: "Political conditions within the disaster area should permit Oxfam America to serve its basic goals through a disaster response." Applying this standard would mean that Oxfam America would refuse to work in partnership with parties to conflict that are manipulating the relief effort to serve strategic ends. This would risk condemning disaster victims by denying them assistance because aid on their behalf is being manipulated. Experience shows, however, that this very manipulation causes more human suffering in the long term. If enough agencies refuse to be used for strategic purposes, the parties to the political conflict would lose a significant weapon.

Lack of indigenous institutions. Oxfam America's approach to disaster relief depends on the existence of indigenous institutions, close to village level, that can organize and rebuild the capacity of the poor after a disaster strikes. When such institutions do not exist, or when they need strengthening, it is imperative for Oxfam America and other agencies to devote resources to building these institutions. Such support will mean far more to the long-term viability of the local community than the provision of emergency disaster supplies.

Rapid spending of emergency funds. Oxfam America has allowed itself to be swept up in the frenzy of the American public when Third World disasters finally capture their imagination. The agency's least effective work has been done in the name of publicity and "getting the money out the door." Oxfam America, and all relief and development agencies in the United States, need to begin a serious effort to educate the American public about what constitutes an effective long-term response to famine and other disasters.

As long as Americans believe that aid not arriving on the scene within days of the disaster cannot be effective, agencies will be forever wasting resources to meet these expectations. Oxfam America, which has tried to build a strong program of donor and public education about its approach to long-term development, is in a good position to begin this education effort about what constitutes effective disaster response.

Appendix Oxfam America Disaster Response: Principles, Guidelines, Procedures

The Oxfam America's disasters policy dates from 1981 in the aftermath of the agency's response to the Cambodian crisis. There were pressures on Oxfam America to become a more traditional relief agency. The Board of Directors decided that long-term development should remain the cornerstone of the work of the agency and that any response to a disaster must work within that broader context.

I. *Definitions and Principles*

A. A "disaster" shall be considered an emergency, in which there is intense and widespread human suffering due to natural and/or man-made causes. A "disaster response" shall normally include Oxfam America's several activities to respond to a disaster: grants, fund-raising, public communications, education, advocacy, etc. A "disaster project" would be an aid project within the total response.

B. Appropriate responses to assist persons affected by disaster are essential to meeting Oxfam America's main goals:

1. Promoting understanding and support for equitable, self-reliant development among the world's poorest people.
2. Providing material assistance, mainly grants but sometimes materiel, to indigenous agencies, groups, and movements, to meet development and emergency needs.
3. Educating and advocating for equitable, self-reliant development *and* self-help recovery from disasters by the very poor.

It is understood that it is imperative to maintain a strong and influential Oxfam America, with enough financial, constituency, and organizational resources to pursue its other goals effectively and with integrity.

C. It will sometimes be desirable and necessary for Oxfam America to provide "relief" aid (e.g., food), but its primary commitment of funds and other resources will be to help people to help themselves: "reconstruction" and "development." The latter is the primary goal of Oxfam America in any disaster situation.

D. Oxfam America's aid techniques and communications in any disaster situation should reinforce its primary organizational commitment to self-reliant development.

II. *Guidelines/Criteria for Disaster Response*

A. A disaster response should serve the basic goals of Oxfam America.

B. A response or project should enable Oxfam America to make a distinctive contribution.

C. A project should enhance the capacities of people to help themselves and restore their own productive capacities. Oxfam America will sometimes engage in "relief" aid to meet urgent needs in order to leverage a preferred role in reconstruction and development. A relief project may also be conducted in an area where Oxfam America already has significant development projects and commitments.

D. Political conditions within the disaster area should permit Oxfam America to serve its basic goals through a disaster response.

E. Projects should strengthen indigenous organization and participation for responding to the disaster and for continuing in reconstruction and development.

F. Oxfam America should either be able to work through or in cooperation with an existing Oxfam disaster response team; through an indigenous organization; through its own overseas staff; or to otherwise assure appropriate administration of a given project.

Note: Disaster projects will normally be initiated and managed by persons with development responsibilities in the geographic area where the disaster occurs.

G. Responses and projects should represent special opportunities to educate and advocate concerning self-reliant development and should involve particular events, issues or relationships with a potential to advance self-reliance and more equitable relationships.

H. Disaster response should ordinarily promise a net increase of funds sufficient to cover the costs of the response, to minimize the use of unrestricted funds for disasters work.

I. The Executive Director and the Board of Directors should be confident that a particular disaster response (or series of them) is undertaken in a time and manner so as to strengthen the programming of Oxfam America or certainly not to weaken it.

J. Communications about disaster work must generally emphasize self-reliance, the dignity and self-help capacity of people, and Oxfam America's primary role in aiding reconstruction, even when the project may contain subsidiary elements of what would be called "relief." Fund-raising communications should avoid demeaning stereotypes. Communications should also be emotionally and intellectually compelling—the basis of disasters fund-raising is the readiness of people to make an immediate and compassionate response.

Note: This need not preclude the use of simple advertising which appeals straightforwardly for compassionate responses. Overall communications must offset and overcome the tendency of public and opinion-makers alike to interpret every disaster response as a "relief" response.

[The rest of the policy statement addresses internal operating procedures and is not relevant here.]

References

Anderson, Mary B., and Peter J. Woodrow. 1989. *Rising from the Ashes: Development Strategies in Times of Disaster*. Boulder: Westview Press.
Shawcross, William. 1984. *The Quality of Mercy: Cambodia, Holocaust, and Modern Conscience*. New York: Simon and Schuster.

8

Building Capacity in the Countryside

The Role of Sahelian Voluntary Development Organizations

Hussein M. Adam

The Reemergence of African Voluntary Organizations

The Sahel is a vast, semi-arid stretch of land extending through six West African countries: Senegal, Mauritania, Mali, Burkina Faso, Niger, and Chad. The bulk of the population makes a living in pastoral and semipastoral activities and trades its livestock for grain produced by the sedentary farmers of the region. For these people droughts and famine have long been a fact of life. Major droughts have occurred in this century in 1910–14, 1930, 1940–44, 1967–74, and 1980–84 (U.S. Congress 1986). These periods of minimal rainfall, in conjunction with deleterious human practices, have caused serious desertification, a major concern in the Sahel.

The 1967–74 drought devastated herds to the extent that two million pastoral people had no means of subsistence. During the period 1982–84, severe drought again struck most of Africa's Sahel. Pastoralists, who had managed to reconstitute their herds, again lost most or all of their animals. The national and international response to the Great West African Famine of 1968–74 resulted in about 100,000 human deaths (mostly pastoralists) out of a total population of about twenty-five million. International relief efforts had funneled over $360 million of emergency aid to the Sahel by 1974. Even with the effective, though belated, response in the early 1970s, the need to avoid future crises remained an urgent challenge. The main actors who responded to the Sahelian crises, as indeed to similar crises in other parts of Africa, include national governments, donors, intergovernmental organizations, and nongovernmental organizations or private voluntary organizations (NGOS/PVOS).

InterAction, an association of over 100 U.S. PVOs, estimates that 10–15 percent of the $460 to $600 million spent in Africa by U.S. PVOs in 1984 was spent in the Sahelian countries (Table 8.1). African voluntary development organizations (VDOs) lack such resources; and in spite of growing trends on the part of donors wanting to fund development activities through the voluntary, nonprofit sector, it is unlikely that indigenous voluntary development organizations will be able to substitute for their international partners in this role. The primary contribution to development of these indigenous voluntary development organizations is not financial; it is and will continue to be enhancing organizational capabilities and facilitating the process of democratization.

Table 8.1 U.S. Private Voluntary Organizations (PVOs) in the Sahel

Country	Number of PVOs	Number of Projects
Burkina Faso	19	82
Cape Verde	3	12
Chad	11	30
The Gambia	18	39
Mali	22	84
Mauritania	11	34
Niger	13	46
Senegal	24	100

Source: InterAction. *Diversity in Development: U.S. Voluntary Assistance to Africa Summary of Findings.* New York: InterAction-American Council for Voluntary International Action, 1985, 22–23.

This chapter examines the role of selected Sahelian voluntary development organizations as creative institutional responses to the ongoing vulnerability of pastoralists and farmers to drought and famine crises. The focus of VDOs on development reduces vulnerability and creates new capacities very much in the spirit of the discussion in Chapter 6 of this book. They strive to link disaster assistance so that it supports the efforts of people to achieve social and economic development. This chapter considers VDOs' attempts to scale their activities to achieve greater effectiveness. A second theme is the development orientation of the groups discussed, along with the evolution and impact of their vision. Specific focus is given to Sahelian VDOs in Senegal (population 7.0 million in mid-1987), Mali (7.8 million), and Burkina Faso (8.3 million).

A brief description of the role of international PVOs and aid donors is necessary in order to understand the current context of indigenous VDOs. Apart from U.S. PVOs, Africa has witnessed the presence of nonprofit philanthropic organizations from various Western European countries such as France, Great Britain, Germany, Italy, Holland, and the Scandinavian countries, and from Canada and Australia. Some of these groups came determined to build local institutions to continue their work after they have withdrawn from the scene. Others assist local institution building for secondary pragmatic reasons. For the most part, the presence of international PVOs and their activities in various sectors, including famine relief, food production, health and education, water development, income generation, and the environment, have created an enabling context for the revival or birth of national indigenous VDOs.

The growing amount of financial resources channeled through PVOs flows mostly through international PVOs. The U.S. government, for example, obligated $270 million to Africa in 1984 through PVOs. This funding represented 60 percent of all U.S. PVO aid to Africa. Nearly half of that support came in the form of food aid. The largest two international PVOs, Catholic Relief Services (CRS) and CARE, together provided two-thirds of all PVO aid to Africa (U.S. Congress 1986).

The trend of channeling official aid funds through PVOs is bound to increase. In fact, the growth process of the PVO/NGO sector is characterized by an increasing dependency on government aid. This has brought about a scramble by official donors and Western PVOs/NGOs to fund nonprofit-sector projects in Africa and elsewhere in the Third World. African VDOs with a strong identity and self-determined role in national development are able to benefit from this situation. On the negative side, the scramble tends to suffocate indigenous VDOs that are relatively weak; it also sponsors artificial VDOs that lack a vision of their own and possess questionable local legitimacy and accountability. These trends will be further elaborated upon in the course of this chapter.

During the heyday of colonialism, the 1930s and 1940s, Africans began to form various types of voluntary associations: educational, religious, economic, welfare and mutual aid, sports-cultural, and—later on—semipolitical. Nearly all nationalist organizations and parties in post–World War II Africa built upon the rich experience of earlier voluntary associations. Thomas Hodgkin (1957, 84–85) describes the contributions of voluntary associations thus: "They have given an important minority valuable experience of modern forms of administration—the keeping of minutes and accounts, the handling of records and correspondence, the techniques of propaganda and diplomacy. . . . In this way they have made it possible for the new urban leadership to acquire a kind of informal professional training. . . . Third, in periods of political ferment and crisis, these associations provide the cells around which a nation-wide political organization can be constructed." In Tanganyika, for example, Julius Nyerere served as the head of the Tanganyika African Association (TAA) before going on to launch a full-fledged nationalist party, the Tanganyika African National Union (TANU) in 1954.

After independence, ironically, African governments across the political spectrum took steps to severely restrict and, in many cases, abolish voluntary associations. In several instances this came about as part of the transformation of African states from multiparty to one-party regimes. The top-down technocratic approach to development adopted by African governments soon after independence, and supported by the major donor organizations, viewed the state as playing a dominant, even monopolistic, role in development. Central planning machineries were created with a strong emphasis on the word *central*. From the mid-1960s to the 1980s the state was encouraged to expand into all sectors of society. This approach turned out to be convenient for the numerous military regimes that took power during this period. They regarded central planning as but one aspect of a military command approach to societal development.

Similarly, radical African regimes, from the Marxist to the African socialist variety (as Mali was under President Modibo Keita), have tended to abolish voluntary associations by merging them into "artificial" mass organizations launched by the state. Goran Hyden (1989, 7) has noted: "Wherever the state arrogated to itself the role of the sole initiator and executor of development in a society where a peasant mode of production still prevails, local institutions derived from this mode continue to protect member interests but are halted in their growth and hence make no or little contribution to national development."

In rural areas especially, mass organizations often atrophied or reverted to defensive, highly informal modes of operation. Nevertheless, in a majority of African countries, VDOs have experienced a resurgence in recent years. Among the reasons are a decline in the confidence and capabilities of most African states, the debt crisis, and related donor pressures against state expansion and for privatization. Other factors include the crisis facing food and agriculture, drought, famine, and desertification as well as military conflicts and refugee crises. Even in the former socialist states of Eastern Europe and Asia, one notices civic associations emerging to fill the growing gap created by the withdrawal of the state's financial and organizational support in areas such as social services, education, and culture. Following the 1960s and 1970s, we seem to be entering a period of global state sector retrenchment and therefore possibilities of a greater role for civil society and its associations.

Not all African states have a tolerant view of PVOs/VDOs. Until recently, Ethiopia, and to some extent Angola, continued to view voluntary organizations as "imperialist tools" and as a "hidden arm of the CIA." By contrast, the 1967–74 drought obliged most Sahelian governments to accept aid through Western NGOS/PVOS and induced them to tolerate the more or less permanent presence of foreign and indigenous voluntary organizations in relief and development programs. For example, by 1984 once-radical Mali with its narrow public sector orientation had come to rely on international PVOs in most of its relief and development programs. The postindependence rebirth of African VDOs is relatively advanced and significant in the Sahelian countries. Some of these VDOs possess a strong sense of identity and vision, not only in national but also in pan-African development as well.

African voluntary development organizations may now be broadly classified into grassroots/primary organizations and intermediary or grassroots-support organizations. The current favorable atmosphere allows the former to be formal rather than informal, and it allows the latter to be national and even regional in their scope of activities. National and international voluntary organizations have been discussed at every major international development conference held recently. Most notably, northern and southern PVOs/VDOs alike radiated their growing confidence at the March 1987 London Conference on Development Alternatives: The Challenge for NGOs, reflecting the growing strength of this movement.

This chapter grew out of my research experiences as a senior research associate of the International Relief/Development Project (IRDP) headed by Mary B. Anderson and Peter J. Woodrow. Our project developed a theoretical framework for assessing rural vulnerabilities and capacities related to disaster situations. The IRDP (1986, 2; see also Anderson and Woodrow 1989 and Chapter 6 of this book) utilized two basic definitions: "*Disaster* is an acute crisis or event that outstrips the capacity of a society to cope with it; *development* is a process through which people's vulnerability to crises (material/physical, social/organizational, psychological/motivational) is reduced, or their capacity to cope is increased." The projects chosen for study were those that have more or less successfully linked relief and development efforts. IRDP developed a series of forty-one case histories, out of which at least ten were from Sahelian Africa. After a number of indigenous field researchers were familiarized with the IRDP analytical framework, they went on to prepare the individual case histories analyzed herein. I was in charge of the Sahelian research subunit of IRDP.

I found the management tasks much easier than the intellectual need to analyze isolated case experiences, comparing their similarities while explaining the uniqueness or specifics of each situation. It is especially challenging to be able to develop generalizations that are valid in multiple situations. The terms of reference given to our field researchers were to discuss and analyze the actual rather than potential role of these organizations up to 1988. "Capacities and Vulnerabilities Analysis is not prescriptive. It does not tell what to do in any given situation. It is only a *diagnostic tool* . . . [with the] power to organize and systematize knowledge and understanding" (Anderson and Woodrow 1989, 21). It does encourage a careful analysis of factors and, therefore, facilitates predictions that are relatively more accurate.

Creative Institution Building

An oft-cited paradigm describing development strategies (Korten 1987) portrays a chronological evolution of northern PVOs/NGOs, moving from agencies that dispense disaster and relief assistance, to organizations that manage small projects for development, to institutions that work with colleagues in developing countries to initiate and strengthen the capacity of local organizations to manage their own development. Interestingly, indigenous VDOs have not had to go through these three stages. Most of them have worked and continue to work on small projects within the framework of enhancing local institutional capacities. Accordingly, this chapter bears a developmental flavor only because the VDOs analyzed emphasize development programs as the best long-run means of combatting drought and famine.

In addition to the IRDP framework I used in developing all the case histories analyzed in this chapter, I propose to utilize a tentative classificatory scheme. At this point in its development, the following typology is neither exclusive nor exhaustive. The typology has grown out of readings, observations, and discussions with indigenous Third World NGO/VDO leaders. I began to formulate it during the first-hand experiences I gained as the founder-director of Somalia's first national intermediary organization, the Somali Unit for Research on Emergencies and Development (SURED). During those years, 1981–86, I noticed indigenous VDOs that were oriented to national policy (SURED among them) and others that were more organically connected to civil society (Islamic cooperatives, for example); still others resembled technocratic associations functioning like private consultancy groups. Most of the NGO typologies I have come across have been developed in connection with the more organized and financially richer northern voluntary organizations. Korten's paradigm cited above is a case in point.

My concern is not to refute other approaches but to offer an additional perspective that attempts to understand specific Sahelian VDOs from the perspective of an African insider. This is a complementary typology offered in the spirit of NGO/VDO pluralism. From my own experience, African VDO leaders are significant factors when analyzing what indigenous organizations are and do. At least this is important during the formative years. However, I do not wish to imply that no other crucial forces are involved. The leadership factor is only one among many. Some of the leaders described I have come to know personally during visits to West Africa and as part of my activities as an advisory member of the Forum of African Voluntary Development Organizations (FAVDO). For the others, I had to rely on the case studies prepared by our field researchers. Needless to say, the reports varied; in some the information was extensive, but in others it was sketchy.

Seize the Past to Conquer the Future

The originality of the indigenous voluntary development organizations Se Servir de la Saison Sêche en Savanne et au Sahel (SIX-S) and Groupement Naam lies in their insistence that the courage to look forward to one's posterity must be combined with the humility to look back to one's history. They provide the best examples of this type of VDO. Their founder, sociologist Dr. Bernard Ledea Ouedraogo, received the 1990 Hunger Project Africa Prize for Leadership. During the award ceremony, he stated that his organizational success lay in "profiting from and developing the qualities of traditional African society; by building upon the solidarity and, in particular, the communal tendency" (Ouedraogo 1990, 47). He concluded his acceptance speech with the observation, "While looking forward to political, scientific and technological trends that will bring about the end of hunger, the Third World must invent its own methods adapted to suit the mentality of its people." This emphasis on respecting history and selectively using traditional structures is much more prevalent in Asia than in Africa. In India it is a product of the Gandhian and Vinoba Bhave movements, and in Sri Lanka it inspires the Sarvodaya movement.

Dr. Ouedraogo, a native of Burkina Faso, worked as a teacher until 1961, when he joined a government ministry as a trainee in agriculture for rural youth. He was soon disillusioned by the government's top-down approach to development. He viewed the government's unsuccessful attempts to establish agricultural cooperatives as attempts to force progress on villagers from the outside. This led him to resign from his government job.

> We were inspired by a method created in 1967 by the rural leaders of the Yatenga in the north of Burkina Faso, who have been particularly affected by the drought. Theirs is a method of indigenous development that follows three essential phases: participation; self-motivation; and taking charge of problems. . . . These three stages are rendered possible through the *Naam* peasant movement. The *Naam* movement

. . . derives its energy and motivation from ancestral sources," (Oue-draogo 1990, 47).

The Kombi Naam (or Naam) is a traditional structure of the Mossi ethnic group. Each year young Mossi from all walks of life form traditional work groups who live apart from the adults during several months when there is work to be done. Even though traditional Mossi society is hierarchical and rigid, in Kombi Naam groupings nether caste nor sex is considered. The official leadership positions of these associations are filled according to merit and achievement criteria, not according to ascriptive practices. This allows these structures to combat social inequalities. While this structure is specific to the Mossi people of Burkina Faso, similar traditions have existed in other African societies. Ouedraogo and his colleagues set to work to modify the traditional Kombi Naam into the more modern Groupement Naam. "The prototypical modern Groupement Naam is an evolution of the Kombi Naam. . . . Membership is apolitical, non-gender stereotyped, and non-sectarian. The Groupements learn how to deal effectively with the market economy. They still coordinate village work during the rainy season, but now they go beyond the village to establish relationships with national government and regional officials. They speak for the village with those authorities" (Parker 1989a, 13).

The Groupement Naams are composed of fifteen to twenty people, usually only men or only women, and there are often several groups in a village. After the creation of several Naam structures, Ouedraogo convened leaders from several villages; and their associations agreed to join together to form federations, which led to the *Union de Féderations de Groupement Naam* (UFGN), a nationally recognized voluntary development organization. The Naams represent beneficiary organizations whose leadership positions are held by elected beneficiary members themselves. In 1976, Ouedraogo formed SIX-S as an international nongovernmental organization to raise funds and give technical assistance to the village Naam groups.[1] SIX-S raises unrestricted funds from international donors and channels them to local groups to use as they see fit. The UFGN and SIX-S are separate organizations, although the organizational structure of SIX-S parallels that of UFGN. They share offices in the same large compound in Ouahigouya, a regional capital in Burkina Faso. Bernard Ledea Ouedraogo serves as executive secretary of SIX-S and as founding president of UFGN.

SIX-S grants loans on easy terms to organized groups on the basis of defined projects: cereal banks, grain mills, improved livestock breeding, gardening, crafts, vegetable drying and storing, weaving, and the building of hand carts. Similarly, through subsidies it finances the construction of barriers to hold back water seepage and to fight

bushfires, the construction of improved housing, actions for the conservation of water and soil, reforestation, drilling, nutrition centers,
and training programs. UFGN village organizations deal with multiple
issues: community organization, soil and water conservation, agricultural development, and small enterprise development. SIX-S/UFGN
has used its partnership-building skills to promote training and technology transfers through intervisitation programs, thereby supporting
farmers in research and acquisition of relevant technology.

As of 1988, there were over 3,600 associated Naams joining many
different ethnic groups in five countries: Burkina Faso, Mali, Senegal,
Niger, and Togo. SIX-S' annual budget for that year was estimated to
be in excess of $2 million for the five countries (Parker 1989a). By 1990,
the Naam organizations had come to represent the largest organized
peasant movement in Africa, with more than 4,000 groups in nine
countries: Burkina Faso, Chad, Gambia, Guinea-Bissau, Mali, Mauritania, Niger, Senegal, and Togo. SIX-S/UFGN operations dwarf most
other voluntary development agencies, not only in West Africa but
elsewhere on the continent as well. Dr. Ouedraogo (1990, 47) closed
his Hunger Project Leadership Prize speech thus:

> That is why at SIX-S we have seized the wisdom of the past, values still
> useful in trying to define the present—a vast and complex present.
> The infinite and sombre future frightens the pessimist and the lazy.
> [But for us] it offers a string of perspectives and strategies that one
> must muster, organize and control. Here is to the Africa of tomorrow."

The Action Committee for the Zone of Bamba Thialene in Senegal
is another indigenous voluntary organization that creatively built
itself from existing local structures and traditional practices. The
region within which the Bamba Thialene Action Committee operates
is among the most underdeveloped in Senegal. Sometime before 1977,
young peasants of the drought-prone villages began to hold discussions on issues pertaining to their own development. Coming to the
realization that development takes place within an organizational
framework, they launched the Action Committee for the Zone of
Bamba Thialene in 1977. The Action Committee took time to develop
an action program. Its formation and evolution have been highly
organic, in harmony with the rhythm and speed of the people themselves. There were times when the Action Committee appeared to be
in hibernation and times when it manifested a flurry of activities.
Sometime after it was formed, the Action Committee was joined by an
ex-teacher who brought with him not only experience in development
training but also the networks necessary to form partnerships and to
raise funds. His impact has been catalytic, not dominating. The main
objective is to promote food self-sufficiency through credit and

agricultural development. The group's efforts also involve natural resource conservation and combatting drought and deforestation (Ba 1989). They seek to minimize the impact of droughts by increasing food production and establishing food reserves. Their approach to history and tradition is very similar to that of the Naam movement.

The Tassacht Association of Mali is another young voluntary development organization that concentrates on settlement-oriented projects. The mobilization of tradition to promote evolutionary change came to fruition during the 1982 drought, prompting certain people in the Gao area of Mali to create an informal organization that entered into a cooperative agreement with Oxfam U.K. and changed its name to Tassacht Association. Having established an office at N'Tillit, with main offices in Gao, Tassacht Association began to work with village committees. In 1983, large numbers of drought victims collected in the environs of N'Tillit. The initial project involved provision of stable water supplies to encourage nomads to settle and a gradual reconstitution of nomadic herds. Loaning five animals to each family had the effect of restoring some of the dignity lost by the former herders. In addition, small-scale agricultural plots, fish ponds, and training and organization (including formation of cooperatives) involved nomads in community expansion and institution building.

Tassacht Association encountered certain problems as a result of respecting pastoral traditions. For example, distances between people caused the absence of two-thirds of the members of the implementation committee from demonstration and orientation meetings. Inadequate infrastructures constituted another constraint, including lack of health centers, schools, markets, and other technical structures of the state. Absence of an agricultural extension agent hampered agricultural development activities, while the fisheries promotion aspect of the project suffered from a lack of fishing instructors.

Nevertheless, Tassacht Association was able to evaluate its own capacities and those of the project at the level of social organization and at the level of technical means necessary for further project implementation (Dicko 1989). Their experience so far shows that, with regard to pastoral settlement issues, all interventions, especially state intervention, must remain strictly noncoercive. It also supports the wisdom of opting for a transitional phase permitting a combination of livestock herding and other activities, a way of life that is partially sedentary and partially pastoral and nomadic.

Return to the Source

Three organizations exemplify a second category of VDOs: RADI, Kaya Region Association, and the Yako Region Committee. Amilcar Cabral (1973, 63) discussed the cultural protest (Negritude) movement that manifested itself among members of the colonized elite as a form of "return to the source": "When the 'return to the source' goes beyond the individual and is expressed through 'group' or 'movements,' the contradiction is transformed into struggles (secret or overt), and is a prelude to the pre-independence movement or of the struggle for liberation from the foreign yoke."[2]

During what Cabral termed the postindependence neo-colonial epoch, one notices that for some members of the urban elite, the establishment of national, intermediary voluntary development organizations that service rural grassroots groups is a form of "return to the source." In the Third World there are a number of such organizations formed by those who have delinked themselves from state structures and urban politics. Several such intermediary VDOs have been formed by radical intellectuals who have drawn theoretical strength and "inspiration from sources as diverse as Paulo Freire, the dependency school, Frantz Fanon, Amilcar Cabral, the black consciousness movement and, particularly in Latin America, the radical Catholic theologians (Gutierrez, Cardinal and others) who have contributed to the Liberation theology movement" (Elliott 1987, 58–59).

Mazide Ndiaye is a typical example of a radical intellectual who decided to "return to the source" by founding an intermediary VDO called RADI (in English, African Network for Integrated Development). Upon completing his university education in agriculture in France, Ndiaye returned home to Senegal, where he worked with the Ministry of Agriculture. Later on he and some friends established a journal and became involved in what the government viewed as conspiratorial left-wing politics. They were arrested and jailed for several months. Upon release, Ndiaye was appointed head of an art/theatre school, where he learned many things that were not in his previous training. He also came to appreciate the vitality of rural folk culture. He went on to work in ENDA (a voluntary development organization established by a Frenchman with Senegalese citizenship) before quitting and establishing RADI.

RADI works in various regions of Senegal, mostly with drought-prone communities, organizing irrigated communal vegetable plots, improving marketing systems, and developing cooperative stores, village pharmacies, and paralegal activities (Parker 1989b). RADI is more like SIX-S than UFGN. It is an organization of "technical assistance" rather than a direct beneficiary organization.

In Burkina Faso, a European Catholic priest named Frans Balemans became disillusioned with the conventional priestly role and began to search for a means to link his activities with the socioeconomic activities of rural grassroots organizations. This led him to the creation, in 1972, of the Association for the Development of the

Kaya Region in Burkina Faso (French acronym ADRK). After several stages of evolution, ADRK had by 1988 come to represent 6,000 members grouped in 108 savings and loans cooperatives established in several villages in the three provinces of the Central Mossi Plateau, including fifty-one cooperatives in the province of Sanmatenga, thirty-five in the province of Namentenga, and twenty-two in the province of Passore (Ouedraogo 1989).

ADRK placed most of its initial emphasis on mass literacy and participatory education. It went on to provide agricultural credit to individuals and existing collectives at rates of interest much lower than those for existing individual credit. During 1987–88, ADRK began to intervene in the areas of water, soil conservation, and erosion prevention, reflecting its success in participatory community education. In 1986, it was the peasant members themselves who demanded action in the area of water and soil conservation. Since then, 32.8 hectares of land have been restored. ADRK has solicited assistance from more technically specialized agencies in carrying out its training and functional literacy program.

Two members of the urban elite, a French doctor, François Gouvier, and a local businessman, El Hadj Oumarou Kanazoe, decided to "return to the source" by forming the Committee for the Development of Yako Region (French acronym CDRY) in 1979. Yako is situated in the province of Passore in the middle of Burkina Faso. The majority of the population is ethnically Mossi. The region experienced the divisiveness of postindependence multiparty politics as well as some positive effects of the rural development campaigns launched by the radical regime that came to power in 1983 under the leadership of President Thomas Sankara. The province has been adversely affected by repeated droughts since 1973. The droughts have contributed to soil erosion and exacerbated the migration of men from Yako to the southern regions and to the Ivory Coast and Gabon.

CDRY has followed in the footsteps of the Naam movement in utilizing the traditional Mossi work ethic and spirit of solidarity. However, while traditional Mossi hierarchical structures lend themselves to mobilization, they deny effective participation to lower-ranked groups and especially to women. The creativity in the Naam movement and in CDRY's work lies in utilizing what is positive in traditional structures while combatting and modifying the negative aspects. CDRY has involved the people in communal participatory activities that resulted in microdams and the provision of potable water; food security through the establishment of cereal banks; anti-erosion measures; and health efforts, including the provision of vaccination and nutrition programs, education, and vegetable gardens intended to increase incomes and to improve nutrition (Palle 1989).

CDRY strives to implement projects requested by grassroots organizations. As of 1988, thirty-nine cereal banks had been established. In 1986 alone, twenty-four hectares of land were restored. Water provision projects have permitted the diversification of agricultural production. Food security has strengthened the motivation, determination, and capacities of the people. That the motivation of the people has indeed been enhanced is witnessed by their massive, voluntary participation in CDRY-supported activities.

A review of the literature of voluntary development organizations reveals at least three main tendencies. First, there are VDOs that strive to empower local, village, and regional groups toward establishing an NGO/VDO hegemony in the long run (SIX-S). Second, there are indigenous VDOs that have formed movements struggling to set VDO agendas, taking responsibility for meeting the needs of their grassroots groups and directing their partners in development such as the state bureaucracy, international PVO/NGOs, and foreign bilateral and multilateral donors. They are conscious of their emerging role as advocates for social change interested in bringing about significant policy and institutional changes (Garilao 1987). The VDOs described and analyzed in this section fit into this trend. They, together with the empowerment-oriented group, also manifest the spirit of volunteerism that is crucial to nonprofit initiatives.

The Transmission Belt

The third tendency consists of VDOs that, consciously or unconsciously, become mere vessels—transmission belts—through which other institutional actors (states, international PVOs/NGOs, donor organizations) gain support for their programs with no real regard for the VDOs themselves. Some of these organizations merge their agendas too closely with that of the state, thereby losing autonomy through a process of cooptation.

The Association for Applied Technology and Management in Africa (French acronym AETA) provides a vivid example of a VDO that has been coopted by government and funding agencies. AETA was formed in Bamako, Mali, in 1982. One of its major objectives is to serve as a conduit between international PVOs/NGOs and other international financial institutions and the projects they wish to fund in Mali (Bacoum 1989). It had a permanent staff of ten as of 1988 and had executed about thirty-four projects with strong funding from European and U.S. sources. AETA does not seem to suffer from lack of project funds nor to experience the internal dilemmas in fundraising that characterize VDOs of the first trend—the agenda-setting group.

Among its projects, AETA became involved in introducing fuel-efficient stoves in Kati, Koulikoro region, Mali. Both donors and the

Mali government regard the struggle to conserve forests as a top priority, but the people do not seem to consider fuel-efficient stoves as crucial to this objective. AETA has been unable, or unwilling, to guide the various international PVOs/NGOs involved in fuel-efficient stoves to arrive at one or two standardized models acceptable to women. Like many of the other transmission-belt type of VDO, AETA assumes that projects *are* development. As an example of its cooptative relationship with the government, AETA relies heavily on the state's political organs for youth and women to choose village trainees and demonstration families for the project. This experience shows the incapacity of top-down, official sociopolitical organizations to mobilize people for development. It also shows the limitations of supplying services that the client does not comprehend but does not wish to refuse when they are subsidized or free, often resulting in nonsustainable benefits.

Private initiatives flourished in Mali following the 1982 Donors Conference (Coulibaly 1989). On 1 May 1983, a group formed, calling itself the Mali Association for Development (French acronym AMADE*)*. Due to changes in donor policies, the government of Mali has found itself, since 1982, unable to provide agricultural inputs and other services it provided previously. AMADE, eager to fill such gaps, initiated a seed-bank project to provide seeds to needy farmers in the Kaye region. AMADE has executed projects mostly in collaboration with international PVOs/NGOs, government organs, and public enterprises. AMADE appears to accept governmental cooptation willingly since it works very closely with the Mali government, the ruling party UDPM, and its social organizations for women, UNFM, and for youth, UNJM. For example, AMADE identified the Kaye project, developed the project proposal, obtained aid, and then requested the official cooperative service in the villages, CAC, to implement it on the ground. Having learned from this mistake, AMADE was by 1988 beginning to develop its own seed-bank program.

Groupe Jeunes is another transmission-type VDO. It was formed at the 1986 General Assembly of the Mali PVO/NGO/VDO umbrella organization (CCA/ONG), dominated by foreign PVOs/NGOs that had received numerous applications for employment from educated young Malians. CCA/ONG asked its secretariat to study the problem and find a solution. These deliberations resulted in the top-down formation of Groupe Jeunes as an indigenous intermediary Malian VDO. The idea was to educate young Malians about PVO/NGO activities by familiarizing them with voluntary sector methods of work and to inculcate in the youth a spirit of creating employment for themselves through development work. Groupe Jeunes has raised funds through member contributions, but by 1988 it was relying mostly on funds raised through partnership with members of CCA/ONG.

International PVOs/NGOs seem to have created Groupe Jeunes as a means of deflecting pressure and criticisms from local groups and organizations. "Some government people seemed convinced that external NGOs are essentially 'transferring' unemployment from the industrial countries to their own. A growing number of local university graduates are unemployed, while the NGO's bring in people with entry-level credentials, who, it is thought, couldn't find work at home of comparable responsibility, or who are merely seeking to avoid military obligations, etc." (Johnson and Johnson 1990, 62).

This need to artificially create VDOs ignores a fundamental aspect of the nonprofit sector. The spirit of volunteerism is the first precondition, without which it is not possible to imagine any move toward reliable nonprofit activity. Even though the staff of indigenous intermediary organizations receive pay for their services, their remuneration is usually less than that for those doing similar jobs in the public and private sectors. Moreover, the grassroots organizations supported by such VDOs tend to rely mostly on the voluntary, apostolic drive of hundreds of nonpaid goodwill promoters. A VDO whose leaders are exclusively motivated by the salaries they earn and by the fear of becoming unemployed can hardly inspire energetic volunteerism among thousands of rural and urban poor. Voluntary development institutions cannot be designed, engineered, and built in a prescribed period, like a factory or a machine. As described above under the heading of organizations seeking to utilize the past to build the future and those led by individuals seeking "to return to the source," authentic VDOs have to grow organically like a living thing. An analysis of Groupe Jeunes reveals its lack of values and vision, both of which are crucial to the organizational growth process.

Groupe Jeunes has done some studies and field monitoring as well as consultancy functions for the CCA/ONG. As of 1988, however, it had not been able to function as a viable VDO due to a lack of field projects. Its main project so far has been the construction of a bridge-dam for the agricultural village of Tenkoni in the southern zone of Mali. Tenkoni has a serious problem of water availability. Droughts have decimated livestock and affected both the material and psychological well-being of the inhabitants, although the people remain proud of their traditions and history. In previous disasters, aid handouts had contributed to attitudes of dependence. In this instance, the villagers volunteered labor to construct the dam. Groupe Jeunes used its unemployed graduates for project technical work and as an umbilical cord to CCA/ONG to secure necessary funding. Contributions were also received from some of the area's labor migrants.

Due to misunderstandings, the people neighboring Tenkoni refused to participate in the effort (Diawara 1989). Lacking a participatory community approach to development, Groupe Jeunes was unwilling and unable to resolve this commonplace problem. Typically, problems ensued from the building of the dam, including waterborne diseases. Groupe Jeunes did not try to help the villagers solve these problems. Their narrow project orientation and their technocratic approach precluded them from seeing their mission beyond the engineering of the dam. Nor did they strive to prepare the villagers of Tenkoni to manage the project after the withdrawal of all external assistance. The habit of stretching arms out for "alms" did not disappear precisely because Groupe Jeunes saw its role as strictly an intervention into the physical/material sphere (building a dam), as separated from the social/organizational and psychological/motivational aspects of people's lives.

Development Orientations

Many of the northern PVO/NGOs began their activities in the field of relief and welfare programs; they were not "concerned to establish relationships with local institutions and communities that enable the latter to become empowered to confront the politics and processes that impoverish them" (Elliott 1987, 57; see also Korten 1987). Over time, slowly, some of them moved along the spectrum to a developmental position: "that is to say the support of development projects which have as their ultimate goal improvement in the capacity of a community to provide for its own basic needs" (Elliott 1987, 58). Charles Elliott's contention that southern NGOs/VDOs tend to move along this spectrum faster than northern PVOs/NGOs is confirmed by the experience of the Sahelian VDOs. Even though most of them were established as a result of drought, they do not consider themselves relief organizations. They see their role as that of combatting vulnerabilities and enhancing community capacities in the physical/material, social/ organizational, and motivational/attitudinal spheres. They see themselves contributing to long-term development rather than to short-term relief or welfare.

Though they broadly share a developmental approach, the Sahelian VDOs examined here also reflect basic differences. The first group consists of those that emphasize empowerment and become involved directly in conscientization activities. I shall analyze the developmental approach of SIX-S/UFGN under the subheading "the empowerment approach" and that of RADI under "the structural transformation approach." The third broad group will be analyzed under "the technocratic approach." Again, in the main, those VDOs whose institutional origins were analyzed under the "seize the past to conquer the future" concept tend to reflect an empowerment orientation, those under "return to the source" tend to emphasize structural transformation activities, and those labeled "transmission belt" tend to manifest a technocratic approach. Rhetorically they utilize such terms as *popular participation*, but programmatically they are not much concerned about establishing empowering relationships with local communities. The activities of Group Jeunes described above fit into this category. However, I have drawn a crude picture to illustrate analytical distinctions that are not so clear-cut in real life. I will discuss below at least one VDO that seems to manifest aspects that cut across such categories.

The Empowerment Approach

SIX-S/UFGN patiently works toward long-term development through the incremental raising of living standards. This complex of organizations works by encouraging villagers themselves to identify local needs, choose their own projects, and provide the planning and labor for them. "Above all, what was necessary was to make the populations responsive to their own problems and conscious of the need to exert common efforts to perform simple, concrete and manageable actions that could achieve real and positive results" (Ouedraogo 1990, 47). The method of indigenous development it follows emphasizes active participation, self-motivation, and taking care of problems. As one SIX-S/UFGN organizer remarked (Parker 1989a, 25): "When an intellectual or professional working in a development agency designs the project it looks good but never works. When it starts at the peasant level, it works."

The vision or general philosophy behind the Naam movement argues that it is impossible to achieve future goals unless one starts at some concrete historical time and place. Africa's history and cultural heritage, however distorted, are still alive in the midst of contemporary activities. Therefore, it is not a question of returning to the past (an impossibility). It is a question of critically examining the role of heritage in contemporary life and utilizing it as a springboard into the future. The thrust here is to combat excessively negative attitudes toward African heritage brought about by colonial rule and education. According to the Burkinabe historian Joseph Ki-Zerbo (1990, 93):

> There is hidden treasure in the backlog of social and religious structures, organizational methods, production modes, techniques for handing down knowledge, etc. At any point in a people's history such *precious gems and nuggets* [emphasis added] might break surface again, to serve new purposes. This is already happening in the case of renewed interest in associations, especially popular in the rural areas, precisely because people in the rural areas have no difficulty recognizing them as

familiar types of organization. In effect, they fit in well because, like the *ton* among Bambaras and Dyulas, or the *kombi-naam* of the Yatenga in Burkina Faso, they are custom-made, not cash-and-carry institutions. Here is a magnificent asset waiting for use in a system of education for all.

SIX/S-UFGN and the other VDOs that share its basic approach place a great deal of emphasis on the revival and development of the traditional African norm of solidarity. They strive to transform clan property and solidarity into communal property and solidarity. In their view, values are necessary to set in motion most varied forms of motivated behavior. Authentic VDOs must be value-driven. They are critical of foreign PVOs/NGOs and donors that use funds to create artificial African VDOs. African VDOs increasingly see themselves as representing a VDO sector, a nonprofit (or third sector) in African societies. As African societies strive to promote private sector initiatives, they see the nonprofit sector as vital in counterbalancing the negative aspects of the private and public sectors. Short-term profits for the few may be bought at the cost of long-term public benefits for the many, hence the VDO emphasis on collective development and self-reliance.

In a sense, SIX-S/UFGN and VDOs with a similar orientation have reversed the widely held, if implicit, assumption that economic factors determine cultural factors. Contemporary history has demonstrated the inconsistency of this dogma by showing the resistance of culture to exclusively material determinants. The Naam movement represents this essential dimension of social action encouraging the emergence of "cultures of enterprise." The VDOs under consideration recognize that it is not easy to develop a critical consciousness while managing production relations that increase surplus for the poor. Those VDOs oriented toward empowerment must continue to wrestle with the dilemma that empowerment without production is as futile as production without empowerment.

Like Sri Lanka's Sarvodaya and the Indian VDOs influenced by Gandhi, SIX-S/UFGN reflects an overall philosophy of nonexploitive development. The Naam movement does not believe in the confrontation thesis of development. Accordingly, it seems to coexist in relative harmony with the governments of the nine countries in which it works. Where necessary, it works with government services when these coincide with its own aims and objectives. For example, SIX-S/UFGN brings villagers into contact with existing extension services and, on occasion, has a positive effect on them. The organization tries to deliver services where they do not exist and to maximize others, avoiding duplication where they do. It does not see itself as a parallel structure to government. On the contrary, it holds the governments responsible for imported top-down models of "development," which have effectively numbed the people's ability to reproduce the old and to build creative developing societies.

The Action Committee for the Zone of Bamba Thialene shares the basic development orientation of SIX-S/UFGN. During its formation and early development, Action Committee members held prolonged village discussions dealing with several issues, including the role of religion and tradition. They concluded that religion and tradition have both positive and negative sides. The positive side facilitates communal mobilization with its emphasis on collective effort, solidarity, and the sharing of profits. They decided to search for and utilize positive messages from the Koran and from local tradition to create a contemporary "culture of enterprise" (Ki-Zerbo 1990). On one thing they were absolutely sure: They could not sidestep this religious/traditional heritage and hope to move forward successfully without including it.

The Structural Transformation Approach

RADI and some of the VDOs that share its basic orientation are also involved with the process of empowerment. However, they are less concerned with discovering "precious gems and nuggets" in the historical heritage of social and religious structures, organizational methods, and so forth. Influenced by dependency theory, they emphasize radical training for transformation. Their political education efforts rely less on revitalization of integral African strengths and more on emphasizing the role of outside intervention in the development and underdevelopment of the poor. They want the people to be constantly aware that they are fighting against an internationally well-organized system of domination and exploitation. This vision of development includes the concept of class conflict at national and international levels.

While SIX-S/UFGN and, of course, the Action Committee of Bamba Thialene respect the rhythm of the villagers, RADI manifests the impatience of the development agent who attempts to drive the developing community to the destination that he or she has set. SIX-S/UFGN's insistence on decisionmaking from below makes their approach somewhat biased against confronting power structures and decisionmaking processes at the national and international levels.[3]

RADI, on the other hand, is very much involved in attempting to transform national and international policies and structures. Compared to SIX-S/UFGN, RADI's village-level work is relatively insignificant, but it has high visibility in the policy advocacy arena. RADI has an immediate attitude toward policies and politics, whereas SIX-S/UFGN adopts a historical, long-range conception of politics. The former seems pointed for partisan politics, whereas the latter is interested in creating effective sanctions to mobilize the popular will in civil society without moving too rapidly into explicitly partisan politics or active political management. RADI displays a long-range attempt to create a humanistic hegemony in civil society for the VDO sector.

Both organizations advocate self-reliance. RADI talks about structural transformation and self-reliance, while SIX-S/UFGN emphasizes self-reliance and respect for indigenous values. Yet, both of them, and all the other VDOs discussed here, depend on external funding. This paradox presents several dilemmas of which, fortunately, the most mature African and other Third World VDOs are painfully aware. Can one really build a viable civil society with funding derived from external societies and states? Most Third World VDOs argue, at least at this point, that local, state, or commercial sources of funding would make them lose all autonomy within their systems, obviously an unsatisfactory condition. However, as noted by Godfrey Gunatilleke (Goulet 1981, v), "What is clear is that the outcome fundamentally depends on the ideology of the recipient movement and institution and its intrinsic capacity to define its own goals and pursue them with a profound commitment, to which the means it employs such as external aid becomes fully subservient."

The VDOs discussed in this and the preceding category tend to reflect autonomy in ideology and objectives. From its inception, SIX-S has been able to create a partnership with at least four European funding agencies. They have provided SIX-S with flexible, multiyear program funding rather than the more rigid, case-by-case project funding. This is a good example of development cooperation.

In spite of having to rely on external funding, SIX-S/UFGN is an organization that has had time to sort out its own priorities and, based on its own analysis, to determine how, when, and where it wants to expand. RADI has a reparations theory of external funding conceptually enunciated by Frantz Fanon (1968, 102): "The wealth of the imperial countries is our wealth too. . . . Europe is literally the creation of the Third World. The wealth which smothers her is that which was stolen from the underdeveloped peoples." Some among the international PVOs/NGOs share this view, but many do not. Those who do not subscribe to a reparations view of external aid see RADI as a necessary evil, a vehicle to reach the poor. This one-way relationship considers RADI—and the other VDOs that share similar views—as being the "operational cost" of channeling external aid to the poor.

VDOs with articulated visions, guided by strong values and objectives, have tended to be criticized for an alleged "personality cult" around their founding president or executive director. However, the Sahelian organizations with charismatic leaders that we have examined have been well managed. They have not been simply one-man shows either. At this point, rather than a problem, the undisputed charisma of a Bernard Ouedraogo or Mazide Ndiaye has been an enabling factor in the growth of their respective organizations, an asset rather than a hindrance. It has provided SIX-S/UFGN and RADI with a national and international profile that has protected them in times of difficulty, thereby serving a useful strategic purpose to the extent that charisma has been consciously promoted.

The Technocratic Approach

Certain VDOs define development in terms of empowerment, education for transformation, and conscientization activities. Conscientization cannot be neatly packaged into projects to be "sold" to northern donors. Other VDOs seek to transform policies and structural obstacles. By contrast, the transmission-belt type of VDO often utilizes the rhetoric of self-reliance and interdependency even though its programmatic activities are heavily influenced by the modernization school of development theory. While the other groups see empowerment and structural transformation as processes, this group assumes that projects *are* development. As more funds become available to PVOs/NGOs/VDOs, they prepare more and more project documents to spend the money. They put unrelenting pressure on people to produce results. VDOs of the technocratic group tend to be product-oriented in contrast to the process orientation of the empowerment VDOs. They put a premium on development professionals, whereas the other groups place emphasis on the people themselves. In the long run, some of the technocratic VDOs may transform themselves into private consultancy firms or other forms of for-profit organizations.[4] There is also the problem of "phantom VDOs," though none of those analyzed in this study fit into this category. These are VDOs that do not really exist except on the letterhead used to solicit external funding.

AMADE, discussed above, is an example of a VDO with a technocratic approach to development. To be sure, after the experience gained from the Kaye project, AMADE was by 1988 beginning to develop its own seed-bank program (Coulibaly 1989). However, another initial reaction was to create a "technical structure" of socioeconomic experts to choose projects. This is contrary to the SIX-S/UFGN method of letting beneficiaries choose projects.

AMRAD is a VDO that seems to embody elements that cut across at least two of the categories used to analyze Sahelian VDOs in this section. It was formed in Mali in 1982 and works in urban as well as rural areas (Touré 1989). AMRAD sees itself as an "action-research" organization that intervenes in several sectors, including village water development, agriculture/livestock, and fisheries development, along with primary health, renewable energy, appropriate technology, and training. During a visit to the regions in which the organization works, the vice president of AMRAD was presented with a project proposal prepared by the community of Niafunke, an area that has witnessed religious and ethnic conflicts and has also suffered from severe drought and desertification.

AMRAD decided to intervene and was able to obtain funding from its external partners to start pilot projects in five of the sixty-five villages covered by the project documents. These initiative. have included potable water projects, vegetable farms for six groups of women, and the reconstitution of livestock herds. Pumps have been utilized to provide potable water in selected villages. AMRAD stresses mass mobilization and participation as well as functional literacy, education, and training. The concerned peasants have been grouped under a General Assembly that provides oversight for the project. At each village an implementation committee executes the decisions of the General Assembly. Benefiting from the experience of SIX-S/UFGN, AMRAD remains convinced that it is not there to give the people fish but rather to teach them how to fish.

Discussion of the institutional development of Sahelian VDOs was followed by an analysis of thcir developmental orientations. To a noticeable extent there is a relationship between institutional birth, growth, and developmental orientation or vision. Now we shall turn to their ability to form developmental partnerships, an issue that is more related to creative institution building as a process.

On Scaling and Partnerships

The founding of umbrella organizations and partnerships is an aspect of creative institution building. As Judith Tendler (1982) has argued, PVO/NGO/VDO effectiveness is often an outcome of its catalytic ability to pull together resources from diverse sources, including from the public sector, for the benefit of local communities. Sahelian VDOs have acted as institutional bridges between diverse agencies. They have convened potential partners to examine their common interests in collaboration. They have acted as learning mechanisms to test potential programs and problem solutions that require flexible and adaptive administration. Some of them have helped build critical institutions (umbrella organizations, for example) that enable partnerships to emerge between local organizations, government agencies, and international bodies.

At the 1987 London Conference on NGOs, Sheldon Annis (1987, 129) raised several pertinent issues:

Nongovernmental organizations (NGOs) are so frequently lost in self-admiration that they fail to see that the strengths for which they are acclaimed can also be serious weaknesses.

- In the face of pervasive poverty, for example, "small scale" can merely mean "insignificant."
- "Politically independent" can mean "powerless" or "disconnected."
- "Low-cost" can mean "underfinanced" or "poor quality."
- and "innovative" can mean simply "temporary" or "unsustainable."

. . . . Can that which is local build upon itself so that small is institutionalized and widely replicated?

Annis challenged PVOs/NGOs to improve their impact by increasing their scale and scope of activities. One way this can be done is through the creation of umbrella or coordinating organizations. PVO/NGO/VDO coordinating bodies at the national level are referred to by various names, including councils, groupings, associations, consortia, and apex or umbrella organizations. Among other tasks, they are expected to amplify the impact of small grassroots development activities. Here I shall refer to them as partnership coordinating organizations (PCOs).

Attempts to form a PCO in Mali began in 1976 and resumed after being dormant for six years in 1982 at the initiative of Euro-Action Accord. It was finally founded by twenty voluntary organizations in 1983. As of 1988, this PCO (with the French acronym CCA/ONG) had sixty-eight dues-paying members and an additional thirty-two "partners" who participate in meetings and activities but who do not pay dues or vote. The severity of drought-related problems encouraged the Mali government to be very open and permissive, thereby facilitating the development of CCA/ONG (Johnson and Johnson 1990). As Ron Parker (1989c, 1–2) has observed, "Many countries have attempted to create NGO coordinating commissions, most of which have only been marginally successful. The CCA/ONG in Mali is a bright exception. When the rains began to fall, and Mali no longer faced a disaster situation, the CCA/ONG took a leadership role in restructuring the relationship between Northern and Southern NGOs. The CCA/ONG helped NGOs not represented in Mali to begin programs and/or search for project partners. At the same time, the CCA/ONG assisted numerous national NGOs get started, and it continues to provide a variety of services that contribute to the institutional growth."

CCA/ONG performs functions commonly performed by coordinating organizations, functions that can be grouped into four categories:

1. Increase contact and collaboration among voluntary development organizations.

2. Provide various services to members.
3. Improve links with government.
4. Increase resources available to PVOs/NGOs/VDOs.

As a PCO, CCA/ONG is able to negotiate for relatively more flexible funding modalities. It has placed great emphasis on the promotion of indigenous VDOs, and it has funded most of Mali's newly created VDOs.

CCA/ONG has not succeeded in helping its members develop a common strategy concerning development policy. Nor has it engaged the government and donors in a nationwide socioeconomic policy dialogue. Although able to coordinate NGO activities at the national level, CCA/ONG has not yet evolved mechanisms for NGO coordination at provincial or district levels. It has, however, guided and controlled the growth of its secretariat in proportion to the needs of the member organizations. Tensions between external and national CCA/ONG members have not risen so far mainly because the international organizations seem eager to fund and promote the development of indigenous VDOs.

Although CCA/ONG has helped numerous national NGOs get started, these fledgling institutions are at risk because they may be getting too much international attention and support too soon. As the larger donors such as the World Bank and the U.S. Agency for International Development (USAID) turn increasingly to the indigenous NGOs, embryonic organizations risk losing sight of their original missions as they accept projects beyond their administrative capacity and technical skills just to take advantage of funding opportunities. Many observers believe that Mali needs to allow these organizations a period of slow growth or a whole generation of potentially good NGOs may be lost (Parker 1989c).

The former permanent secretary of CCA/ONG, Mamadou Kone, recognized this problem (Parker 1989c, 22). "In the future," he recommended, "funding should be limited to those NGOs which already have projects, and those whose staff have demonstrated experience. This is where you begin: support the ones who are already working. This is where the CCA/ONG can help. Its staff knows the projects and individuals." Thus, indigenous VDOs with a track record should be given funding priority over those that are newly started. Although well founded, this recommendation need not be implemented in a rigid manner.

CCA/ONG has succeeded as an umbrella organization partly because of the strong support it has received from the Mali government. The government sees it as a form of security to facilitate drought-relief assistance in case of emergencies. It is also viewed as a drought-relief network even though CCA/ONG members see themselves, for the most part, as promoting long-term development to combat drought. The government has not allowed PVOs/VDOs to play any significant role in formulating development plans in spite of the visibility that the CCA/ONG umbrella has given them.

The CCA/ONG experience also illustrates a difference since the drought of 1974, when international PVOs/NGOs felt that they had to do everything by themselves. By 1982–84, they found a number of indigenous VDOs on the ground; and most of them decided, therefore, to strengthen and increase their number rather than substitute for them in field activities.

Within Senegal, RADI has played a crucial role in revitalizing CONGAD, a partnership coordination organization like the Malian body CCA/ONG. During the crucial years of RADI's growth, Mazide Ndiaye also served as the elected head of CONGAD. RADI was able to host, in 1987, the first Dakar Congress, which brought together representatives of indigenous voluntary nongovernmental development organizations from eighteen African countries. The delegates agreed to form a pan-African umbrella organization entitled the Forum of African Voluntary Development Organizations (FAVDO). FAVDO is intended to provide a forum for mutual support and cooperation among African development organizations. RADI under Mazide Ndiaye's leadership has shown itself to be extremely competent in organizing the organizers, the intermediary national or pan-African VDOs. CONGAD and FAVDO tasks take quite a bit of his time, and it may be appropriate to speculate that in the long run RADI might decide to put its energies mostly into global and national policy advocacy with minimum inputs into actual village development.

SIX-S/UFGN face the opposite dilemma. Their insistence on letting villagers speak for themselves and on decisionmaking from below sometimes means that they do not get very far beyond a village view of realities. Nevertheless, creative institution building has allowed SIX-S/UFGN structures and institutions to scale up and to scale horizontally and to begin to have a low-profile impact (especially through SIX-S) on national and regional policies and institutions. As of 1988, SIX-S/UFGN was working in five neighboring West African countries; by 1990 it was working in nine countries with more than 4,000 groups. Its vision of continental scaling or African VDO unity is gradualist and sub-regional in orientation.

Democratization Possibilities

The connection between famine relief and some forms of democracy is bluntly stated by Peter Cutler (Chapter 4 in this book; see also Field 1989): "Without effective sponsors, rural famine victims become asset-stripped and starve. Their best hope is to be born in a country with a reasonably free press, a concerned middle class, and a Western-aligned foreign policy." The emergence of African VDOs means that rural famine victims have influential and concerned urban elites on their side. In a country with a relatively free press (Senegal) these elites have access to the press. In all cases their partnership relations with northern PVOs/NGOs ensure them access to the international media. Thus, the response to the Sahelian drought of 1984 was much faster and more effectively organized than the 1973–74 response. In any future drought, the Sahelian VDOs should effectively serve as conduits for funds and other forms of famine assistance. They are in the best position to be able to implement relief programs within a developmental framework.

These VDOs are a resource in themselves, a form of development investment. Building them institutionally constitutes a strategic form of development assistance. With regard to processes of democratization, VDOs serve as strategic incremental innovators. They also help give mass mobilization organized and relatively nonpolitical forms. Samuel P. Huntington (1968) has theorized that political disorder in the Third World is often a result of mass mobilization and participation's exceeding organizational and institutional capacities. Webs and networks of PVOs are being created where before only discrete organizations existed; and coordinating bodies, or PCOs, have been established at the national level in Mali (CCA/ONG), Senegal (CONGAD), Burkina Faso (SPONG), in other Sahelian countries, and, indeed, in many other African countries.

PVOs whose organizations are capable of sustaining respect and credibility among the local people are also able to create a moral climate supporting enhanced productivity. Urban elites involved in the PVO sector, even those with a narrow technocratic approach, emphasize production and the need to work hard to earn a better living. They are evolving a culture that is anticorruption, answering much that has been written about the corruption and "rent-seeking" activities of many among Africa's ruling circles.[5] VDOs also serve as civic education schools for leaders and masses. In countries that have recently thrown off dictatorial regimes—Brazil, Philippines, and the countries of Eastern Europe, for example—one finds among the newly elected leaders several that received their training within the VDO sector. Within their own projects, the participatory-oriented VDOs promote democratic practices at local levels. They create practical schools of democracy and provide space for intellectual probing on matters of importance. As noted above, the Action Committee for Bamba Thialene held prolonged ideological debates on the role of religion and tradition and on developmental orientation.

VDOs maintain democratic space even under dictatorial regimes: within their projects, in their institutional functioning, and/or with the international solidarity that they stimulate by their existence and activities. They also contribute to democracy by helping dissidents stay in their own countries. Committed members of the intelligentsia can thus remain in their own societies and be usefully employed instead of having to emigrate, pushed out by the authoritarian regime in power (Padron 1987).

African democratic participation will be meaningless without the active participation of African women. In the sample of case studies on Sahelian VDOs, a discussion on gender role is provided in some cases but missing in others. With regard to Groupement Naam and SIX-S for example, traditional Kombi Naam structures of the Mossi ethnic group did not transcend the gender gap. In the past, young male Mossi from all walks of life formed gender-restricted work groups who lived apart from adults during several months when there was work to be done. Modernized Kombi Naam structures transcend both caste and gender barriers. Is the VDO able to project this transformation beyond itself and into surrounding institutions? There is partial but not conclusive evidence to suggest modest success. Credit-oriented activities involve women and men, although there is impressionistic evidence to suggest that women are more reliable and have higher repayment ratios than men. The migration of able-bodied men from critical areas of the Sahel as a result of the drought has left women, children, and elders behind to assume extra burdens.

A technocratic-oriented organization like AETA sees its relation to women as one of organization. The introduction of fuel-efficient stoves involves women. AETA chose women and demonstration family trainees by relying on the top-down methods of the ruling party and its so-called mass organizations. AETA missed the opportunity to engage in an empowering dialogue with the women to arrive, for example, at one or two standardized models of cookstove acceptable to women. In their critical modernization of religion and tradition, the Action Committee has tried to show that oppression of women has nothing to do with religion properly understood. To prove their point, they have searched for positive messages from the Koran and sayings of the Prophet Muhammad. RADI has a striking team of women in the ranks of its senior staff. A few of them are extremely vocal and convincing in their advocacy of women's emancipation. Nevertheless, the limited observations of their actual field operations conducted by the case history researcher and this author do not permit us to conclude that RADI has carried out outstanding work on the gender gap.

Generally speaking, most women's organizations in Africa tend to be at the regional or local levels. An interesting example of this type is the Nigeria-based Country Women Association (COWA) headed by Mrs. Bisi Ogunleye. It is involved in promoting revolving credit schemes for women. There are few national intermediary women's organizations. There are, however, significant pan-African women's organizations. At least two are headquartered in Dakar, Senegal: an organization dealing with women in the media, and the African Women Research and Development (AWORD) voluntary association. The field researchers we collaborated with did not choose to study any specific women's organizations.

Apart from being more sophisticated and better organized, African PVOs have become more aware of their power; and inspired by recent events in Eastern Europe, they have increased their prodemocratization militancy. Certain Western countries and donor organizations have begun to include a pro–human rights/democratization conditionality to their foreign aid package.[6] A respected African leader, ex-President Julius Nyerere of Tanzania, who championed one-party states in the past, has publicly stated that, in light of the events in Eastern Europe, Africa should be open to experiment with multiparty states.[7] Thus, PVOs, in addition to combatting famine through development programs, are also in a position to open up possibilities for democratizing Sahelian states and societies. Moreover, the apparent exhaustion of authoritarian routes to "developmental dictatorship" in Africa, as evidenced in democracy movements across the continent, obliges those concerned to search for democratic forms of accountability as the best means of disciplining ruling classes and regimes.

Conclusion

Sahelian PVOs have risen and flourished mostly as a response to the drought and famine emergencies that have afflicted the region. They have manifested remarkable creativity in institution building. A number of them are still in the formative and developmental stage of organizational building (for example, Groupe Jeunes). Others have attained the second level, the consolidation stage (AMRAD), while still others have moved to a third level, the institutionalization stage (SIX-S/UFGN; RADI).

An analysis of the dynamics of PVO formation has enabled us to put them into the groupings of "seize the past to conquer the future," "return to the source," and "transmission belt." Their development orientations are summarized in Table 8.2. There is a relationship between institutional formation and development orientation. The "seize the past" cluster, with its empowerment approach, assumes that one does not develop anyone else, but instead develops oneself.

Table 8.2 Classification of Sahelian VDOs

VDO Grouping	Development Orientation
Seize the past	Empowerment approach
Return to the source	Structural transformation approach
Transmission belt	Technocratic approach

Some go further to maintain that even correct and socially sensitive ideas should not be imposed on rural villagers by urban elites (planners, researchers, activists). They want development to come from below. They believe that empowerment cannot be passed on through projects. Rather, it is a process to be learned. The dilemma they face is that, so far at least, they have not been able to go beyond a village view of realities. Paradoxically, this sounds more like accommodation than empowerment. However, SIX-S leaders, in the tradition of Gandhi, argue that only by pursuing bottom-up development over a long period of time can one achieve hegemony. Once hegemony is achieved, the question of structural transformation will be easier and can be attained without confrontation.

The "return to the source" cluster, with its structural transformation approach, emphasizes the policy-framework aspect of development. VDOs in this cluster stress the need for national and international structural transformations, whereas the clear-cut empowerment-oriented VDOs stress the need for self-reliance and respect for indigenous values. While the former conduct most of their policy education programs within national and international contexts, the latter focus on grassroots conscientization activities. The dilemma the former face is that, while giving most attention to matters pertaining to development policies, village-level development work becomes superficial.

The "transmission belt," technocratic VDOs seem content to serve as extensions or conduits for First World aid flows into the Third World. Obviously, the relative ease with which international assistance is granted provides disincentives for indigenous PVOs to seek and mobilize local resources. The technocratic VDOs want to implement discrete projects; the empowerment and transformation VDOs want to go beyond projects to become involved in the overall process of development. The "transmission-belt" VDOs lack their own clear-cut identity, vision, and self-determined role in national development. Should they be allowed to dominate the scene, they would pose a serious threat to the task of establishing an effective, authentic nonprofit sector that contributes to Africa's internally driven development. They remain content to organize the people for drought relief, while the empowerment and transformation VDOs strive to promote long-term development as the best means to combat drought and famine.

Sahelian VDOs have played a significant role in the creation and maintenance of local partnerships and of national (CCA/ONG) and continental coordinating bodies (FAVDO). In spite of differences in development orientation, most have striven to ensure that "that which is local" can "build upon itself so that small is institutionalized and widely replicated" (Annis 1987, 129). With regard to scaling, the Sahel countries have experimented with forms that seem to be more advanced than those found in other parts of Africa. Nevertheless, even the CCA/ONG umbrella organization has yet to prove effective in promoting development policy dialogues between voluntary development organizations, donor representatives, and government.

Concerning drought and famine, Sahelian VDOs feel that they are making a significant contribution simply by organizing the victims. In his New York acceptance speech referred to earlier, Dr. Bernard L. Ouedraogo (1990, 46) quoted an African farmer who stated: "Hunger disgraces the individual and does not fear the Lord. It only recoils before organized and conscientious work."

One of the key elements of democracy is freedom of association. PVOs are exercising this basic right by their very existence and activities. Webs and networks of VDOs have been created, as have PVO/NGO/VDO coordinating bodies. National and grassroots popular organizations have become increasingly aware of their power and of the direct and indirect roles they can play to enhance the worldwide process of democratization in their particular country and region. Recent events in parts of Asia, Latin America, and particularly Eastern Europe and Southern Africa have strengthened their resolve to promote democratization. The creation of a viable nonprofit sector even in authoritarian African countries would have consequences far beyond the effectiveness of particular VDOs and even beyond this sector itself. As de Tocqueville (1966, 255) said addressing American society more than 150 years ago:

> Democracy does not provide a people with the most skillful of governments, but it does that which the most skillful government cannot do; it spreads throughout the body politic restless activity, superabundant force and energy never found elsewhere which, however little favored by circumstance, can do wonders. Those are its true advantages.

Notes

1. SIX-S stands for "se servir de la saison sêche en savanne et au Sahel" ("using the dry season in the savanna and the Sahel").

2. Cabral was the only genuine revolutionary theorist among the African leaders who spearheaded independence movements.

3. This position is similar to that of the Sarvodaya movement in Sri Lanka; see Goulet 1981.

4. On this point Alan Fowler (1989, 15) writes: "Uncritical promotion of NGDOs as the new institutional solution to poverty alleviation can and has led to abuse. One example in Kenya is the Full Salvation Ministry which sought to import over one hundred prestigious motor cars—Volvos and Mercedes—for resale in order to help it fight against 'demons of poverty' (*Daily Nation*, 14 August 1988), an enterprising innovation for Southern NGDOs whose purpose is poverty alleviation!"

5. "Rent seeking" is the private use of public resources through administrative mechanisms. See Bates 1981.

6. The *New York Times*, 22 June 1990: A3, reports President François Mitterand as stating that French aid would in the future flow "more enthusiastically" to those countries that take steps toward democracy.

7. See the *New York Times*, 27 February 1990. For heated debates about Kenya's one-party state see the *New York Times* Sunday, 6 May 1990: 12–13. The *Christian Science Monitor*, 22 February 1990, has a long article entitled "In Africa, Glasnost . . . and Perestroika," which shows that in countries such as Algeria, democratization trends actually preceded the events in Eastern Europe. Pressures to transform single-party states into multiparty systems have been felt in several countries, including Kenya, Ivory Coast, Niger, Benin, Zaire, Gabon, and Cameroon.

References

Adam, Hussein, and L. David Brown. 1987. "Forum of African Voluntary Development Organizations." *World Development* 15, Supplement: 251–253.

Anderson, Mary B., and Peter J. Woodrow. 1989. *Rising from the Ashes: Development Strategies in Times of Disaster*. Boulder: Westview Press.

Anderson, Mary B., and Peter J. Woodrow. 1993. "Reducing Vulnerability to Drought and Famine: Developmental Approaches to Relief." In *The Challenge of Famine: Recent Experience, Lessons Learned*, edited by John Osgood Field, 131–146. West Hartford, Conn.: Kumarian Press.

Annis, Sheldon. 1987. "Can Small-scale Development Be a Large-scale Policy? The Case of Latin America." *World Development* 15, Supplement: 129–134.

Ba, Moussa. 1989. "Food Self-Sufficiency in the Villages of Bamba Thialene" (in French). International Relief/Development Project, Harvard University. Mimeo.

Bacoum, Amadou. 1989. "Fuel Efficient Stoves for the Sahel" (in French). International Relief/Development Project, Harvard University. Mimeo.

Bates, Robert H. 1981. *Markets and States in Tropical Africa: The Political Basis of Agricultural Policies*. Berkeley: University of California Press.

Cabral, Amilcar. 1973. *Return to the Source: Selected Speeches*. New York: Monthly Review Press.

Coulibaly, Dada. 1989. "Seed Bank Project in Kayes, Mali" (in French). International Relief/Development Project, Harvard University. Mimeo.

Cutler, Peter. 1993. "Responses to Famine: Why They Are Allowed to Happen." In *The Challenge of Famine: Recent Experience, Lessons Learned*, edited by John Osgood Field, 72–87. West Hartford, Conn.: Kumarian Press.

de Tocqueville, Alexis. 1966. *Democracy in America*. New York: Harper and Row.

Diawara, Adam. 1989. "Using Unemployed Young Professionals in Drought-Prone Rural Villages" (in French). International Relief/Development Project, Harvard University. Mimeo.

Dicko, Baba Abdou. 1989. "Helping Nomadic Populations During Drought" (in French). International Relief/Development Project, Harvard University. Mimeo.

Elliott, Charles. 1987. "Some Aspects of Relations Between the North and South in the NGO Sector." *World Development* 15, Supplement: 57–68.

Fanon, Frantz. 1968. *The Wretched of the Earth*. New York: Grove Press.

Field, John Osgood. 1989. "Beyond Relief: A Development Perspective on Famine." Paper presented at the Fourteenth International Congress of Nutrition, Seoul, Korea, 20–25 August. Mimeo.

Fowler, Alan. 1989. "New Scrambles for Africa: Nongovernmental Organizations and their Donors in Kenya." Paper presented at the Thirty-second Annual Meeting of the African Studies Association, Atlanta, Georgia, 1–4 November.

Garilao, Ernesto D. 1987. "Indigenous NGOs as Strategic Institutions: Managing the Relationship with Government and Resource Agencies." *World Development* 15, Supplement: 113–120.

Goulet, Denis. 1981. *Survival with Integrity: Sarvodaya at the Crossroads*. Colombo, Sri Lanka: Marga Institute.

Hodgkin, Thomas. 1957. *Nationalism in Colonial Africa*. New York: New York University Press.

Huntington, Samuel P. 1968. *Political Order in Changing Societies*. New Haven: Yale University Press.

Hyden, Goran. 1989. "Food Security, Local Institutions and the State: Two Tanzanian Case Studies." Paper presented at the Second Annual Hunger Research Briefing and Exchange, Brown University, 5–8 April.

International Relief/Development Project. 1986. "Project Summary." Harvard University. Mimeo.

Johnson, Willard, and Vivian R. Johnson. 1990. *West African Governments and Volunteer Development Organizations: Priorities for Partnership*. Lanham, Md.: University Press of America.

Ki-Zerbo, Joseph. 1990. *Educate or Perish*. Paris: UNESCO-UNICEF.

Korten, David C. 1987. "Third-Generation NGO Strategies: A Key to People-Centered Development." *World Development* 15, Supplement: 145–159.

Ouedraogo, Bernard Ledea. 1990. "West African Villagers Fight Hunger." *African Farmer* 3 (April): 46–47.

Ouedraogo, Moussa. 1989. "Struggle Against Environmental Degradation" (in French). International Relief/Development Project, Harvard University. Mimeo.

Padron, Mario. 1987. "Nongovernmental Development Organizations: From Development Aid to Development Cooperation." *World Development* 15, Supplement: 69–77.

Palle, Bernadette. 1989. "Yako Regional Development Committee" (in French). International Relief/Development Project, Harvard University. Mimeo.

Parker, Ronald S. 1989a. "Organization Building to Fight Drought." International Relief/Development Project, Harvard University. Mimeo.

Parker, Ronald S. 1989b. "A Long-term Approach to Drought in Thies." International Relief/Development Project, Harvard University. Mimeo.

Parker, Ronald S. 1989c. "The Coordinating Council of NGO Emergency Activities." International Relief/Development Project, Harvard University. Mimeo.

Tendler, Judith. 1982. "Turning Private Voluntary Organizations into Development Agencies: Questions for Evaluation." Program Evaluation Discussion Paper No. 12. Washington, D.C.: USAID.

Touré, Miriam O. 1989. "Development in the Circle de Niafunke: An Integrated Approach to Drought and Famine Relief" (in French). International Relief/Development Project, Harvard University. Mimeo.

U.S. Congress, Office of Technology Assessment. 1986. *Continuing the Commitment: Agriculture Development in the Sahel—Special Report.* OTA-F-308 (August).

Part IV

Improving Famine Detection and Response

Introduction

The Challenge of Famine concludes with three quite different assessments of early warning and response.

Chapter 9 by William I. Torry examines the Sudan Red Crescent Society's Food Crisis/Drought Monitoring Program in North Darfur, a vast, underdeveloped, ecologically marginal, and intensely famine-prone province of Sudan. The Sudan Red Crescent Society's Drought Monitoring Program (SRC DMP) was established in 1985 to provide the data required to discern a deteriorating situation so as to allow for an early and well-targeted response. The hallmark of the SRC's surveillance system is recruitment of local volunteers to monitor conditions and gather information for provincial and national authorities. Torry's study of the SRC illuminates the difficulties of participatory monitoring and identifies barriers to converting early warning into early response.

Chapter 10 by Paul Ulrich focuses on the most recent experience assessed in this book, the massive drought-induced famine in North Kordofan province, Sudan, in 1989–90, when Ulrich worked for the American voluntary agency CARE. In the hope of expediting food aid to afflicted communities in the region, Ulrich decided to test a relatively simple technique for detecting impending famine and guiding a timely response. His chapter presents a terms-of-trade index between livestock and grain prices and reports quite spectacular findings. What emerges is a promising alternative to most existing early warning systems, including the one in neighboring Darfur analyzed by Torry in the previous chapter.

The Challenge of Famine concludes with Chapter 11 by the editor. "Beyond Relief: Toward Improved Management of Famine" highlights several paradoxes in famine management. These paradoxes identify both opportunities for improving performance and formidable obstacles—mostly in the way we think and function—to converting opportunity into achievement. Chapter 11 goes on to distinguish among *famine process*, *famine conditions*, and *famine* itself, suggesting that a conceptual understanding of these distinctions could determine the appropriate timing and the very purpose of intervention. A simple model of famine dynamics is also advanced.

India's approach to famine management, as it has evolved over more than a century, is contrasted with the situation in much of Africa today. India has long relied on ground observation and decisionmaking by local officials, with a clear mandate to intervene early—declare famine so as to prevent famine from occurring—with a well-conceived strategy and the means with which to activate it. The contrast between India and Africa etched in Chapter 11 occasions both despair and hope. The obstacles in Africa are formidable, but solutions exist. These are to be found more in political processes and administrative capacities than in technology. They call for diplomacy and a conscious redirection of development thinking and policy. The good news is that with effort, ingenuity, and luck the elimination of famine in Africa is a realizable goal. The final chapter of *The Challenge of Famine*, like the book as a whole, identifies both constraints and pathways.

9

Information for Food

Community Famine Surveillance in Sudan

William I. Torry

Like many sub-Saharan countries, Sudan has suffered recent crippling droughts. Drought and other factors made 1988 another year when several hundred thousand families in Sudan required emergency food aid. Donor and government agencies took a cautious approach and planned relief consignments on a targeted basis so that only the neediest peasants would benefit from food intervention programs. Effective targeting supposes the timely monitoring of local food conditions. However, for much of the 1980s the food aid establishment in Sudan lacked a developed surveillance and early warning capability. An experiment in North Darfur, initiated in 1986, was designed to put aid agencies in possession of the facts by involving members from local communities in the surveillance process. As emergency food welfare assumes an expanding role in the survival options of dryland populations inhabiting half the surface area of Africa, the concept of participatory famine surveillance should come into prominence. This chapter examines Sudan's only participatory system, set up by the Sudan Red Crescent (SRC), and offers lessons about what such systems are capable of achieving.

Background

Africa's Sudano-Sahelian region crosses nineteen countries lodged between and including Cape Verde and Somalia. The population of some 300 million persons consists predominantly of farmers and herders occupying expansive drylands (some 415 million hectares) classified as at least moderately desertified and drought-ridden (Mabutt 1984; Milas 1984). These dryland zones, and preponderant rainfed areas particularly, are becoming less livable with the passage of each cropping season. Impoverishment spurred or hastened by the 1984–86 famine has been undercutting traditional land use capabilities so boldly that peasant livelihood, in a significant number of cases, can be sustained no longer without emergency food provisions. Food welfarism is evolving into a crucial policy tool deployed by governments and international agencies, while becoming an important subsistence prop for farmers and pastoralists struggling for economic survival. In regard to a sizable group of Sudano-Sahelian societies, it can be argued with justification that an ecological or economic study lacking an account of food welfare influences would be incomplete.

Aid agencies deem food emergency welfare programs at best a necessary evil. Food welfarism, they suppose, will foster dependency of the African villager on his government and dependency of the latter on the foreign donors. This dependency is considered inimical to development initiatives. Sudan's national leaders in the latter 1980s held their own fears about food welfare evils in abeyance, recognizing that rural development efforts would go nowhere if peasants parted with livestock, cash, land, and labor every few years in exchange for food. Sudan's government faced the dilemma with large-scale targeted emergency programs meant for the neediest rural families. Selective assistance supposes cutoff points where monitored conditions will trigger alarms for emergency intervention. Famine surveillance and warning systems developed during drought years to the point of linking many Sahelian populations to their food supplies and of informing national food security policy (Food and Agriculture Organization 1987).

Sudan had the largest famine-affected population reported anywhere in Africa during 1984–86 (Devres 1986), and it benefited from the continent's most costly and far-reaching relief campaign (International Institute for Environment and Development 1986). Darfur and Kordofan regions received commanding slices of Sudan's total aid allocations. Emergency operations started up again in these western areas as a result of poor 1987 crop yields and the slow pace of recovery following 1984–86. Over this span of drought years, surveillance and warnings were carried out at three organizational levels in the western regions.

National and regional consignments originated from central government and donor agency food balance estimates broken down by region. Supply and deficit figures came from assorted sources. Nongovernmental organizations (NGOs) got involved farther down the distribution chain. Their job was twofold. They rationed bulk dispatches to villages and village clusters and transported supplies to end-line drop-off points. The lead NGOs engaged in food relief exercises included Oxfam, Save the Children Fund–U.K., Save the Children Federation–U.S., CARE, and SRC/LRCS (Sudan Red Crescent and League of Red Cross and Red Crescent Societies). NGO surveillants monitored food requirements and deliveries by means of four survey protocols during 1984–86.

1. *Food Production.* The relief agencies occasionally ran pre- and/or postharvest crop surveys supporting appeals formatted for bulk donors. These data also helped target distribution. "Objective" crop-cuts were rejected in favor of more convenient windshield assessments and farmer interviews.

2. *Availability.* So-called socioeconomic markers were the indicators monitored most frequently. Many substituted for actual and procurable food stock measurements. Cereal and livestock prices, home granary levels, income, migration, wage rates, and wild food consumption were calculated.

3. *Consumption.* Weight/height measurements of children under six came to be standard procedure for all agencies monitoring nutritional status.

4. *Food Allotments.* This is where agencies require delivery-against-receipt checks at central or down-line depots.

While donor and government agencies targeted regions, and NGOs selected recipient village populations, final allocative decisions devolved upon community leaders who targeted household units and individuals (Save the Children U.S. 1987; Save the Children U.K. 1986; SRC file notes; CARE 1987). Regional governments insisted on this policy, which several NGOs supported, on the principle that beneficiaries alone command the right and knowledge to make such life-and-death decisions for themselves. Community representatives conducted microlevel surveillance with little or no formal information gathering.

NGOs came to rely heavily upon informant interviews to size up conditions in their outreach areas. Virtually all food production and availability, and some allotment monitoring, registered information furnished exclusively by villagers and townspeople. Agency field officers put great stock in local knowledge. Respect for indigenous expertise combined with their hallmark avowal of participatory development moved some NGOs to voice encouragement for data gathering and diagnosis by grassroots organizations (for example, International Institute for Environment and Development 1986). Researchers also lent support to this concept (Oguntoyinbo and Richards 1978; Campbell

1986; Berry and Ford 1978; Borton and York 1987; York 1985; Currey 1984). Certain advantages posited were:

- Data would be richer since locals detect and diagnose risk and need thresholds within their communities more thoroughly than expatriates.
- Data analysis would be less susceptible to biases introduced by expatriate cultural categories.
- Locals know what to find out, will spot errors more readily, and in short order forge bonds of trust with people of similar cultural backgrounds.
- Data could be relayed quickly and regularly to regional collection points through networks of in-field monitoring stations.
- The systems could be run with small overhead costs if piggybacked onto other programs by the organization.

Enthusiasm for participatory monitoring systems must be seen against not only the background of NGO development mandates and the respect conferred by NGOs upon indigenous systems of knowledge. In addition, it is known (Torry 1988) that sophisticated, high-tech national surveillance was practically useless during recent famines in eyeballing local food situations in order to target and keep track of food flows.

Participatory famine monitoring and warning systems take a couple of possible forms. They may feed data directly to a donor mission or department of local government or hitch onto an NGO surveillance unit. Such systems might accomplish data procurement, diagnosis, and/or warning functions. These characteristics are mainly hypothetical for the present, given that few indigenous famine reporting systems operate in Africa; certainly the research literature makes no mention of them.[1]

Early in 1988 I conducted a field study of Sudan's sole participatory monitoring system to help remove this knowledge gap. Findings from the project are discussed below. It is important for NGOs, donors, and other users of locally generated food crisis information to understand what these systems can actually accomplish and under what circumstances they achieve certain levels of performance. The SRC study offers some guidelines.

The SRC Monitoring System

A remote region as big as France, Darfur is divided into southern and northern provinces. All but one of SRC's sixty-five or so Darfur branches were situated in semi-arid North Darfur. Provinces segmented into area, rural, and village council divisions of local government. Each administrative cell headquartered at a market town. Every area council, most rural council, and some village council administrative posts hosted an SRC branch chapter. Unlike elements forming the local government bureaucracy, branches were not related hierarchically, by size, function, or influence. They operated autonomously within the hinterland of their market hubs.

The North Darfur society, SRC's largest regional entity, was formed in 1986. It came into its own by multiplying branches during the 1984–85 famine. Initially, SRC/LRCS brought the branches up as conduits for emergency food distribution. Late in 1986, when emergency relief activities shut down in Darfur, the chapters resorted to planning, and in many instances actually implementing, small-scale development projects. Still, the overwhelming benefit people associated with membership was one of special access to emergency food assistance. Food welfarism had evolved into a survival prerequisite for most of North Darfur's ecologically marginal farmers and herders (numbering, at the time, over one million persons).[2]

Membership was voluntary and open to anyone, even youths. Branches ranged from 50 to over 2,000 members. An executive committee of about fifteen individuals handled branch business with regional headquarters in El Fasher (the regional government capital), collected dues, planned development projects, supervised project implementation, and oversaw chapter relief work. SRC employed four field officers for North Darfur, and all but one held college degrees. Their jurisdictions encompassed one or two area councils, and they maintained communication links between branch and regional compartments. They acted as chief relief officers for their areas and helped branches steer development proposals through SRC/LRCS channels.

With SRC approval, a Sudan-based British Red Cross delegate approached London's Relief and Development Institute (RDI) early in 1984 for help with developing a Food Crisis Drought Monitoring Program aimed at famine-ravaged North Darfur. RDI complied and sent one researcher out to produce a questionnaire form and organizational blueprint. The program would test the idea of a famine early warning system (extending through a famine cycle) managed by a Sudanese NGO and staffed substantially by volunteer monitors. There were many unknowns. Would a low-budget participatory surveillance apparatus work? Would donors take it seriously and even buy into it? Could monitored economic data facilitate the planning of development projects on which the society was about to embark? The lead objectives for SRC were to alert donor agencies to extraordinary local needs so that assistance during poor growing years could arrive before migration and other costly adjustments had to be activated by villagers. It was further reasoned that the program would be an impetus for an SRC famine-preparedness capability. Its tie-in with Red Crescent's development plans and the elevation of SRC's profile would be bonuses.

Fourteen branches were participating in this experimental program by 1988. Each branch recruited from its ranks one or more persons who, monthly, gathered data and filled out the monitoring forms in Arabic. Monitors tended to be hometown grade school teachers and public health workers, so they were both numerate and literate. Field officers supplied cooperating branches with forms and helped train local monitors; but that was the extent of their involvement. Every month monitors were to send the completed forms to El Fasher and retain a copy for their records.

The regional office discharged only one function related to this program. It collected completed forms and distributed processed summaries to local organizations. A monthly collection was made by the Drought Monitoring coordinator, who flew in from Khartoum and returned there to analyze the data and to prepare English and Arabic summaries. Sometimes he would stay on for a week or two, visiting monitoring branches and spot-checking survey information, in addition to ensuring that proper procedure was being followed. Select donor agencies, NGOs, and the Sudanese Relief and Rehabilitation Commission obtained the English summaries. Central headquarters ran off many Arabic copies, of which each participating branch was supposed to receive a full set monthly. SRC expected that disseminating situation reports among scattered branches would furnish chapter members with useful intelligence for making labor migration, livestock sale, and other scarcity adjustment decisions. Departments of central and regional government also obtained the Arabic forms. SRC's Drought Monitoring coordinator, who assumed responsibility for data analysis, prepared an occasional three-to-five-month trend synopsis and situation outlook.

The survey came in six short sections. The first asked for sorghum and millet prices collected weekly at local markets. Both cereals constitute the region's staple foodstuffs. Part two called for seven types of livestock data. Numbers of deaths compared to figures for the year and month before, prices per livestock class, and general observations were recorded. Several questions considered in- and out-migration (that is, numbers of families, individuals, and livestock entering and leaving area villages). And there was more. Monitors reported wage rates (compared to the preceding month), wild food consumption levels, relief food intake, and crop and weather conditions. Most answers entered as interval data (high/average/low; decreasing/increasing; yes/no).

The Famine Response System

Compared with participatory development projects, a participatory reporting system mainly serves external users. Local systems are meant to be components of more inclusive networks of information. SRC branch-based information had to make its way up two ladders of organization to elicit prescribed reactions. Its foremost aid suppliers functioned within Red Cross/Red Crescent's international family. An elaborate command structure regulated resource and information movements in this system (Figure 9.1). The second hierarchy embraced regional and national government regulatory agencies and donor missions other than LRCSs (Figure 9.2). Both structures are outlined so we can evaluate the SRC monitoring program's effectiveness from the standpoint of the impact it exerted on food supplier decisionmaking. The effectiveness issue will be dissected by two criteria: program linkage with food aid organizations and usefulness of the data provided. Later in the chapter, a third criterion is marshaled; it concerns data quality, irrespective of the uptake of the data by relief suppliers.

The SRC/LRCS Information Pyramid

The Sudan Red Crescent began in 1965 as a British Red Cross Society affiliate and became an independent national society in 1957. During the late 1980s, it numbered among 137 national Red Cross and Red Crescent chapters worldwide. SRC operated, at the time, under the patronage of the head of state; and the minister of Health was honorary chairman. The society worked closely in many ways with government departments in Khartoum and Darfur. However, the wellspring for resources needed to fight famines was predominantly SRC's parent organization, the League of Red Cross and Red Crescent Societies (LRCS), based in Geneva. The League delegation in Khartoum served the SRC in an advisory role, helping strengthen the national organization and assisting with relief and development planning. When a famine was considered imminent, SRC's secretary general consulted on a disaster preparedness plan with the League's chief delegate. This plan had to detail supply and personnel requirements, steps and timetables of action, and budgetary proposals.

Ideally, League and SRC officers were to commence intervention planning in Khartoum months in advance of the November-December harvest season. SRC's food crisis monitoring system was to deliver its real payoff during this lead-in phase. In conjunction with other agencies' reports, monitored information pinpointed trouble spots. By the time preliminary harvest survey results were available, a famine relief plan should have been well in hand. Then, if conditions warranted,

Figure 9.1 The SRC/LRS Information and Food Pyramid

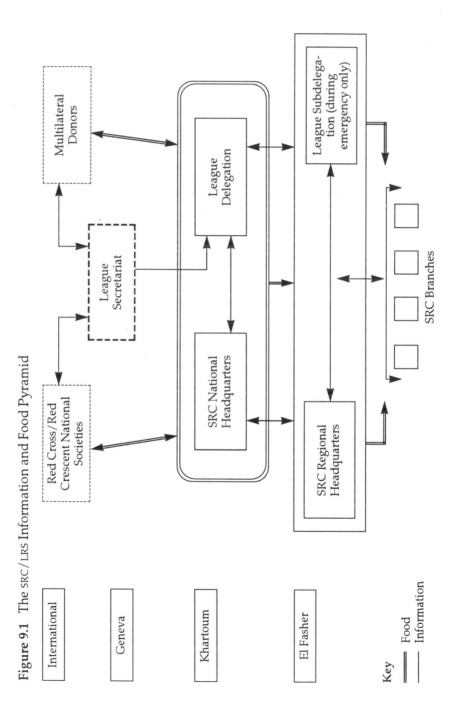

International

Geneva

Khartoum

El Fasher

Multilateral Donors

League Secretariat

Red Cross/Red Crescent National Societies

League Delegation

SRC National Headquarters

League Subdelegation (during emergency only)

SRC Regional Headquarters

SRC Branches

Key
=== Food
─── Information

Figure 9.2 Information Uptake in the SRC Participation Monitoring System: The Regional and National Structures

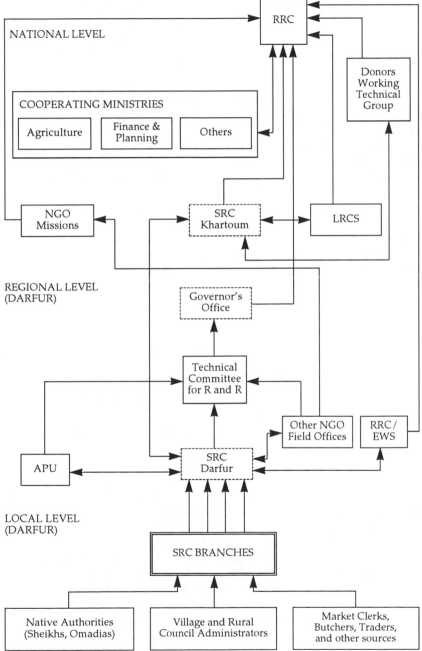

the chief delegate and SRC executive staff would submit a joint appeal to Geneva for assistance.

The League secretariat coordinated appeals and pledges between member societies and dispatched SRC requests to multinational donors, such as the European Economic Community (EEC) (Cutler 1986; SRC file papers; Price-Waterhouse 1986). Only under exceptional circumstances could a soliciting society approach a donor directly for support. Geneva and donor society delegates were free to visit Khartoum and Darfur on independent tours of inspection. All League operations in Sudan came under supervision of the chief delegate's office. If the League took action and set its relief machinery in motion, it would establish a subdelegation in El Fasher vested with a fair degree of autonomy in its cooperative association with SRC's regional staff.

The following are some important features of this system.

- The SRC and LRCS were separate organizations working as a team. SRC's limited experience and resources in the realm of famine management accounted for the strong role played by League delegates during food emergencies in the 1980s (York 1986).
- SRC-Darfur alone conducted prerelief monitoring exercises through its participatory reporting network and its harvest field surveys.
- SRC and League staff converted branch-monitored data into forecasts and alarms. Grain, oil, beans, rice, blankets, clothes, and other goods distributed during famines came from external donations for the most part.

We know that during 1986–88 the SRC and League drafted and implemented procurement and distribution procedures internally, aided by intraagency surveillance reports. These activities coexisted with programs undertaken by many other organizations participating in the famine relief field. SRC gave reliable external reports serious attention; authoritative nutritional, meteorological, and crop production statistics were prized particularly. Other agencies also made use of the SRC's data. Once a relief campaign got going, SRC/LRCS, the government, and expatriate NGOs stayed in continuous contact, each adjusting its maneuvers, day to day, to flashes of news disclosing shifts in population, logistical hitches, supply anomalies, and other exigencies demanding intraagency flexibility and interorganizational coordination. During 1984–86, for example, Save the Children Fund and SRC/LRCS tried to keep each other briefed about breakdowns in distribution so that one organization could step in, temporarily, to pick up the slack left by the other's disability. Figure 9.2 displays agencies other than LRCS over which SRC's monitoring program could exert influence. Functions of the most important of these bodies, in the scheme of SRC's reporting system, are described next.

The Darfur Technical Committee (TC) for Relief and Rehabilitation

The TC constituted Darfur's axis of emergency food policy. It laid down general guidelines and procedures for procuring, storing, distributing, and monitoring food consignments for which the regional government had been delegated responsibility. Local government bodies estimated nine-to-twelve-month food aid requirements when their constituents suffered substantial harvest losses. From these figures, and data supplied by SRC and other groups, TC staff was to decide whether an appeal for assistance from outside the region would be in order and could withstand external scrutiny. TC officials communicated with the Regional Ministry of Agriculture's Agricultural Planning Unit and the Governor's Office; and if the governor were to give the go-ahead, an allocation plan would be forwarded to the Relief and Rehabilitation Commission (RRC) in Khartoum. This proposal stipulated metric tonnage requirements (in sorghum) for Darfur's thirteen subregions (area councils) for so many months, and recommended an allocation mode (free, subsidized sale, or both). A detailed execution scheme was to accompany every official appeal, but implementation would fall to NGOs and local administrative units; the TC charge just bound it to policy decisions. The fourteen-member cell consisted of regional ministry executives and SRC's regional director. No other voluntary organization sat on the TC.

The Agricultural Planning Unit (APU)

The APU, ensconced within the Regional Ministry of Agriculture and Natural Resources, started up in 1986 as relief operations wound down in Darfur. APU advised on all aspects of food security in Darfur. Supported by ODA funding and staffed by expatriate consultants, the APU inaugurated research, convened conferences and workshops, and maintained a library facility. The better-financed APU enjoyed a respected advisory role with regard to the TC, feeding the latter data and framing recommendations in support of emergency and long-term food and agricultural policies. The TC's framework of emergency preparedness owed much to APU counsel. APU kept up regular data-sharing arrangements with NGOs. In fact, APU and SRC staffs collaboratively prepared and analyzed SRC's annual harvest survey forms. TC members thus plugged into the SRC's surveillance apparatus through the APU and by virtue of having impaneled SRC's regional director.

The Relief and Rehabilitation Commission (RRC)

Sudan struggled through 1984–85 hampered by imposing handicaps. Notably, it managed without effectively evolving the central coordination and masterplanning capabilities needed to regulate relief programs and agencies, rally and guide donor inputs, and tie relief and rehabilitation together to the country's seemingly indomitable desertification problems. Sudan's RRC emerged in April 1986 to meet these pressing needs (Gavaghan 1987; Relief and Rehabilitation Commission 1986). Its constituted powers ranged widely before the organization's demise, but these powers concern us only insofar as they supplied part of the institutional framework for the SRC's monitoring activities.

The RRC was to some extent a national version of Darfur's Technical Committee. Two outstanding differences involved its links with donors and NGOs. Darfur's TC did not intervene in NGO functions, whereas the RRC carried a statutory obligation to coordinate NGO programs of emergency relief. Moreover, statute enjoined the TC from entering aid negotiations with *Western* donors.[3] In contrast, donor emergency operations in Sudan had to be channeled through the RRC. RRC officers were the nexus between international donors and regional governors and their TCs.

When Darfur's leaders turned outside for food assistance, they knew their fate depended on two major food grain suppliers: Western donors and the Agricultural Bank of Sudan (ABS). If the TC could pay its own way or count on Ministry of Finance credit relief, it would almost certainly buy sorghum straight from the Bank. Regional authorities resented going the donor route, as many strings were attached to donor contributions. The regional government had nowhere but the RRC to turn to, and the RRC did not have finances to buy ABS grain for Darfur. That is what the donors agreed to provide.

Donors, in short, served as major paymasters while RRC officers brokered compromises between expatriate suppliers and regional authorities. In Darfur's case, TC appeals went through the RRC's Technical Committee and its Darfur desk, then moved on to the donors for a hearing. The TC's chairman and Governor Office executives argued their proposals before RRC chiefs and at joint RRC-donor meetings, which ran through several rounds before differences were settled. RRC deliberations took some account of SRC monitoring reports. They were routed to RRC headquarters from SRC's Khartoum office and utilized in RRC monthly Early Warning System (EWS) bulletins, and the EWS consultant stationed in El Fasher studied these documents in the course of preparing his own food outlook summaries.

The Donors' Working Technical Group

Donors divided their operations along functional and territorial lines throughout 1984 and 1985. Greater unification of donor relief plans had been called for by the government since the RRC's inception. Lead donor agencies, including the World Food Programme (WFP), the U.S. Agency for International Development (USAID), the EEC, and the German and British governments, had been appraising the food situation in Darfur and other regions and laying the foundation for an intervention strategy during a series of meetings inaugurated in September 1987. As of October of that year, their Working Technical Group began holding weekly sessions with RRC's Technical Committee officers under the chairmanship of a WFP representative. High-ranking bureaucrats from key central ministries and Darfur administrative heads were in attendance more occasionally.

The Impact Of SRC's Participatory Reporting System

Was SRC's famine monitoring system effective? The answer is affirmative if the monitoring surveys were digested by food relief decisionmakers and, more importantly, if they helped donors and government regulators decide what to do. SRC's system apparently passes the weaker test of proficiency but comes up short on the stronger one. Many reasons account for the system's mixed performance.

Key organizations, beyond question, gave the monitoring reports a reading. Monitored data entered major regional information channels, thanks importantly to the influence wielded by SRC's respected regional director. He was a native son on familiar terms with regional power brokers who worked at SRC on secondment from the Regional Ministry of Information, where he put out news releases publicizing government activities. Top officials asked him routinely for food situation advisories, and he aired SRC's viewpoints at TC meetings. APU economists engaged him regularly in brainstorming sessions. The RRC's Early Warning System consultant in Darfur used to stop by SRC regional headquarters often and maintained a warm friendship with the Drought Monitoring Program's coordinator.

In Khartoum, similarly, SRC data interested regulatory and donor agency decisionmakers. Two examples will suffice. Sudan's largest food donations in the late 1980s came from USAID, which also bankrolled a short-term return of the League delegate who conceived SRC's monitoring program. At USAID's behest, he began working again at SRC, in part to perfect the organization's monitoring procedures. The RRC's Early Warning System staff and SRC's Drought Monitoring coordinator, furthermore, talked almost weekly. EWS occasionally incorporated SRC surveillance into its monthly bulletins circulated among almost all mainline expatriate donors.

SRC merits praise for having entrenched its participatory reporting system in the food emergency infrastructures of Darfur region and the capital. Yet, branch-level vigilance produced no significant policy impacts even within SRC/LRCS circles. Evidence for this claim is overwhelming. Take, for example, the pivotal report written by the monitoring coordinator immediately after his 14 September–7 October 1987 tour of North Darfur, which coincided with the end of the 1987 summer growing season (Mukhier 1987, 1):

> 1987's rainy season . . . started too early—in April-May—and there was a very long gap from mid-June to mid-August. By the time most of the people lost hope in a harvest. Grain prices increased dramatically from an average of 70 SL [Sudanese pounds] for a [90 kg] sack to 135 SL in the whole of North Darfur. The people planted at least 4 times and few of them succeeded in growing millet [the province's food staple].

Monitoring branches reported virtually no cereal crop production in the large, semidesert Mellit and Umm Kedada Area councils (subprovinces). Local markets offered little millet for sale, and peasants were by then consuming wild plants. Crop failure in El Fasher was also evident, except in certain pockets, although more farmers there still possessed carryover grain stocks. The coordinator (Mukhier 1987, 3) went on to remark:

> I think Umm Kedada and Mellit areas need urgent assistance, otherwise the people are going to desert their villages seeking food. Other agencies like Oxfam are ready to support such assistance which can take the form of food-for-work projects. . . . I think such a program needs further discussion and coordination between all NGOs, including SRC, and the RRC in El Fasher.

This and subsequent monitoring releases did not fall completely on deaf ears. The RRC, exceptionally, devoted almost the entire October EWS Bulletin to coverage of Darfur and neighboring Kordofan regions. The Darfur prognosis echoed SRC's October cautions (Relief and Rehabilitation Commission 1987, 3):

> Outside El Fasher to the north no stocks of millet in houses, and only small quantities on sale. Price of millet high. Unusual movement of people from North to South Darfur in search of food. Umm Kedada and Mellit areas requesting urgent assistance—i.e. relief food—otherwise 2 areas will be deserted. El Geneina [the most populace Area Council in North Darfur] a potential trouble spot needing monitoring.

The APU's September, October, and November food situation prognoses for Darfur leaned on an amalgam of reports incorporating SRC's monitoring surveys. APU analysts projected production shortfalls at several points spanning North Darfur's agricultural grid. Concern that another crisis was in the offing prompted APU investigators to prod their TC counterparts and the governor's people into moving forward with an operational relief strategy before the December and/or January harvest surveys ended. Red flags unfurled in a 16 November APU memo entitled "Notes on Harvest Assessments and Relief Grain Requirements for Darfur 1987" and in the 7 December APU paper, "Proposals for Relief Grain Distribution in Darfur (1987)," prepared specifically for TC consumption.

As late as early January 1988, when my field study concluded, not one agency had completed a plan of emergency intervention. SRC and LRCS were nowhere near ready to take action, and at their offices an air of urgency was conspicuously absent. Red Crescent staff occupied itself with December's anniversary festivities, and plotting tactics for January's constitutional assembly meetings overshadowed other concerns. Three of the four field officers stayed in Khartoum for most of the month, forcing a postponement of the crucial SRC harvest survey for Darfur. APU, TC, and League analysts required the harvest data for their 1988 food aid calculations. SRC staff doubted a full state of readiness could be attained before April.

Without an emergency apparatus in place, a monitoring system's essential purpose is defeated, as nothing exists for it to trigger. A crisis was definitely taking hold by mid-planting season 1987 in substantial portions of North Darfur. Why precautionary planning lagged despite abundant early warning comes down to two related factors. There was unquestionably bureaucratic sluggishness to blame on staff at the TC, League, and SRC-Khartoum. But signals that suppliers and planners were prepared to respond to also slowed reaction time considerably. What looked at first like apathy was, in cases, cautious waiting for the right signals to appear, although inaction sometimes masqueraded as seasoned caution.

In hunting for explanations, we have to recognize the climate of opinion looming large at donor and RRC offices at the time. Everyone was fed up entirely with famine relief and dreaded immersion in yet another full campaign so close on the heels of the last one. Moreover, inevitable exertion and costs aroused worry. Decisionmakers felt ambivalent about the very prudence of relief. They grappled with many questions. Would food aid defy ecological wisdom by sustaining farming systems on degraded parcels of land? Would it glut local grain markets and cut farmers' earnings in zones of surplus production? Would that diminish cereal production and open new vulnerabilities to future droughts? Concerns such as these ruled out premature action. A commitment to relief would hinge on hard evidence entailing conclusive rather that premonitory signals.

There were three warning categories for which the agencies were genuinely primed. Significantly, SRC surveillance covered just one. Harvest data constituted the primary intervention trigger. Production figures were a cornerstone of the food balance sheet calculations that donors employ to reckon consumption needs (Food and Agriculture Organization 1987). Crop yield surveys normally furnish analyzed data sometime late in December or thereafter. Two other signals would be studied as checks that conditions were not getting out of hand before then. Excess starvation mortalities and unusual population movements could produce action for food releases. Some RRC and donor analysts acknowledged the possible validity of conditions portrayed in SRC reports and in other food intelligence sources, but underscored the lack of proof that villagers were bearing unacceptable costs. Migration, which SRC did monitor, was *alone* of incidental importance to donors and the RRC, and the impressionistic quality of such evidence presented in SRC documents robbed it of compelling force.

Evidently, SRC's famine monitoring unit and technicians from the food aid establishment were failing to speak each other's language. SRC was not worried enough about its program's clout to reformulate questionnaire data into donors' warning categories. Those exercises would not have been excessively difficult; the APU had done somewhat as much, with little effort, in response to a TC request in November. Adjusting 1983 census data for an estimated population growth rate of 3.2 percent per year, and assuming a standard 400 gram ration of sorghum per person per day, APU's economists estimated total consumption requirements in metric tonnage for each area council in Darfur. Preliminary relief requirements were derived from the percentage of population estimated to warrant relief (30–70 percent), multiplied by the months that relief would be required (ten months for all of North Darfur). The final preliminary call-in came out to 105,741 metric tons, or 46 percent of North Darfur's postulated consumption requirements. The APU did not go into how its beneficiary population figures were derived, but the authors by all accounts distilled their numbers from a welter of socioeconomic information of the very kind gathered by the SRC.

Debate over these figures bounced back and forth between Darfur and Khartoum for weeks before the RRC opted for halving TC's request (111,865 metric tons for the whole of Darfur) until the harvest production picture became clearer. The League bided its time waiting to see what kind of pledge the RRC and other donors would announce. An opportunity may have beckoned SRC and the League for a more aggressive course of action. With some help from League delegates, the SRC could have drafted figures of its own that were no less plausible than what the APU proposed, put them in food balance sheet format, and readied them by September or early October.

I have branded the SRC's monitoring program ineffectual on two accounts. More could have been expected from the SRC and League directorates. Essentially, they were disregarding their own warnings while remaining aloof from disaster planning throughout the harvest season. The TC showed more concern but dragged its heels all the same. RRC and the Donors Working Technical Group demonstrated serious commitment but could not get much direction from the *type* of information SRC was issuing.

Data Quality and Participatory Reporting

Facts supplied to outsiders by branches had high arousal value, but divining from them what would be in store foundered, nevertheless, on data quality problems. Perhaps the data might have had relevance but lacked credibility or intelligibility. In this section, the quality of participatory reporting is examined irrespective of uses to which it was put.

Welinksi (1967) designates high-quality intelligence as clear, timely, reliable, valid, adequate, and wide-ranging. We will adopt three criteria from his list and add one of our own. *Validity* denotes congruence between branch reporters' observations and accepted independent accounts of the objects observed. *Reliability* signifies consistency between different reporters' observations. *Timeliness* reduces lag in crisis recognition. *Accuracy* pertains to the precision or exactness of representations of reality. If data turn out to be poor, we must know why and remedy the problem. Constraints on data quality considered here include deceptions and ignorance. Deceptions show themselves when a monitor falsifies evidence deliberately, and ignorance appears with the unintended commission of errors.

NGOs in Darfur operated on the front lines, sizing up peoples' requirements during the famine. So donors presumed that NGOs were conversant with local reporting capabilities. We take interest, then, in how these voluntary groups judged information from local sources during their needs assessment missions in Darfur.

Relief workers—expatriate and national—espoused respect for local knowledge. Folk botany and native plant use made a big impression. Skilled farming on grudging soils evoked respect. So did the practice of matching elastic herd requirements and variable water and fodder supplies. Foodgrain movement through intricate kinship networks was something to behold. Allegedly, community leaders had it in their power to come up with accurate census profiles and reckon with reliability differentials in wealth in their villages. Field staff, nevertheless, were not always confident that the data supplied to them by informants could be trusted. They could not pretend indifference to certain tendencies. Underreporting household food stores and asset wealth and inflating family size and destitution margins went on routinely. Nomads and merchants came across as inveterate liars.

Most revealing is the rationale for NGO misgivings. Qualms concerned informant truthfulness (and occasionally expatriate language proficiency) more than anything. Suspicion that "natives" lacked command of facts did not show up often in confidential file reports or interviews arranged with agency field officials. Essentially, attitude rather than ignorance was held to sabotage data quality. This perception, we now show, is far from valid.

About half of Darfur's monitoring branches were visited, and in interviews monitors discussed survey methodology and data interpretation. What came out of the interview sessions was fairly surprising. SRC left monitors pretty much to their own devices, pursuing facts with negligible rigor. Collectors avoided surveys in out-of-the-way locations even though most Darfurans inhabit outlying villages and camps. Any sampling procedure utilized was thoroughly ad hoc. Two monitoring teams allowed a loose sampling tactic in which informants were picked, when it was convenient, from among villages lying in three or four of the cardinal directions. Subjects could be anyone known and respected by the monitors. Further, monitors mistrusted or placed little stock in ideas held by women and nomads and preferred passing over such persons when choosing subjects for a meeting. This insouciant attitude prejudicing the data collected merits examination.

First, collectors did not care about precision. Their instruments just registered approximate information. Even if the program designers demanded accurate detail, they would probably not get much as the system stood, except for prices gathered readily from the market. (See Chapter 10 for confirmation of this observation.) Most importantly, no incentives were introduced for motivating collectors to work harder at their monitoring tasks. They gathered the data as a service to SRC and realized fully that the product held no intrinsic value for their people. Peasants employed monitoring and warning protocols of their own, and an external system of surveillance would prove no match for their enormous information requirements. Locals argued, further, that one look at a village would sufficiently demonstrate whether people were going hungry. Fine scrutiny of who had how much of what wasted time and confirmed the obvious, they reasoned.

Logistical difficulties would have threatened sample representativeness if it were made a survey goal. Certain monitors said village surveys were fine, provided SRC supplied the vehicles. But foot, don-key, or camel travel was out of the question. Besides, they insisted, village headmen (*sheikhs*) and local government administrators often came to town. "They are easy enough to get hold of and discuss circumstances in their communities freely. We can put complete faith in their reports, for our leaders are people we trust." Many monitors, it was discovered, did not go to much trouble in this respect. They contented themselves assembling responses for survey forms from recollected conversations and observations, conferring now and again with a trusted colleague.

A lack of universal standards of comparison casts a shadow of doubt over reporting accuracy and reliability. Take the question: "For this time of year are the number of animal deaths high, average, low?" Group interviews coaxed out widely disparate answers. What one monitor would rate high, another would rank low or average, and large ranges of variation fell within each ranking. Some would count cattle only, but some thought otherwise and averaged across classes of livestock. Going around and around on this in interviews with monitors and their associates might lead the group toward an average, but any such figure would have to go on record as an invention of circumstance. Heterogeneous responses arose in these and other answers because units and magnitudes of value could vary greatly between households, regions, and historical periods. One program monitor, for example, was not sure if time of year referred to that not-so-distant past when his people (the Berti) owned lots of cattle, or today, when most Berti herds have been destroyed as a result of drought ordeals.

Another tendency detracted from the mining of quality information. Specialty data are the province of persons and corporate groups whose mantles of authority cloak these facts and figures in legitimacy (and finality). For instance, monitors had to enumerate in- and out-migrating households by their ethnic identity, size, location, composition, and livestock holdings. These data, we know, derived from "armchair" investigation. The best sources, the monitors contended, are rural and village council administrators, who distributed government-subsidized sugar. A village's sugar ration depended on its size. Village leaders were required by law to keep a running census. They were only too happy to inform the authorities when newcomers arrived, for this influx enlarged their sugar subsidy. But out-migration was reported less assiduously. Rather than going out and searching actively for drought migrants, monitors who exerted themselves would consult with their local administrator. The same local authorities, it should be added, managed food relief dispatches at the community level. What they did with donated sorghum did not always accord with announced distribution rules, but the reports they supplied often concealed irregular practices and became part of the record that SRC monitors accepted.

Monitors acquired a certain amount of livestock ownership data from village sheikhs. Responsibility for collecting annual tribal livestock taxes rested with the sheikhs. These taxes were levied at a fixed rate for each class of livestock, and liability estimates came up for revision every three years. Sheikhs had no means of estimating the number of livestock belonging to each herding unit with any accuracy, and they were mindful of local sentiment about the tax. Consequently, native leaders would typically underreport the animal wealth they believed was actually owned. One of the few reports to discuss this subject (Huntington Technical Service 1974) suggests that estimates equaled as little as 20 percent of total livestock numbers. Another document (Holy 1974, 147) states that "the number of domestic animals on which a *sheikh's* followers pay taxes varies from about 6 to 100 percent of the number they own," with the majority of households paying in less than full compliance of the levy. Therefore, for the questions the monitors needed answers to, local administrative and native authorities were not altogether reliable sources of information. Yet, monitors drew on them unflinchingly.

From accuracy of sources we move to the problems of recall and normative inference. Several items on the questionnaire and interviews by touring SRC staff elicited subjective estimates of quantities— for example, livestock mortalities, stream levels, and wild food sold at local markets. But the surveillance system was not equipped with controls for corroborating subjective estimates with "objective" checks. Confidence in these estimates requires canons of verification. Jebel Marra Rural Development Project's 1986 findings aptly dramatize this fundamental problem. Farmers from several ethnic groups within the region were asked to estimate their plot dimensions. Comparing farmers' estimates of plot areas and measured plot areas revealed (Jebel Marra Rural Development Project 1986, 10) that "farmers tend to overestimate their farmed areas by 100%." Accuracy of crop yield estimates is about 40 percent better. These findings are worrying and raise doubts about estimation error in SRC data for periods, volumes, and distances of all kinds.

Subjective estimates of quantities, and practically all responses, depend upon recall. Even "exact" survey categories, such as market prices and wage rates, were not necessarily recorded on the spot, and notes taken were not always examined when monitors did get down to filling in their forms. It was unusual for government officials to have had files handy when monitors quizzed them about migration and other matters. These conversations took place often in crowded market settings. Great reliance, in short, was invested in memory. The literature on informant recall is extensive. One highly regarded literature review (Bernard et al. 1984, 503) reaches a conclusion that decisionmakers who utilize SRC and similar data should bear seriously in mind: "About half of what informants report is probably incorrect in some way."

Data quality would suffer if variations in individual circumstances were missed by famine monitors. Their surveys would encapsulate glaring inaccuracies and appear unreliable against outsiders' judgments. A reason this problem suffused the SRC's monitoring system involves a normative inference syndrome rooted in small community experience almost everywhere (Freeman and Romney 1987; Cancian 1975). This cognitive mode found many different forms of expression in Darfur. Basically, monitors did not dwell much on irregularity or stay on high alert for unexpected tendencies. Their situation models did capture nuances, but averaged them into generalized, stereotypical impressions blended from much presupposition about what ought to be and some casual observation. This is one explanation for why monitors professed sufficient if not complete knowledge without bothering to survey households and villages for signs of unusual suffering. And that is why survey input was not submitted to colloquy. Monitors, in fact, initiated little or no discussion of findings among themselves or with other members of their branches. What is the point, they said, when no basis exists for disagreement. And that may be why persons who harbored alleged aberrant points of view, such as women and nomads, seldom were called upon for information.

It is conceivable, too, that different groups within these societies did not uniformly assign the same degrees of danger to one another's circumstances. Monitors were male elites whose scales of risk might rank women, poor nomads, and drought refugees at lower levels of danger than these persons would rank themselves or the population segments classified as high risk by the monitors. Practically nothing is known about the cultural construction of risk in the western Sudan, but its study would almost certainly illuminate socioeconomic correlates of the alarm cues to which the monitors responded.

Officials in the relief administrations of government found little fault with the program of participatory monitoring run by the SRC. Only the lateness of arrival of the reports evoked fairly consistent critical responses. More than five or six weeks often elapsed between the date a branch completed its form and the time finished reports traveled the loop back to Darfur. Forms got lost en route to Darfur from the branches, and some branches skipped a month or two every so often. The rains could slow conveyance to El Fasher by weeks, and processing work in Khartoum added to the wait.

The preceding analysis of data quality advances the conclusion that participatory famine monitoring produced low-grade information in the formative state it achieved at SRC. The data were decidedly impressionistic, and monitors made uncritical use of local expertise. Along with that, conceptual and sampling biases of some importance colored the evidence. We cannot agree with those who blamed poor-quality data almost wholly on deceptive practices.

Indigenous monitoring systems will serve their essential purpose, some argue (Borton and York 1987; Wiley 1978), without employing sophisticated methods, simply by eliciting more rigorous and expensive surveillance from the outside. Nutritional and crop surveillance would be of this nature. Whether or not such is or should be the case, there are still internal standards of competency that ought to form a basis for evaluating a monitoring system's performance. In all likelihood, a system that meets high standards of quality will have an edge at triggering action from decisionmakers, provided it can deliver the type of information desired.

Discussion

Weak social service bureaucracies and frequent ordeals with drought define the conditions for which participatory famine surveillance is designed. The people of western Sudan should have benefited enormously from this kind of surveillance if only because it filled such a vacuum. The extension worker to farmer ratio in Darfur had been put at 1:30,000, against a rule-of-thumb guideline advanced by the World Bank of one worker to 600 farmers (Trail 1985). It is also significant that an Agricultural Statistics Unit was not contained in the regional government structure. Moreover, regional health and social service ministries suffered acute shortages of all basic resources. Neither regional bodies nor central ministries, the RRC, or donor agencies could staff a program for monitoring even one major famine indicator systematically and with good geographical coverage. Some international agencies fielded small, occasional crop assessment teams; and the Ministry of Agriculture, with short-term USAID backstopping, ran crop surveys annually. All of this surveillance, though, missed large areas of human settlement. It depended, in part, on subjective farmer reports and released processed data in mid-January or later. Two large agricultural corporations administered detailed farming systems surveys, but their command areas were in South Darfur.

The food aid establishment required better warning information than it could gather itself. Sudan's first major international relief experience, during 1984–86, saw NGOs strengthening the establishment's diagnostic capabilities very considerably. Counting on NGOs again, to this extent, may be unwise. A danger arises because all NGOs active in Darfur, except for SRC, are, or have been, expatriate groups pursuing community development objectives. Famine monitoring programs, ostensibly, reward the expatriate NGOs and their backers with few development dividends; and effective programs would be costly, labor intensive, and time consuming. As expatriate NGOs do not stay on indefinitely, they would be obliged to implant a surveillance cell into some existing structure rather than spend a lot of time starting one from scratch. That can only mean working within the fold of district and regional government. Such a prospect would not fire up much NGO enthusiasm. A risk is run of being closely identified by community leaders with government interests and of coming under uncomfortably close official scrutiny. Surveillance fuels peasants' expectations of ready benefits in exchange for information and, at times in Darfur, excites rumors of foreign espionage. Scarce resources, furthermore, are diverted from the village sector. Finally, the vexing question of whether bureaucratic inertia will reassert itself after it withdraws from a monitoring project is hard for an NGO to dispel.

What the problem would apparently call for is the good work of an NGO willing to stay put in an area, make relief activity a first order of business, and create an organization from the grassroots that stands outside of, but interacts smoothly with, institutions under the government's umbrella. Taking all of these desiderata into account would give the impression that SRC was made to order.

Unless the national society goes under, the regional subsociety in Darfur is there to stay. Disaster relief is of foremost concern to the League federation even though rehabilitation and development goals are gaining in importance. Branches do not rein in their emergency work completely when famine relief comes to a halt. Routinely they answer appeals from victims of floods, fires, thefts, and other disasters, whether or not an afflicted party holds membership in the branch. With some assistance from SRC's regional office, branch volunteers furnish labor, blankets, food, clothing, and even cash. Schools, prisons, and clinics, as well as individuals, can be eligible for charitable aid.

SRC officials are aware of the close linkage of public charity with the fate of the society and its branches. Many branch members interviewed said they joined the organization and would have their memberships renewed primarily because of succor expected when they fall on difficult times, especially during droughts. Neither indigenous institutions nor the government, they confided, could offer famine insurance comparable to SRC's. And relief binds branch and parent organization and augments SRC's resources, as the agency retains equipment and supplies left behind by donors once an emergency program is concluded.

SRC's membership crosscuts Darfuran social divisions. Every branch reached on visits could boast tribal leaders (sheikhs and omodiya primarily), civil servants from sundry occupational classes, and ordinary farmers and herders. According to prevailing opinion, branch projects complemented work done by other local groups. Only traders vending cooking oil and foodgrains portrayed the SRC as a competitor. Any expatriate NGO ingrained this firmly in community living arrangements would be a very rare case indeed. SRC's excellent working relationship with community leaders and its grasp of local requirements prompted an important invitation from the regional government of Darfur. Officials in 1988 hoped that SRC would take charge of North Darfur's targeted free food aid program.

With all of this going for it, SRC should be a ready beacon for famine early warning. The reasons it retreated from this promise warrant a little additional light. Within SRC's operating structure, the program was a disembodied element, since the lack of an early response instrument at SRC obviated its designated function. SRC's response failure went beyond inertia at the top. Red Crescent and LRCS's centralized approaches to preparedness played a part. The regional office functioned solely as an information clearinghouse, devoid of diagnostic and decisionmaking powers for precautionary action. Whether anything would have changed radically if El Fasher lobbied more aggressively for faster reaction time from Khartoum is an open question.

SRC executives had not incorporated branch leadership into the policy process at the time of the study. That may have to wait until the SRC matures. The branches elected officers, designed projects, and targeted and distributed rations. But they lacked the leverage to pressure SRC into taking precautionary steps. Isolation from power centers inside the organization, on top of the low priority that peasants conferred on the program, help explain why monitors put out little effort and were lackadaisical about getting their reports to El Fasher safely and on time. For the monitors, the program played the symbolic role of reminding El Fasher that the branch was still alive and performing services *for the* SRC. This weak embrace of program tasks may reflect aspects of participatory reporting setting it apart from participatory development. Participatory reporting does not rally an entire community to action; it coopts select individuals. It creates a product for export, but its connection with a specific local payoff is not obvious or usually demonstrable. Certainly this surveillance plays no part in the community's own reactions to scarcity.

Participatory reporting is not limited to famine early warning, although that function was stressed by the SRC. "Early" in the Sudanese context signifies a period antecedent to harvest survey wrap-ups circa January. Early warning should create an environment for decisions about commitment. Ordinarily, such commitments will stop short of food intervention measures. Commitment applies to information and organization more commonly. Levels of readiness are elevated with more finely tuned probes of highly liable areas and the formulation of a central plan. None of this is cut-and-dried procedure. What constitutes a warning and an appropriate response for most famine indicators will be subject to varying interpretations.

Warning diagnostics hinge importantly on what aid administrators, remote from actual situations and actors, preconceive to be abnormal conditions. Numerous donor government officials interviewed shared the conviction that drought-prone populations are in possession of immense powers of resilience and make do, despite unpromising harvests, by migrating toward employment poles, consuming wild plants, borrowing necessities, and liquidating assets. Suffering, officials frequently asserted, was a regrettable but not an abnormal, and hence dangerous, state of affairs at the time. Yet, downtrodden groups were manifesting weakened vital signs fully three to four months before the harvest season started, and the crop prognosis for their districts was looking grim.

The aid managers may have been correct in thinking of hardship this grave as the norm for very vulnerable areas. But they lost sight of the fact that *the norm now signaled danger*. Risks to human lives and to economic recovery were climbing toward alarming levels in these sizable pockets of hardship. That is the danger that lurked. The aid establishment needed to know prior to harvest outcomes what was the norm, whether to tolerate it, and how far conditions could veer from it before a relief trigger had to be pulled. And their data suppliers needed to understand the cue structure by which the aid managers saw and solved problems.

Proficient early warning mechanisms should present Khartoum decisionmakers with a version of social reality converted to the coarse cereal cues they can assimilate. That is, the state of a social system should reduce to a statistic. A system of equivalencies in which so much migration, livestock loss, indebtedness, and so forth translate into costs that so much grain can obviate or diminish to some estimated control level would stand a chance of putting early warning onto the agenda for emergency planning. SRC did some of this but not enough.

Lessons for Future Planning

SRC's architect for the monitoring system had in mind that "the major issue is, perhaps, not whether the data can be collected, or how much warning they can give—but how swiftly and to how small and remote an area can an agency . . . bring, or be willing to bring assistance" (York 1985, 178). The delegate who thought up the program was under the impression that it will require very little maintenance and could be sustained by SRC regional officials. As regards participatory reporting functions, it was noted that "many [NGOs] suggested that NGO staffs . . . and village leaders be trained to report against a simple set of indicators that show a strong possibility of food shortages" (International Institute for Environment and Development 1986, 283), and that "local views may form a useful early indicator which triggers a more detailed monitoring of other indicators" (Borton and York 1987, 185).

These observations had been made without the benefit of case study documentation of systems that were going concerns. Our study is now available, and in light of it earlier assumptions might be revised. York may want to rethink her claim and allow that the collectability of reliable and accurate data and their warning potential *are* major issues. These issues, moreover, cannot be resolved if we examine monitoring systems in isolation. The requirements of data users are relevant determinants and must be fully ascertained by those who build and evaluate participatory reporting programs. Surveillants' skills enter into the issue, and so do linkages with emergency assistance measures. These factors and others also decide if a simple set of indicators will sound an alarm compelling enough to activate additional and more thorough surveys. Finally, the premium that should be put on better training and task incentives challenges the notion that indigenous reporting systems are cheap and easy to run.

Agencies should come to realize this axiom: Participatory reporting programs with impact are not cost free and take time and trained staff to develop and manage. Failing the application of this lesson, the best result that can be expected is a shell of a system manifesting impressive form but little content. Turning again to SRC, it is well to reiterate that an effective system should come wired to a disaster readiness plan. In conjunction with this capability, a decentralized analytical unit, set up in El Fasher, would have been advisable, if not imperative. The unit would subsume several upgraded functions, including: (1) actively retrieving data from branches; (2) collating the data, when possible, with information furnished by other regional agencies; (3) spelling out more completely what dangers the data signal; (4) converting these danger markers into grain demand statistics;

and (5) recommending or modifying SRC/LRCS disaster contingency plans in accordance with the arrival of fresh information.

The supervisory staff consisting of four field officers should at least have been doubled and a small core of local nutrition advisers (such as were recruited during the famine) added. The field officers *and* monitors required training in basic social survey methods, with stress laid upon critical judgment. Little progress will be likely in future monitoring efforts unless the SRC can find transport for its monitors throughout their surveillance zones. Travel and interviewing demand time and effort that should be remunerated by the SRC. If the monitors had been delegated a role in the diagnosis of their data, that might have enhanced their appreciation of program participation. And program benefits to their communities might have become clear if more intrusive surveillance, such as surveys of nutritional, income, and preharvest crop yield indicators, had been used. For tapping into these parameters SRC surveys might have coordinated with those of other agencies operating in the region.

All things considered, the SRC participatory monitoring system was off to a reasonably good start. It will be a pity if it fails to add more to the foundation it has admirably put down. What, after all, are the alternatives? As long as over one million Darfurans cannot get by without food assistance every few years, and external agencies are not about to blanket the region with supplies, if that can be helped, timely surveillance is required for screening areas and groups at risk. Otherwise, too little may come too late, and Darfur will fall further behind in embarking on a path to economic recovery. Taking a measure of everyone's interests confirms the proposition that information should be valued as much as food in terms of screening and targeting beneficiaries. For now, only voluntary organizations emanating into or from Darfuran communities have the human resources for this type of work. Our study has shown that opportunity exists for such local participation in one of dryland Africa's poorest and remotest regions. And it has indicated what steps must be taken if this opportunity is to be fulfilled.

Notes

1. York's (1985) report on the Sudan Red Crescent Society's monitoring system, which is the subject of this chapter, may be the only exception.
2. Over two thirds of North Darfur's land surface is mantled with relatively infertile sandy soils which will not sustain a full cereal crop under rainfed cultivation if annual rainfall drops below 250 millimeters (Ibrahim 1984). Over the past decade, several locations in North Darfur have absorbed a 31–53 percent reduction in annual rainfall from the ten-year mean of 1946–55

(Clift-Hill 1987). Scarcely a year has gone by since 1979 without the advent of severe crop failures associated with sub-250-millimeter totals and poor intraseasonal distributions. Since the late 1960s, drought and desertification have contributed to the settlement of most of the region's nomadic populations, and large stretches of land lying to the north and east are practically devoid of plant growth. Except for some individuals owning alluvial plots near larger intermittent streams (*wadis*), few peasants can survive from year to year entirely on what their farms produce.

3. Aid dispatches from Libya and the Gulf states can and do involve direct contacts with Darfur government leaders. Darfur officials consider these gifts minor. The small volumes of foodgrains consigned tend to consist of wheat, which must be exchanged outside Darfur for the preferred sorghum and millet staples.

References

Bernard, H. R., Peter Killworth, David Kronenfeld, and Lee Sailer. 1984. "The Problem of Informant Accuracy: The Validity of Retrospective Data." *Annual Review of Anthropology* 13: 495–517.

Berry, L., and R. B. Ford. 1978. "Networks and Information Systems for Dealing with Drought." In *Symposium on Drought in Botswana*, edited by M. T. Hinchey, 165–172. Hanover: University Press of New England.

Borton, J., and S. York. 1987. "Experiences of the Collection and Use of Micro-Level Data in Disaster Preparedness and Managing Emergency Operations." *Disasters* 11, 3: 173–181.

Campbell, D. 1986. "Coping Strategies as Indicators of Food Shortage in African Villages." Paper presented at the Annual Meeting of the American Anthropological Association, Philadelphia. Mimeo.

Cancian, F. 1975. *What Are the Norms: A Study of Beliefs and Action in a Maya Community*. Cambridge: Cambridge University Press.

CARE. 1987. "Kordofan Emergency Feeding/Drought Relief Program, Final Report." Khartoum: CARE. Mimeo.

Clift-Hill, A. 1987. "Darfur Rainfall Records." Overseas Development Agency, London. Mimeo.

Currey, B. 1984. "Issues in Evaluating Food Crises Warning Systems." *Food and Nutrition Bulletin* 6, 2: 7–17.

Cutler, P. 1986. "A Review of the Drought Relief Operations of the League of Red Cross and Red Crescent Societies in Sudan, 1984–86." Institute of Development Studies, University of Sussex. Mimeo.

Devres, Inc. 1986. *Evaluation of the African Food Assistance Program in Sudan 1984–85*. Washington, D.C.: Devres.

Food and Agriculture Organization (FAO). 1986. *Establishing or Strengthening National and Regional Early Warning and Food Information Systems in Africa*. Global Information and Early Warning System on Food and Agriculture. Rome: FAO.

Food and Agriculture Organization (FAO). 1987. *Methodology for the Assessment of the Food Supply Situation and Requirements for Exceptional Assistance*

Arising from Crop Failure or Unusual Crop Surplus. Global Information and Early Warning System on Food and Agriculture. Rome: FAO. Mimeo.

Freeman, L., and A. K. Romney. 1987. "Words, Deeds and Social Structure: A Preliminary Study of the Reliability of Informants." *Human Organization* 46, 4: 330–334.

Gavaghan, T. 1987. *Disaster Preparedness: A Plan Formulated for the Government of Sudan Relief and Rehabilitation Commission.* United Nations Disaster Relief Organization, Geneva. Mimeo.

Holy, L. 1974. *Neighbors and Kinsmen: A Study of the Berti People of Darfur.* New York: St. Martin's Press.

Huntington Technical Service, Ltd. 1974. *Southern Darfur Land-Use Planning Survey: Annex 6, Economics and Project Evaluation.* London: Huntington Technical Service.

Ibrahim, Fouad N. 1984. "Ecological Imbalance in the Republic of the Sudan— with Reference to Desertification in Darfur." *Bayreuther Geowissenchaftliche Arbeiten* 6.

International Institute for Environment and Development (IIED). 1986. *Report on the African Emergency Relief Operation (1984–86) with Particular Reference to the Contribution of Non-Governmental Organizations.* London and Washington: IIED.

Jebel Marra Rural Development Project (JMRDP). 1986. *Annual Report 1985–86. Annex II, Monitoring and Evaluation Department.* Zalingei, Sudan: JMRDP.

Mabutt, J. 1984. "A New Global Assessment of the Status and Trends of Desertification." *Environmental Conservation* 11, 2: 103–113.

Milas, S. 1984. "Population Crisis and Desertification in the Sudano-Sahelian Region." *Environmental Conservation* 11, 2: 167–169.

Mukhier, Mohammed Omer. 1987. "North Darfur Trip 14th September to 7th October." Sudan Red Crescent Drought Monitoring Program Report. Mimeo.

Oguntoyinbo, J., and P. Richards. 1978. "Drought and the Nigerian Farmer." *Journal of Arid Environments* 1: 165–194.

Price-Waterhouse. 1986. *Review and Evaluation of the Leagues' Africa Drought Operations 1984–86.* Zurich: Price-Waterhouse. Mimeo.

Relief and Rehabilitation Commission (RRC). 1986. *Policies, Strategies, and Programs.* Khartoum: RRC. Mimeo.

Relief and Rehabilitation Commission (RRC). 1987. *Sudan Early Warning System (EWS) October 15 Report.* Khartoum: RRC. Mimeo.

Save the Children Federation U.S. 1987. *Emergency Feeding Program Um Ruwaba District [Kordofan Region] July 1985 to December 1986.* Khartoum. Mimeo.

Save the Children Fund U.K. 1986. *Draft Report: Free Grain Distribution in Darfur 1985–86.* Khartoum. Mimeo.

Torry, W. 1988. "Famine Early Warning Systems: The Need for an Anthropological Dimension." *Human Organization* 47, 3: 273–281.

Trail, T. F. 1985. *Extension in Darfur Region, Sudan.* Western Sudan Agricultural Research Project (WSARP), Government of Sudan, Khartoum.

Welinski, H. L. 1967. *Organizational Intelligence: Knowledge and Policy in Government and Industry.* New York: Basic Books.

Wiley, E. 1978. "An Aspect of Warning Systems for Drought: Information Collecting in the Districts." In *Symposium on Drought in Botswana*, edited by M. T. Hinchey, 210–217. Hanover: University Press of New England.

York, S. 1985. "Report on a Pilot Project to Set Up a Drought Information Network in Conjunction with the Red Crescent Society in Darfur." *Disasters* 9, 3: 173–178.

York, S. 1986. *An Evaluation of the Use of Human Resources During the League of Red Cross and Red Crescent Societies' Program of Activities in Sudan 1984–86 with Particular Reference to the Case of Darfur, Western Sudan.* Institute of Development Studies, University of Sussex. Mimeo.

10

Using Market Prices as a Guide to Predict, Prevent, or Mitigate Famine in Pastoral Economies

A Case Study from Sudan, 1989–90

Paul Ulrich

Prolonged drought in Sudan in the early 1980s led to a major famine in 1984 and 1985. Soon after, the Sudanese government established a famine early warning system; and since then indigenous and international nongovernmental organizations (NGOs) have helped monitor agroclimatic, socioeconomic, and nutritional conditions in North Kordofan, North Darfur, and the Red Sea Hills—the three provinces of Sudan most susceptible to drought.

Despite exceptionally good rains in Sudan during 1986 and 1988, drought recurred with ever increasing severity in 1987, 1989, and 1990. Current indicators now predict a famine on an even larger scale than a decade ago. As a CARE employee in 1989 and 1990, I participated in two missions to assess the drought in North Kordofan. This chapter presents my refinement of a technique for detecting early signs of famine and for guiding a response.

Background

Famine Early Warning Systems

Like other countries prone to famine, both Sudan and Ethiopia have systems for collecting information on any dramatic drop in the production or consumption of food. Periodic surveys of the planting, growth, and harvesting of crops; estimates of public and privately held food stocks; measurements of the level, distribution, and timing of rainfall; and remote satellite sensing of vegetation help predict the likely level of food output. And monitoring of rural wages and prices, reporting of unusual activities or migrations, and surveys of nutritional status in vulnerable groups help show who has access to the current stock of food.

Early warning indicators should be accurate and timely, inexpensive to collect, and easy to interpret (Swift 1988). Of the indicators currently used, only one—the terms of trade between livestock and grain prices—fulfills all these criteria.

Information on current or future levels of food production and stocks is often inaccurate. Whether from an aversion to taxes or an expectation of food aid, farmers and semipastoralists tend to underreport their private holdings of grain or livestock and their expected harvest yields (see Chapter 9). The success or failure of harvests may depend upon late-season rains that give only a few months' lead time for gearing up an emergency relief operation. Moreover, the quantity of rainfall in a particular area does not translate into the size of harvest likely to result. Satellite imagery of ground cover is expensive and sometimes ambiguous. Yet, even with improvements in accuracy, cost, timeliness, or interpretation, indicators that measure the production or supply of food can point only to a potential problem inasmuch as a decline in the availability of food is neither a necessary cause nor an inevitable result of famine.

Famine results from a failure of entitlements, or access, to food (Sen 1981). The proximate indicators of this access, therefore, should offer more certain predictions of famine. Unfortunately, the clearest indicator of insufficient consumption—measurements of nutritional status—come far too late to ward off hunger. They show that famine is underway, not that it is about to occur. Likewise, reports of unseasonal migrations in search of work, distress sales of assets, and consumption of unusual "famine" foods often occur late in the chain of events leading to famine.

A fall in the price of livestock typically accompanies an increase in grain prices, as herders must sell more of their animals to purchase the increasingly expensive grain. Recent research has suggested that routinely monitoring the terms of trade between these livestock and grain prices can provide the most timely and unambiguous early warning of pastoral famines, granted that an effective famine early warning system for pastoral areas will combine several of the above indices (Swift 1988).

Data on livestock and grain prices are routinely collected, readily available, and easy to analyze because changes in relative prices lead to predictable responses. Looking at the shifts in livestock-to-grain prices rather than just measuring the increase in price for livestock or grain separately enables the analysis to control for the effect of inflation—a secular rise in the general level of prices. It is important to isolate a rise in prices caused by scarcity from one caused by inflation. Similarly, the analysis should compare terms of trade at the same seasons of different years to remove the potential for bias introduced by the normal seasonal rise and fall of agricultural and livestock prices. Discussing the changes in the pastoral terms of trade during the 1984–85 famine, one researcher has proposed that a fall in the livestock-to-grain price indices by 50 percent should act as a trigger for administrative concern and action, while also predicting that mass distress migrations would have already begun by the time the index had fallen to 25 percent or less of its predrought value (Cutler 1986).

The famine early warning systems in Sudan and Ethiopia collect many different types of data but have not developed a system for prioritizing the information to enable policymakers to act decisively or knowledgeably to stave off a crisis once they have made a commitment to providing relief. Much of the more compelling data on coping strategies present only a qualitative picture; the quantitative figures on crop production and rainfall give only a broad overview of the situation; and detailed, objective price data, even when conscientiously collected, escape any rigorous analysis that might draw out the appropriate conclusions.

A typical early warning report compares this month's increased grain prices to those of the preceding months without noting that routine storage costs make Sudanese grain prices rise in normal years by as much as 50 percent prior to harvest. A slightly more sophisticated analysis will illustrate the changes in pastoral terms of trade, but will again compare them to those of previous months without accounting for the seasonal price changes that distort indices compared across different times of the same year. For example, in the drought-prone areas of Sudan, grain prices drop precipitously after the harvest in December and gradually rise again until just before the following harvest a year later. The price of livestock, however, depends on the availability of water and fodder and peaks in May just before the start of the rainy season. Thus, *even in normal times* during the summer and autumn, a decline in livestock prices accompanies an increase in the price of grain, and the terms-of-trade index falls from one month to the next. In this case, the index actually compounds the seasonal bias in any time series of monthly, rather than annual, livestock-to-grain price changes.

North Kordofan

The province of North Kordofan consists of five districts subdivided into twenty-nine rural and town councils. The last government census in 1983 identified approximately 3,800 villages in the province and a total population of 1.8 million persons, of whom only 13 percent lived in urban areas. Most of the indigenous population is Arab. Nearly half of the population in the northern-most district of Sodeiry is nomadic, while a smaller but still significant percentage of the other four districts consists of semipastoralists practicing a mix of agriculture and livestock herding. The 1983 census listed 27 percent of the province as nomadic and 73 percent as settled. Most settled farmers own at least a few goats to supplement their incomes, and goats or sheep comprise the majority of livestock in the area. Nomads to the north tend to own most of the camels. There are few cattle.

The province lies in the center of Sudan and extends between the twelfth and sixteenth degree north latitude and from the twenty-eighth to thirty-eighth degree east longitude. Although largely deforested, the southern half of the province can still be considered woodland savanna. It has some ground cover of drought-resistant trees, shrubs, and grasses on predominately sandy soils; and its annual rainfall averages between 200 and 450 millimeters per year. The northern half is mostly desert; soils are sandy, ground cover is sparse, and annual rainfall ranges from 0 to 200 millimeters per year.

North Kordofan has no paved or improved roads nor any links to the Sudanese rail network. The almost nonexistent transportation infrastructure and consequent high costs of transport have created large variations in the price of basic commodities. Livestock and grain prices may vary by more than 100 percent between villages of one district and those of another.

While Sudan as a whole has often produced grain surpluses and exported up to a million metric tons of sorghum per year, the irrigated and mechanized rainfed agriculture in the country's eastern and central regions produces almost all of the surplus. By contrast, North Kordofan province is perennially in deficit. Its agriculture consists entirely of traditional rainfed farms that even in good years market only about 20 percent of their grain, with the remainder grown for subsistence (Food and Agriculture Organization 1986).

The size of the food deficits shown in Table 10.1 is probably overstated because the amounts of grain held in private storage are usually underestimated, and the deficits assume an ideal whereby in a constant population of 3.23 million persons each individual consumes 500 grams of grain per day. Nevertheless, the figures are illustrative of the relative harvest sizes in recent years. No postharvest data are yet available for 1990–91, but preharvest indicators point to a harvest even worse than the one in 1989–90. North Kordofan province has over half of the region's total population but produces less than 30 percent of its grain harvest. From the end of 1984 to mid-1986, North

Table 10.1 Cereal Production and Structural Food Deficits in Kordofan Region

Year	Harvest (metric tons)	Deficit (metric tons)
1984–85	112,000	477,000
1985–86	400,000	189,000
1986–87	382,000	207,000
1987–88	270,000	319,000
1988–89	389,000	200,000
1989–90	105,000	486,000

Source: General Director of Kordofan Ministry of Agriculture, verbal communication, 14 December 1989.

Kordofan province received over 200,000 metric tons of emergency food aid. Again in 1988, the poor harvest of 1987 prompted a Western relief operation with pledges of 51,000 metric tons, although actual deliveries came to only 13,500 metric tons of sorghum (Borton and Shoham 1989). The regional government's 1989 postharvest survey requested 100,000 metric tons of food aid for 1990. Donors responded with just over 11,500 metric tons of free grain and 35,000 metric tons for subsidized sale. Distribution of donated grain did not begin until the end of July 1990, and conservative estimates for 1991 put the need at about 200,000 metric tons. If past patterns provide any indication of the likely response to this and future situations, donors' pledges will lag behind the estimated need, and their deliveries will fall short of their pledges.

Methodology for Drought Assessment in North Kordofan

Since 1986, the Kordofan Food Aid Administration and the regional Ministry of Agriculture have conducted quarterly or annual surveys to monitor agroclimatic and socioeconomic data in the drought-prone areas of Kordofan. In November 1989, survey teams randomly selected two or three villages in each of the twenty-nine rural and town councils of North Kordofan. It was not possible to interview any nomadic communities. Field surveyors collected information through private interviews of individual villagers, group discussions with the village sheikh and assembled community, talks with rural government officials, and personal observations of crop conditions.

As a supplement to the standard questions on rainfall, agricultural production, pasture, and livestock conditions, the survey placed an increased emphasis on socioeconomic indicators. In order to calculate relative changes in the pastoral terms of trade, surveyors asked about current livestock and crop prices and had villagers recall prices for the same period in 1988. The surveyors also reported on a rise in petty commodity production and trading, distress sale of household assets, unseasonably early or large migrations in search of work, levels of grain stocks remaining from previous harvests, increased demand for credit, consumption of famine foods, and wage rates compared with the rates of previous years. In September 1990, as the regional government received reports of complete crop failure and unusual migrations, it conducted another rapid but less comprehensive survey of the province.

Findings

Most answers to the survey questions were necessarily subjective or affected by uncertainty in estimates and the respondents' ulterior motives. By contrast, villagers had little trouble in recalling and agreeing on current and last year's prices for the staple grains—sorghum and millet—and various livestock prices.

Villagers in North Kordofan have received food aid in four of the last six years. It might therefore be reasonable to expect that they would see a connection between the size of their reported harvests and the amount of free food they are likely to receive. However, few— if any—villagers seemed to recognize the significance of relative prices. Their clear, prompt answers and lack of incentive to distort responses made the information used to calculate changes in pastoral terms of trade the most reliable and objective indicator of the survey.

Though consistent *within* villages, prices varied considerably between communities and reflected the extremes in variability to which even nearby, but isolated, areas can be affected by crop failure.

Table 10.2 shows calculations of the change in pastoral terms of trade. Prices are in Sudanese pounds (LS).

The first column of Table 10.2 lists the capitalized names of the five districts in North Kordofan, followed by the names of the rural or town councils surveyed in each district. The table treats separately the eastern and western parts of the two worst-affected districts of Bara and Sodeiry to show that the eastern areas suffered the most severe declines in the terms of trade. The second, third, and fourth columns present the average price of a female goat divided by the cost of one *malwa* (3.2 kilograms) of grain at three points: November 1988, November 1989, and September 1990. The data for November 1988 represent the predrought prices as recalled by the interviewees

Table 10.2 Indexed Livestock and Grain Prices in North Kordofan, 1988–90

District	Livestock-to-Grain Price Index (Sudanese pounds)			Index Ratio (%)	
Rural/Town Council 1990–88	Nov 88	Nov 89	Sep 90	89–90	90–88
Bara (East)					
Um Siyala	380/3.5	300/7.5	125/40.0	36	3
Gereighekh	250/4.5	210/8.5	120/40.0	44	5
Um Garfa	350/4.0	250/8.0	215/35.0	36	7
Bara (West)					
Taiba	170/2.6	280/8.5	250/45.0	50	8
Mazrub	200/3.5	250/9.0	100/50.0	49	4
Um Kreidim	160/3.0	250/8.5	150/40.0	55	7
Bara Town	200/6.5	225/9.5	150/40.0	77	12
Sodeiry (East)					
Gebrat El Sheik	425/3.5	340/8.0	150/35.0	35	4
Sodeiry (West)					
Hamrat El Sheik	250/5.0	550/12.5	240/40.0	88	12
Sodeiry	200/5.5	310/9.7	160/40.0	88	11
En Nahud					
El Odeiya	200/5.2	450/9.5	140/25.0	123	15
Ghabeish	250/3.3	500/8.3	275/25.0	78	15
En Nahud	280/5.0	570/9.0	175/25.0	113	12
Abu Zabad	200/5.0	380/10.3	100/35.0	92	7
El Khuwei	330/6.0	370/5.5	150/33.0	98	8
Suq El Gamal	210/4.0	430/8.3	175/25.0	99	13
Wad Banda	200/5.0	350/10.0	130/10.0	88	33
El Obeid					
El Obeid Town	150/8.0	270/11.0	600/55.0	131	58
Um Ruwaba					
Avg. of 5 rural councils	240/4.1	255/6.7	105/45.0	61	4

Source: Field data collected by the author and Kordafan government officials in surveys, November 1989 and September 1990.

in November 1989. To illustrate actual average price quotations and their variance among councils, price indices remain in the form of a fraction with the average female goat price as numerator and average grain price as denominator.

The survey chose an amount of grain that individual villagers commonly purchase (one *malwa*) and selected the most prevalent form of livestock that the poorest livestock owners hold (goats). Questions also specified the animal's gender because of a difference in price for the female and male of each species.

These three columns show the mean of the goat and grain prices recorded in each rural or town council's randomly selected villages. On average, a rural or town council contains 100 villages and a total population of 60,000 inhabitants. Data on the two districts of El Obeid and Um Ruwaba were less complete and have been averaged across the entire district or, in the case of El Obeid, just presented for the town. El Obeid is the capital of Kordofan region.

The index ratios in the last two columns of the table show the change in the terms of trade over twelve and twenty-two months. In the fifth column, the 1989–88 ratio comes from dividing the price index in the November 1989 column by the corresponding index in the November 1988 column, and the sixth column derives its ratio in like manner, dividing the September 1990 price index by the November 1988 index. For example, in Um Siyala one goat would buy 108.5 malwa of grain in November 1988 prior to the drought (380/3.5). By September 1990, it would fetch only 3.1 malwa of grain (125/40). The 1990–88 ratio of the sixth column divides the 3.1 by 108.5 malwa, yielding .03 or 3 percent. In other words, goats in that particular rural council had lost 97 percent of their predrought value, as reflected in the index ratio of 3 percent.

The terms-of-trade indices for 1988 and 1989 record the prices of one malwa of millet. The September 1990 figures, however, show the price of one malwa of sorghum, because by that time most areas no longer had any millet available. Previously, millet had been 15–25 percent more expensive than sorghum, so the 1990–88 ratio slightly understates the true decline in terms of trade. Also, the urgency of the situation in 1990 necessitated a survey in September rather than in November. Since livestock prices typically fall and grain prices rise between these months, the 1990–88 ratio further underestimates the severity of the decline.

The last two columns of Table 10.2 show a striking pattern. By November 1989, at the time of the first failed harvest, the pastoral terms of trade in most of the rural councils of Bara and the eastern part of Sodeiry districts had dropped to below 50 percent of their predrought exchange rate. These two districts had also been hardest hit by the 1984–85 drought and have the most degraded land in the province. The surveyors in 1989 found only the aged and women with small children still in the villages. Expecting little or no harvest, the men had left earlier than usual to look for work elsewhere—in the cities or as farm laborers in the eastern and central regions. Many had to sell household possessions, and the two villages with the sharpest decline in terms of trade reported that entire families had left. Some remaining residents had tried to supplement their income by collecting more wood to make charcoal for sale. Yet, there was no clear pattern of a fall in charcoal prices, as one might have expected, possibly because the increasing scarcity of wood offset any increases in the output of charcoal. With no harvest and plummeting livestock values, some villages reported to be surviving on remittances that amounted to as much as 90 percent of their present income.

In November 1989, the decline in terms of trade for a given area corresponded fairly closely with the degree of failure in that area's harvest. The isolation of most village markets—the unusually high cost of rural transport, poor communication networks, and the lack of nearby marketable surpluses—meant that trade with better-off areas could not readily offset the falling livestock-grain rate of exchange caused by the failed harvest. The isolation also explains how adjacent districts—or even villages—could experience vastly different effects on the prices of their grain and livestock, depending on whether or not they had any harvest and grain stored from previous years.

A prolonged dry spell in 1987 had left Bara, Sodeiry, and the northern part of Um Ruwaba with little or no harvest. Despite good rains the following year, these areas again fared poorly when locusts destroyed about half the crop. By the time another harvest failed in 1989, it was not surprising that the pastoral terms of trade had fallen considerably further than in other less affected areas.

The drought of 1989 continued right through 1990. By September many areas had received only a third of the normal amount of rain, and what rain they did get was badly distributed, as only 1 or 2 percent of the normal amount came during a vital growing period in the last week of August and first week of September. Much of the country was affected, and widespread crop failure was reported in several regions, including the normally productive central and eastern regions. Government and donor grain reserves had fallen to a dangerously low level.

The last column of Table 10.2 shows the extent of the collapse in pastoral incomes. The terms of trade in virtually every rural council plummeted. By the autumn of 1990, the livestock-for-grain exchange rates in the worst-affected areas of 1989 were down to less than 10 percent of their predrought value, while the rates in the areas that had been slightly better off before were rapidly falling to the same low level.

Only the city of El Obeid still had an exchange rate above 50 percent of its previous value in September 1990. Its access to government grain stocks and its having more types of employment than the rural areas might explain the slower decline in its terms of trade. Otherwise, the speed of collapse in the terms of trade was remarkable. In just one month's time between July and August at Um Ruwaba, the exchange rate fell by 75 percent as grain prices doubled and goat prices dropped in half.

Expectations of grain and livestock traders may have contributed to the suddenness of the change. July and August are the crucial months of rain for rainfed agriculture in northern Sudan. As the drought continued, reports of crop failure began coming not just from Kordofan, but from the surplus producing areas of eastern and central Sudan as well. Moreover, in an effort to improve a trade imbalance, the central government had been allowing private exports of several hundred thousand tons of sorghum.[1] Its strategic grain reserve had almost disappeared. Traders, accustomed to the upward movement of prices during grain shortages, probably began accumulating supplies, and the effect of their actions magnified the price changes. Research on one recent famine reveals that a 10 percent change in traders' expectations led to a 90 percent change in market prices (Ravallion 1987).

The unambiguous and dramatic nature of the shifts in terms of trade underscores an important advantage that the indicator has over other techniques for monitoring famine; namely, that one need not be overly concerned with errors in measurement. A concern for minimizing errors can, for example, hamper nutritional surveys that measure the weight, height, and mid–upper arm circumference of children.[2]

A study of the effects of the 1984–85 famine in Red Sea Hills province found a drop in the pastoral terms of trade very similar to those recorded in the worst affected areas of this survey. By January 1984, the goat-to-sorghum exchange rate had fallen to 57.5 percent and by January 1985 to 4.5 percent of its predrought value (Cutler 1986). That the terms of trade in September 1990 had already fallen to as low as 3 percent by September is perhaps indicative of the even more severe situation prevailing at the time. In the fall of 1984, the surplus areas of the east were still able to offset partially the deficits in the other areas, and the central government was in a stronger position economically. Whether or not the terms of trade continued to fall to even lower levels at the end of 1990 is no longer of much importance, since pastoralists had already lost over 90 percent of their purchasing power and seen the dissolution of their assets and ability to acquire food.

In August 1990, hundreds of families began migrating from eastern Bara and eastern Sodeiry districts to relief centers in Omdurman, outside the country's capital of Khartoum. Livestock were dying from lack of pasture and water. Hungry inhabitants slaughtered their animals for food when grain, a much more efficient source of calories, became too expensive and they could no longer find buyers for their animals at the small village markets. Local health workers reported that the nutritional status of children in Bara district was very poor and that the incidence of vitamin A deficiency, a sign of acute malnutrition, had reached alarming levels of as much as 10 percent, far above the World Health Organization's acceptable threshold of 0.4 percent. Health authorities also verified the first cases of death from starvation in isolated areas of Sodeiry district.

Discussion

The fact that mass migrations of entire families had begun only in areas where the terms of trade had fallen to below 10 percent may suggest that coping mechanisms allow famine victims to hold out longer than previously supposed. At least this may be true in Sudan, where unreported remittances from workers in the Gulf states play a large role in rural incomes. Studies of famine in pastoral areas in Ethiopia—in Harerghe in 1973–74 and Borena in 1984–85—have both shown that the terms of trade in that country dropped to about 25 or 30 percent of their predrought values (Sen 1981).[3] The size of the decline may depend on an individual country's economy, but the repeated pattern suggests that a government's early warning system should set its thresholds for specific actions and interventions to past patterns of price changes in the same or similar regions of the country.

Implementation of Relief

Having tracked the change in the pastoral terms of trade, relief agencies were in a position to target their food aid to areas most in need. From the district to the rural council and finally to the level of village clusters, relief planners could follow the terms-of-trade indices and know which areas had suffered the most and were in urgent need of assistance. Scattered nutritional surveys and more qualitative warning signs of distress confirmed the data already provided and quantified by the terms-of-trade index.

The time needed to get food to famine-stricken areas after an appeal for aid can stretch to six months or more. While some food may be in the "pipeline" or diverted relatively quickly from other uses, there is never enough to cover the entire need. In such circumstances, having a way of assigning priorities for the available aid assumes added significance.

The terms-of-trade data enabled planners to target emergency food aid geographically. Since 1985, drought relief programs had brought food to drop-off points at hundreds of village clusters or rural council headquarters in North Kordofan, and then let the village representatives themselves distribute the food as they saw fit. A proposal for the 1990 relief operation called for doing the same, but with some added features to improve targeting to both drop-off centers and individual recipients.

The terms of trade indicated that the degree of need among districts and rural councils varied, that some communities could hold out longer than others until relief arrived, but that eventually they would all need help. The plan assumed that the same held true for villages within councils and for families within villages. Before receiving food aid, village representatives would have to provide a list of inhabitants, differentiated into four groups: (1) able-bodied adults interested in food for work; (2) the sick, the old, pregnant and lactating mothers, and children under five years of age (under 115 centimeters in height), that is, those eligible for direct feeding at special centers; (3) the names of households, not already included in the other categories, who wanted to get grain in exchange for slaughtering a certain number of their livestock and drying the meat; and (4) those not in need of assistance.

The program would determine fair market exchange rates of donated sorghum (or wheat) for various types of livestock and base the rate on 1988 predrought values, with adjustments according to location and time of year. The activities of the livestock exchange would help support the free market price of livestock, while the introduction of grain rather than cash as payment would dampen the inflation in grain prices. The use of food payments in relief works would have a similar effect, and the dried meat would be used in the direct feeding centers as a source of protein. An additional activity to support the livestock price through the culling of herds would include stepped-up efforts by the government's livestock and meat marketing corporation to export live animals to urban markets in Khartoum and to Saudi Arabia. Traditionally, North Kordofan has been the prime source of sheep exports to Saudi Arabia, and its sheep have fetched higher prices per pound than European breeds shipped from Australia (World Bank 1989). Sheep are also the form of livestock most vulnerable to drought and, therefore, the most obvious choice for removal.

Throughout the implementation of the relief operation, periodic monitoring of the terms-of-trade indices would inform planners of the effect of their program. The planners could set specific index levels for discontinuing or phasing out various aspects of the operation in a given location. The monitoring would be quick, cheap, and easy. Local government representatives could take responsibility for collecting and relaying local market prices. Already, under the auspices of the

Sudan Red Crescent Society, rural communities in drought-prone areas of North Darfur and Red Sea Hills have been collecting and sending in much more elaborate data for years.

Knowing when to stop a relief program is almost as important as knowing when to start. Too often, relief continues after the need has passed, creating a dependence on free food, competing with local agriculture, and undermining future developmental efforts. Using an index level of the predrought terms of trade as a trigger for stopping the relief program would ease the planner's dilemma in deciding when the operation had met its objectives.

Emphasis on Terms of Trade

Famine early warning surveys rarely, if ever, deal effectively with nomadic populations. Although vulnerable to drought, nomads have no fixed residence, which makes it difficult for outsiders to monitor their condition. Since pastoralists come to rural markets to sell and exchange livestock, such centers offer the best information on how nomads are faring.

Freely fluctuating prices in undistorted markets act as signals of relative scarcity and provide an objective indication of the current economic situation, along with expectations of future levels of demand and supply. If a government imposes fixed price levels or sets a ceiling or floor to price fluctuations, prices have little information to impart, and analysts must look to the black or parallel markets. In Sudan, the government does not control most grain and livestock prices, but other famine-prone countries may have marketing boards that do. Nevertheless, even the most efficient systems for price fixing often do not extend to remote rural markets and, if nominally in place, are easily circumvented. Reasonably informative prices should almost always be available, and the likelihood of finding them increases with the remoteness of the market and the severity of the scarcity.

Since prices give the most objective, reliable, and readily available information on famines, their collection and interpretation should become the central component of any system to detect and avert famine. Other indicators, like crop and rainfall figures, can corroborate the conclusions drawn from price data but do not require the prime emphasis in famine early warning reports.

Price changes also provide a timely warning. Data gathered in November 1989 already specified which areas were badly affected long before the "conclusive" evidence of deaths from starvation and mass migrations began in the latter half of 1990. Unfortunately, an early warning system only sounds an alarm. Others must act upon it. As governments and relief agencies learn to interpret the mass of data that comes in, they can respond with more confidence that their efforts are needed and will succeed.

Notes

I would like to thank Mr. Mohammed Ibrahim of the Kordofan Ministry of Agriculture for his tireless and conscientious collection of data under difficult circumstances. His efforts over the past few years made this study possible.

1. This information was provided to the author by the Famine Early Warning System (FEWS) representative in Sudan. See Jane Perlez, "U.S. Bars New Aid in Sudan Famine," *New York Times*, 5 October 1990, 2.

2. One authority on famine in Sudan has gone so far as to call such nutritional surveillance "technically almost useless" (de Waal 1989, 225).

3. See also an unpublished study on Ethiopia by the International Food Policy Research Institute, 1989.

References

Borton, J., and J. Shoham. 1989. "A Review of the Sudanese Red Crescent Society's Drought Monitoring Programme." Research and Development Institute, London (February). Mimeo.

Cutler, Peter. 1986. "The Response to Drought of Beja Famine Refugees in Sudan." *Disasters* 10 (October): 181–188.

de Waal, Alexander. 1989. *Famine That Kills: Darfur, Sudan, 1984–1985.* Oxford: Clarendon Press.

Food and Agriculture Organization (FAO). 1986. *Mission to Sudan, November 1986.* Global Information and Early Warning System. Rome: FAO.

International Food Policy Research Institute. 1989. Unpublished study on Ethiopia.

Perlez, Jane. 1990. "U.S. Bars New Aid in Sudan Famine." *New York Times*, 5 October, 2.

Ravallion, Martin. 1987. *Markets and Famines.* Oxford: Clarendon Press.

Sen, Amartya. 1981. *Poverty and Famines: An Essay on Entitlement and Deprivation.* Oxford: Clarendon Press.

Swift, Jeremy. 1988. "Notes on a Sahelian Pastoral Famine Early Warning System." London: Relief and Development Institute. Mimeo.

Torry, William I. 1993. "Information for Food: Community Famine Surveillance in Sudan." In *The Challenge of Famine: Recent Experience, Lessons Learned,* edited by John Osgood Field, 209–238. West Hartford, Conn.: Kumarian Press.

World Bank. 1989. Stock Routes Project Memorandum. Washington, D.C.: World Bank. Mimeo.

11

Beyond Relief

Toward Improved Management of Famine

John Osgood Field

It's not easy to tell whether college applicants are late bloomers or non-bloomers if they haven't bloomed.
—Directors of Undergraduate Admissions
Stanford University, 1989

"Famine is like insanity, hard to define, but glaring enough when recognized" (Taylor, quoted in Devereux and Hay 1986, 4). This apt analogy speaks to a characteristic of famine that has bedeviled governments and international agencies. Not only is famine hard to define, its emergence is hard to detect and harder to forecast. Yet, when in full bloom, famine is dramatically clear even to the naked eye. The camera records the obvious, galvanizing sympathy and support for the afflicted; but the camera cannot record what does not yet exist.

How to recognize famine before it becomes obvious is the dilemma around which this final chapter is constructed. The dilemma typically leaves those who would respond to famine responding after the fact rather than preemptively. Even though the international community has learned how to provide famine relief, only a few members of the international community have learned how to prepare for famine and to intervene early enough to prevent its emergence.

This chapter first addresses famine dynamics, pointing to opportunities as well as difficulties in detection and to the often tenuous relationship between detection and response. It then explores some significant differences in how famine has been managed in India over the past century as against how it is typically managed in Africa at the present time. This is followed by a return to the process that leads to

253

famine and to reconsideration of how that process can help crystallize more appropriate objectives for famine early warning systems than relief alone.

Famine Dynamics, Detection, and Response

Unlike such quick-onset disasters as earthquakes, floods, and typhoons, famine is a slow-onset disaster. Because famine does not happen suddenly but instead has a lengthy gestation, it is helpful to chart the dynamics disposing to famine. Doing so is more than a theoretical exercise, for it suggests indicators appropriate to detecting the process as it unfolds. To the extent that early detection facilitates early response, detection becomes an important element in any strategy of famine prevention. The several famine early warning systems now in use are based on the proposition that information is the key to action (a half-truth only) while also inferring, and at times testing, the dynamics and indicators in question.

Analyses of famine over the past decade have greatly enriched understanding of famine dynamics, but at the same time they have confounded the quest for effective early warning by expanding enormously the type and number of variables to monitor. When famine was attributed primarily to natural causes (drought, flooding, locusts, etc.), one could focus on them and work at preparing for their emergence. When famine was interpreted as reflecting a downturn in food availability, it was possible to concentrate on crop failure and then attempt to counter local shortfalls with supplies brought in from outside. Indeed, the two perspectives went nicely together: Climatic instability explained variations in food production, with famine resulting when shortfalls were not matched by imports.

While this simple dynamic remains basic to famine, it is now clear that two other factors are equally important. One is that vulnerability to famine is not simply a function of the weather; it is embedded even more in political economy relationships (Lofchie 1975; Franke and Chasin 1980; Bates 1981; Watts 1983; Lipton 1986; Devereux and Hay 1986; Drèze and Sen 1989 and 1990a; Downs, Kerner and Reyna 1991; among many others). In modern times, in particular, much famine is man-made, a product of economic marginalization, population pressures on land, environmental stress, and political struggle (Independent Commission 1985). Similarly, famine is not simply a crisis of supply (crops fail and there isn't enough food); for most of its victims famine is really a crisis of demand (Sen 1981). Food exists or might be obtained from elsewhere, but people who have lost employment or whose income fails to keep pace with rising food prices cannot command it.

Indeed, even fairly modest declines in food availability can trigger massive declines in effective demand, or "exchange entitlement."[1]

A more complete and accurate understanding of famine causality, therefore, requires the monitoring of not only natural forces, but also social systems, and food entitlement decline (FED), as well as accurate food availability decline (FAD).[2] The practical challenge is not merely to anticipate a famine before it occurs, a daunting task in its own right, but to locate it spatially and socially so as to intervene on behalf of the people who most need protection.

Figure 11.1 represents one way of conceptualizing the events leading to famine. As with any such diagram, this one is selective. It does not feature processes of environmental deterioration (overgrazing, overcropping, deforestation, soil erosion, desertification, and the like) which accentuate vulnerability to famine (Franke and Chasin 1980; Timberlake 1985). These are long-term processes that call for remedial attention in their own right, quite apart from their secondary effects. Important contextual variables (the presence of insurgency, military conflict, political suppression) are omitted for the same reason. What the figure does is highlight key endowment and exchange relationships while acknowledging that the trigger mechanism disposing to famine is usually some kind of natural disturbance.

Figure 11.1 posits that "entitlements/exchange relationships" and the "employment and income" flowing from them are filters through which shocks ("drought," etc.) spread, adversely affecting the normal, precrisis equilibrium and threatening different types and degrees of "collapse." When unchecked, the dynamic can result in "famine."[3]

Several insights germane to detection and response are suggested by Figure 11.1.

- Notwithstanding the complexity of famine and the multiple factors underlying it, the principal indicators are few and manageable.
- The earliest indicators (rainfall, crops) warn better than they predict.
- Prices, employment, and income are the major catalyzers of famine. When these are seasonally abnormal, intervention is necessary to protect direct and exchange entitlements.
- Social disintegration, the explosive spread of infectious disease, starvation, and excess deaths are the clearest signs of famine; but they appear very late in the overall dynamic. Similarly, the mass migration of hungry people is a "terminal indicator of distress" (Cutler 1984, 55).[4]
- Whether famine occurs or not depends critically on the timing and effectiveness of governmental action to avert or minimize the trauma.

Figure 11.1 The Famine Dynamic: Key Indicators and Predictors

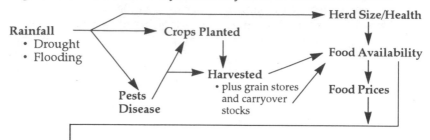

Entitlements/Exchange Relationships
- Ownership of land and other assets
- Availability of credit, loans, and other supports to farmers
- Terms of trade among farmers, herders, fisherpeople, artisans
- Rural-urban terms of trade
- Government procurement, price-fixing, taxation

Employment and Income
- Vulnerability/viability
- Capacity to cope in times of stress

Collapse
- Unusual food outflows; rural to urban
- Failure of deficit areas/people to attract food
- Consumption reduced to enhance future survival/recourse to inferior "famine foods"
- Search for alternative employment
- Hoarding/black market profiteering/smuggling
- Looting/other crime
- Marked declines in nutritional status
- Breakdown of social reciprocities/unusual social conflict
- Distress sale of productive assets
- Seed grain consumed; next harvest not planted
- Abandonment of wives/children
- Abandonment of land/out-migration

**Marked increase in
STARVATION
DISEASE
DEATH**

"FAMINE"

Note: Government intervention is possible at any point on this diagram with the potential, at least, of preventing the dynamic from resulting in famine.

Several inferences are suggested as well.

- The best indicators with which to monitor the famine dynamic will be contextually grounded and hence will vary from place to place. In each instance, however, a relatively concise number of key indicators should suffice so far as systematic data gathering and analysis are concerned.[5]
- By extension, elaborate modeling and data-generation exercises, the vacuum cleaner approach to early warning, are a diversion of scarce time, talent, and resources better spent on preparedness and prevention. Comprehensiveness is neither necessary nor desirable, a more appropriate objective being effective parsimony.[6]
- One reason why focused monitoring is preferable to extensive data acquisition is that early response is necessarily launched before the fact of famine is incontrovertibly clear. More data does not obviate the need for judgment. Indeed, the need for judgment is especially acute in early response and does not disappear thereafter. Moreover, detection and decision are not the same thing, granted that detection can aid, even prod, a decision to act. So no matter how comprehensive data gathering and analysis may be, they are at most technical inputs to a political process. The quest for certainty as the key to decision converts early warning into late warning and even later response.[7]
- Except when curtailed consumption of food is an early adaptation to anticipated scarcity (Corbett 1988), nutritional status is not an optimal early warning indicator because its movement downward comes quite late in the overall dynamic. Declines in weight relative to height, the usual diagnostic for famine, serve better to confirm what is happening than to anticipate future events.[8]
- Concerning intervention, the earlier the better, prevention being preferable to cure (and much less expensive). On the other hand, the earlier the intervention the less clear it is that a famine will actually occur. The fact that false positives abound (de Waal 1988) is a political disincentive to act preemptively.
- Early and late intervention are both likely to be supply oriented, whereas intervention in between is more likely to be demand oriented. When governments choose to act in the face of actual or anticipated food shortages, the logical thing to do is to import grain both to ensure an adequate domestic supply and to contain inflationary pressures on food prices in local markets.[9] Similarly, famine relief is usually a matter of providing food and medicine to displaced people at risk of death. In between, the

focus appropriately shifts to enhancing employment opportunities and other ways of maintaining income so as to preserve
market access.[10]

- Effective early warning means sounding the alarm and inter-
vening before entitlements collapse and the distress disposal of
productive assets, abandonment of land, and out-migration
occur. Early warning solely for relief is not only a contradiction
of terms; it is a cop-out. Intervention at this point may be better
than no intervention at all, but it is "too little, too late."

If the purpose of monitoring famine indicators is detection, the
purpose of detection is to facilitate a more timely response. Similarly,
if the stated purpose of famine early warning systems is to improve
detection, an objective of equal importance is to reduce ambiguity and
thereby overcome inhibitions to taking action.[11] On the one hand, the
assumption of early warning systems is that lack of information is the
principal constraint to early response, and that governments and
international agencies would respond better if forecasting were
improved. On the other hand, early warning systems have the political role of spurring action; the need is not just for information but for
information that is definitive, clear, and compelling. The dilemma facing early warning is that it is very difficult, perhaps impossible, to be
definitive, clear, and compelling about something that does not yet
exist. Ambiguity is inherent in famine prediction. That, in turn, means
that political decisionmaking will come into play. Early warning does
not eliminate the politics; it tries to harness politics to construc-
tive purpose.[12]

One can take the argument a step further. Of the three broad types
of famine early warning—political, administrative, and technical—
timely and effective state intervention is related more closely to the
first two than to the third. This observation is illustrated in the next
section, and there are two reasons for it. First, even technical detection—satellite imagery, remote sensing, etc.—requires administrative
interpretation and political decision to stimulate action; and these
often depend on "ground truthing" as well (that is, confirmation of
growing stress on the ground using other indicators). Second, political
incentives to state action derived from democratic institutions and
processes usually trigger an early, preemptive response because of the
accountability to the public that these institutions and processes
impose on those in power.[13] Administrative early warning—detection
and decision by government officials—serves with equal effectiveness
in spurring action while also encouraging preparedness. However,
administrative early warning presumes a political environment favorable to early intervention; and the further removed administrative

decisionmaking is from the scene of stress, the more likely delays in response will occur. Nevertheless, both political early warning and administrative early warning—when they exist—have much better track records in inducing early decision and response than does technical early warning to date.[14]

India Historically Versus Africa Today

The difficulty of linking detection and response, along with the effectiveness of administrative and political early warning in doing so, is best conveyed by contrasting India's experience with famine management and the situation in much of famine-prone Africa at the present time. India developed its celebrated Famine Codes as early as 1880 and has used them and descendants of them to considerable advantage ever since. In Africa, only Botswana has something similar (Drèze 1990b).[15]

In India, detection and response were the responsibility of the same individuals, who typically were district-level officials.[16] For Africa, detection and response are the responsibility of different individuals, the most authoritative of whom are usually located far from the scene of stress. The leading detectors today are the Global Information and Early Warning Unit in the Food and Agriculture Organization (FAO), Rome; contractors for the Famine Early Warning System (FEWS) project of the U.S. Agency for International Development (USAID); some units of national governments such as the Relief and Rehabilitation Commission (RCC) in Ethiopia (replicated and then abandoned in Sudan); interstate bodies like the Comité permanent interétats de lutte contre la sécheresse dans le Sahel (CILSS) in the Sahel; and various PVO/NGO bodies with a presence in famine-prone areas. Unfortunately, the power to act definitively diminishes with closeness to the problem.

In India, the basis for both detection and response was the exercise of human judgment informed by on-the-ground observation and contextual understanding. While monitoring market prices (especially for grain and livestock), the crime rate, migration, and deaths, "intelligent apprehension" was clearly preferred to "too mechanical obedience to rule" (Orissa Enquiry Commissioner's Report 1867, quoted in Currey 1981, 20). Famine detection for Africa relies heavily on satellite surveillance combined with computer processing of quantitative data from the field. Detection is grounded in the analysis of vast amounts of data derived from multiple sources, all of which must somehow fall into place and provide a clear, coherent picture of what is happening. It seldom does. Moreover, those who detect must persuade those with the authority to sound the alarm, while those who sound the alarm must persuade those empowered to authorize a response. The key detectors, alarm sounders, and response decisionmakers are located in national capitals at best, more typically in donor agencies and governments outside the country.

The divorce of detection and response in Africa today, along with the removal of both from the afflicted area, leaves response at the mercy of political considerations that go far beyond famine itself. In effect, famine response gets embroiled in and subsumed under broader diplomatic and strategic relationships informing the international system (Shawcross 1984; Gill 1986; Jansson, Harris, and Penrose 1987; Bonner 1989; Giorgis 1989; see also Chapters 4 and 5 in this book). In colonial India, by contrast, preventing famine deaths became a stated objective of government policy, with a clear mandate given to district and presidency officials to intervene as necessary, no questions asked. In independent India, notwithstanding some retreat from rhetorical commitment, the existence of an open, competitive political process, representation of rural areas and interests, unfretted parliamentary debate and disclosure, and a free press serving as watchdog and instrument of accountability have perpetuated the incentives to detect, acknowledge, and respond earlier rather then later, with the government's reputation at stake based on how well it performs.[17]

In India, it became the responsibility of local government to prepare for incipient famine by designing interventions (notably public works to shore up employment and earnings, food relief, and loans to farmers) and to stockpile the materiel necessary to activate them in advance.[18] Little such preparedness planning exists in Africa today. Famine-prone African countries are painfully dependent on international sources of supply for food, medicine, transport, and intervention management. These usually arrive on the scene after famine has already peaked.[19]

In India, the response to famine was early and preventive in character, with relief being provided only to the truly destitute and dependent. In Africa, the emphasis is on relief (understandably given the lateness of the response). By the same token, development in India became quite explicitly oriented to the prevention of famine, as illustrated in construction of the South Maratha Railroad a century ago.[20] In Africa, development policy is only tangentially related to famine, notwithstanding a growing interest in "food security." Attention to vulnerability to famine—who, where, when, why—by most African governments is nascent, as is the intent to build capacities to intervene to prevent famine. International assistance to famine-prone African countries has been too niggardly (and off the mark) to be of much help (Timberlake 1985; Independent Commission 1985; see also Edelman 1986).[21]

In India, rehabilitation was built into famine intervention. In Africa, rehabilitation is contingent on favorable circumstances (such as people being able—and willing—to return to their homes), institutional mandates, and the necessary resources. Rehabilitation often does not happen.

India's overall record in dealing with famine is as good as its record in dealing with chronic malnutrition is poor.[22] Africa's record and that of the international community tend to be quite dismal except in the provision of relief.[23] The reasons are not difficult to fathom, and they go beyond India's impressive development of infrastructure and operational capacity. In India, problem and solution have been closely linked, with both being local. India has been prepared to intervene against famine early and fast. Historically, the authorities declared famine to prevent famine from occurring.[24] The decision to intervene was and, to a lesser extent, still is made by responsible officials on the scene, while the criterion for decision remains human judgment, not vast amounts of quantitative and scientifically derived evidence based on high-tech methodologies, which in practice tend to be treated as substitutes for judgment as much as aides to decision.[25]

These observations are summarized in Table 11.1. Ironically perhaps, the burden of the historical record is that effectiveness is inversely related to technological sophistication. India historically has made the best of poorly developed technologies, vast and varied areas of responsibility, and the need for considerable devolution of discretionary latitude onto local officials. Africa's dilemma is that it confronts the persistent specter of famine at a time when everything —detection, decisionmaking, response—has been internationalized, to say nothing of computerized and politicized. As a solution of the last resort, this is a major asset. As a solution of the first resort, it is a major liability.

The Objectives of Famine Early Warning Reconsidered

If the monitoring of famine dynamics remains confounded by still inadequate technologies, by the growing gap between detection and response, and by weak political incentives and administrative capacities, it is also confounded by conceptual confusion concerning what to monitor, the purpose of monitoring, and the very nature of famine. Uncertainty as to whether famine is a discrete event or a process (Currey 1992) compounds the inherent difficulty in distinguishing famine from nonfamine. The latter is made all the more difficult if one accepts de Waal's argument (1989) that widespread hunger and destitution

Table 11.1 Famine Detection and Response in India and Africa

	India Historically	Africa Today
Detection		
Mode	Ground observation	Satellite imagery complemented by ground observation
Who's responsible	Local officials	International agencies; in some cases national governments, in others NGOs on the scene.
Technology	Human judgment	Computer analysis of GIS and other quantitative data
Response		
Preparedness to intervene	Yes, both strategically and materially	Very limited in advance; reliance on ad hoc marshaling of resources once crisis is clear
Who's responsible for response decision	Local officials initially; state and national officials subsequently	National governments and international agencies in either order
Response in relation to detection	Very rapid, often immediate	Slow; time lag for international shipment, amassing resources, and establishing organizational capacity on the ground
Resources to apply	Local initially, national and international subsequently as necessary	Mostly international, some national, almost none local

Table 11.1 continued

	India Historically	Africa Today
Type of response	Prevention primarily, relief as necessary, rehabilitation built into both	Relief primarily, rehabilitation as possible
Effectiveness in preventing/mitigating famine	Very effective typically	Not effective at all: assistance after the fact
Effectiveness in curbing famine deaths, restoring health	Modest to considerable	Considerable to exceptional
Effectiveness in rehabilitating famine victims	Considerable, part of intervention strategy	Varied, often left to chance or a function of circumstances
Perceived relation of famine response to development	Close relationship in terms both of prevention and restoration	Tangential relationship, relief seen as a discrete agenda
Actual relation of famine response to development	Close: development protected and promoted	Marginal: development returned to after relief completed

constitute famine even when people do not die. Even if one restricts famine to starvation, disease, and death (as in Figure 11.1), it remains a judgment call as to what magnitudes of starvation and disease, and how many people are dying as a result, constitute "famine." The dividing line, if there is one, between famine and nonfamine is so blurred that, on the margins, the existence of famine is a matter of interpretation. It is no wonder that the response to famine by national governments and international agencies, given their penchant for clarity, is typically so late and one-dimensional (relief).

Although the burden of interpretation will continue in most live situations, some degree of conceptual clarification is possible that should prove helpful in crystallizing the objectives both of monitoring famine dynamics and of policy response to the signals received.[26]

Famine is indeed an event that happens episodically and, when in full bloom, is easily recognized as a discrete outcome. That said, famine is the end point of a process leading to it; and so it is also meaningful to refer to famine as a process disposing to and shaping the outcome. Doing so has intellectual value but, more importantly, is central to detecting incipient famine so as to respond preemptively to it.

One way of sorting out the elements involved is to distinguish between *famine process, famine conditions,* and *famine.*

- *Famine process* is the process of stress and destitution that can result in a famine outcome.
- *Famine conditions* are that stage in the process when destitution—defined as the involuntary disposal of productive assets—occurs. It often culminates in distress migration.
- *Famine* itself is the final but not inevitable stage of the famine process in which people starve, suffer disease, and die in unusually large numbers. It may accompany or follow destitution.

Consistent with Corbett's analysis, the famine process is a downward progression in which people first attempt to cope with adversity, then successively lose their ability to cope, and finally succumb. How far the process goes depends both on the severity of the disruption setting the process in motion and on the subtle interplay of people's vulnerability and capacity to cope (Anderson and Woodrow 1989; Chapter 6 of this book). This view of the famine process parallels the one emphasizing loss of entitlements, although the latter is more an explanation of the process than an account of the process itself.

Before turning to the objectives of famine early warning systems, it might be useful to expand briefly on this skeletal framework of the famine process, famine conditions, and famine.

The initial phase of the process is when people react to or anticipate a decline in their entitlement to food and modify normal practices in an attempt to cope. Examples of behavior modification at this stage include altering cropping and planting strategies, seeking alternative employment, reducing current consumption of food to safeguard future survival, disposing of small livestock, selling jewelry and other household possessions, gathering wild foods, and borrowing money or food from relatives. Corbett calls this the stage of insurance mechanisms, for the practices engaged in are precautionary and relatively low cost; more importantly, they are reversible if the coping is successful. The goal that people pursue in this initial phase is to protect their livelihood and avoid destitution. The immediate objective is to hold onto productive assets in order to maintain the means of livelihood so as to return to normal economic enterprise when conditions improve.

The famine process continues—and intensifies—when these insurance mechanisms no longer suffice and when coping behaviors give way to behaviors implying failure to cope. The key to this second stage is the disposal of productive assets on which household livelihood depends: larger livestock such as oxen or water buffalo, farm tools and other implements essential to economic performance (looms for weavers, nets and boats for fishermen), and land itself.[27] This stage entails a process of destitution. It is high cost and increasingly irreversible. It represents a deepening crisis in which each step exerts a ratchet effect downward in terms of livelihood and potential survival. This is the stage where social structures and reciprocities erode, where dependents are sold or cast adrift, and where desperate efforts at current survival mortgage future well-being.

An exhaustion of options accompanies the marginalization occurring; and while famine in the conventional sense—starvation, disease, and death—may not yet exist, "famine conditions" do. As Corbett (1988, 1108) notes, "When large numbers of households reach the stage where maintaining current food consumption levels has to take precedence over their future income generating capacity then famine conditions are created." The end point of this stage is the grim reality of destitution, distress migration, and acute dependence on whatever relief is available. Accompanying or emerging from it are the four hallmarks of famine itself: widespread starvation, rampant disease, and excess deaths in large numbers, along with even greater vulnerability to future adversity on the part of thousands, even millions of survivors.[28]

This progression is relevant to the objectives of famine early warning systems. The usual objective is to warn of a famine outcome by monitoring the process leading to it and thereby marshall relief to salvage people on the verge of bottoming out. A related objective is to identify which groups in society are most vulnerable should famine occur (Sen 1981; de Waal 1988; Downing 1991). These are minimalist objectives at best.

If the focus of early warning is on a famine outcome, the actual objective should be to prevent that outcome through preemptive action. The purpose of early warning is not to mobilize relief when famine happens; it is to trigger an early response that effectively breaks the dynamic before famine becomes a reality. This is the essence of effective drought management in India and several African countries (Drèze 1990a and 1990b). It is a higher level of accomplishment to which most famine-prone countries and their international benefactors should aspire.

As impressive an accomplishment as preventing famine would be, as an objective it is confined to changing the outcome and says nothing about altering the process. It addresses famine but not famine conditions. It seeks to prevent death, not destitution; and by virtue of ignoring the latter, it tends to isolate famine management from development. Hence, more and more analysts, myself included, regard the ultimate objective of detection as discerning a famine process in the making so as to intervene early enough to avoid destitution. As Walker (1989, 70) notes, "If famine warning is tied solely to mass starvation, it is, in effect, accepting the process of deprivation." The real objective should be to preserve livelihood as well as lives. It is not only to predict mass starvation and death; it is also to warn of famine conditions, the erosion of people's productive capacities and their resource base. The key to early warning is not to cue off of destitution to prevent death; it is to cue off of coping—especially the entitlement failures that influence coping—to prevent destitution.

Moreover, the logic of this conception of famine early warning extends to what might be termed the Currey corollary (Currey 1992). The objective of monitoring is not only to protect the downside of destitution; it is to track strengthening the upside of resilience. This is not a mere rhetorical twist. It speaks to the essence of development by linking early warning to the development process as it informs vulnerabilities and capabilities in the countryside. It also speaks to sustainability over time (Walker 1989), because ultimately societies end famine by preventing famine conditions. This is the real lesson of India and Botswana.

Conclusion

Short of nuclear war, famine is the ultimate scourge of human populations. Short of physical torture, it is the cruelest way to die. Famine is an unnecessary tragedy that simply should not be permitted to happen in an interconnected world of plenty. Yet, happen it does, and with no end in sight.

Ultimately, famine will be eliminated when a political consensus emerges, both within famine-prone countries and internationally, that famine is unacceptable regardless of circumstance; when priorities in development are directed to reducing vulnerability to famine as an explicit goal; and when building capacities in society, economy, and government to cope with famine stresses become central to the development agenda.

For the foreseeable future, improved early warning can help but is not enough. For detection to trigger timely and effective action, there must be a capacity to act in the form of preparedness plans and stockpiling of the material resources required to activate them. Building and/or strengthening national and regional capacities to detect famine dynamics early in the process and then to act quickly in a manner appropriate to the situation, based on response options that have been well thought out in advance, are essential to arresting the dynamic before it gets out of control. Early warning that is not well integrated with decisionmaking and response mechanisms, especially within famine-prone countries, is unlikely to achieve its objectives. Without preparedness plans, everything is ad hoc. Without materiel and the administrative capacity to move quickly, preparedness plans are just good ideas on paper.

In sum, early warning is only the beginning. The major agenda that necessarily follows is to build the human and institutional capacity to plan for famine and, when the alarm sounds, to implement a well-conceived response for which the appropriate preparations have already been made. Strengthening mechanisms to facilitate timely decisionmaking and developing national preparedness plans are the critical next steps if detection is to result in action. If these things do not happen, the countries in question and the international donor community will benefit little from improved early warning.

Notes

This chapter is adapted from a larger paper, "Beyond Relief: A Developmental Perspective on Famine," presented at the Fourteenth International Congress of Nutrition, Seoul, Korea, 20–25 August 1989. An earlier version appeared in *Bayreuther Geowissenschaftliche Arbeiten* 15 (1991): 151–166. Portions also appear in "Famine: A Perspective for the Nutrition Community," *Nutrition Reviews* 49 (May 1991): 145–153.

1. The consumption decelerator is a function of production and market release on the supply side and reduced employment and income—and rising food prices—on the demand side. (See Sen 1981; Greenough 1982; Ravallion 1987; Drèze and Sen 1989 and 1990a.) For an excellent account of how these factors interplay, see Devereux 1988. The concept *entitlement* as applied to

chronic malnutrition and episodic famine comes from Sen and is summarized in Chapter 1 of this book, note 16.

2. These terms are Sen's, 1981. See also Drèze and Sen 1989 and 1990a.

3. Although based primarily on Sen 1981 and subsequent analyses of famine dynamics, Figure 11.1 is consistent with the three stages of household coping strategies identified in Corbett 1988; see also Walker 1989 and Cekan 1990. These stages of coping are discussed later in the text.

4. By contrast, migration by individual family members—men especially—in search of employment is an early form of coping (Vaughan 1987; Drèze and Sen 1989), as is early migration by pastoral nomads (Timberlake 1985).

5. For example, an animal-grain terms-of-trade-index in pastoral areas (Sen 1981; see also Chapter 10 in this book), unemployment rates for landless laborers and artisans, and a grain-wage (or grain-fish) exchange rate as appropriate (Cutler 1985). Because increases in grain prices associated with famine are usually massive (two to six times normal, occasionally more), monitoring grain prices is a promising way of detecting accelerating stress unless, of course, price movements are inhibited by demand failure or by the opportunity costs of provisioning (Sen 1981; Devereux 1988). The point here is that indices such as these should serve as very reliable barometers of a crisis in the making. In concert with meteorological and crop data they are pretty much all one needs for effective early warning.

Cuing off of household coping strategies to prevent drought—or any other disruption—from becoming famine is an alternative idea for early warning (see, for example, Corbett 1988). The idea is that early warning systems should be based on coping strategies or at least should incorporate them into a broader arsenal of data. Although it is an attractive proposition, to be applied effectively it requires considerable contextual understanding of behavior modification, its meaning, and probable success. Moreover, it is not clear that human responses to stress are better indicators than the stresses themselves unless, of course, they precede them by way of anticipation. The best indicators for famine early warning may well be different from the best indicators for verification, with coping strategies more typically being among the latter.

6. Complex data gathering and analysis tend to become self-fulfilling exercises and, by virtue of being divorced from decision and response, are often self-defeating as well, as was true in the case of multisectoral nutrition planning (Field 1987). USAID's Famine Early Warning System (FEWS) project, "conceptually and operationally the most sophisticated effort of its kind" (Agency for International Development 1986, 1), is a good example of the vacuum cleaner approach, alas without allowing for original data generation in the field to date.

7. As Currey 1981 has noted, the politics of information is more important than its accuracy. Indeed, many analysts believe that the real issue in famine management is political (early response), not technical (early warning). On the other hand, how early warning might promote early response is addressed below.

8. Drèze and Sen 1991 concur with this inference, as does Cutler 1986 and 1987; but see Shoham 1987. A rapid nutritional assessment in southern Iraq in June 1991, ten months after the trade embargo was imposed and three months after the Gulf War ended, revealed considerable stunting and underweight among children but very few weights below normal for established height

(Field and Russell 1992; see also International Study Team 1991), and this despite 1991's being called a famine year in Iraq (Drèze and Gazdar 1991).

9. In 1984–85, the Government of Kenya successfully averted famine by importing 647,000 metric tons of maize and 251,000 metric tons of wheat to compensate for sharp declines in domestic production (35 percent and 40 percent respectively) attributable to drought. With aggregate supply protected, the government stabilized food prices and enabled normal market channels to continue functioning (Downing 1990; see also Drèze 1990b).

10. Strategies of entitlement protection are assessed in Drèze and Sen 1989, while Corbett 1988 offers a helpful typology of the phases of famine in terms of household coping strategies. The task remains of developing a typology of the specific policies and interventions that are appropriate to each phase.

11. As Carlson (1982, 9) has observed, "One of the most strikingly predictable responses by government officials has been to deny and suppress famine reports as long as possible." Among other reasons, "government officials feel that famine conditions indicate somehow that they have not properly performed their public roles. They are faced with actual or potential loss of power, as an individual, a party, or a government. This . . . possibility is very real, and like death, is often easier to deny than to face." Examples may be found in Shepherd 1975; Gill 1986; Jansson, Harris, and Penrose 1987; and Bonner 1989.

12. Another assumption of early warning systems is that all is well until something goes wrong, the task of early warning being to detect that something. Yet, as Anderson (1985, 50) has noted, for many people normalcy is "the condition of vulnerability that allowed the crisis to become a disaster." Moreover, the "pre-crisis equilibrium" mentioned in the text is itself often a period of immizeration that over time increases vulnerability (Greenough 1982).

13. Regime ideology disposing to early intervention, something quite independent of regime type, is also important (Drèze 1990b), as are calculations of the government's capacity to respond.

14. Helpful analyses of famine early warning systems include Cutler 1985; Walker 1989; Drèze and Sen 1989; Drèze 1990a and 1990b; and Chapters 9 and 10 in this book.

15. Kenya, Zimbabwe, and Cape Verde are making good progress (Hay 1988; Drèze 1990b). Technical early warning systems have sprouted in profusion in the Sahel region. Niger is one country that has tried to intervene to protect pastoral nomads in times of severe drought; see Chapter 3 in this book. Indigenous voluntary agencies have been important to drought management/famine prevention efforts throughout the Sahel; see Chapter 8 in this book.

16. References to India are in the past tense only because they reflect the historical period.

17. These political attributes are no guarantee that the government will intervene in time. Drèze 1990a argues that the response in Bihar in 1966–67 was tardy, although it still averted outright famine. The Orissa state government flatly refused to acknowledge famine conditions in certain tribal areas in 1987, only to be overruled by the central government after considerable delay. The press played a catalytic role in this episode, as it has on other occasions (Palmieri 1982; May 1987; Penrose in Jansson, Harris, and Penrose 1987; Ram 1990).

18. India's several Famine Codes varied over space and time but typically featured four types of intervention: (1) provision of employment on public work schemes, with compensation calibrated to food needs based on age, sex, pregnancy, and lactation; (2) a village dole for those unable to work or without support, with village headmen held responsible for any deaths among them; (3) *takavi*, or loans to agriculturalists to stay in production, provide employment, protect livestock, and improve production potential through leveling, bunding, well digging, and the like; and (4) more *takavi* for purchase of seed and cattle so that farmers could recover from protracted drought and rebuild working capital. Over time, *takavi* became the preferred approach because of its effectiveness and low administrative costs (McAlpin 1983; see also Drèze 1990a). In effect, the Famine Codes sought to protect market demand for food by sustaining purchasing power, and to preserve, restore, and enhance productive assets. Since independence the arsenal has been expanded to include food subsidies through Fair Price Shops, child feeding programs, health interventions, and—more recently—guaranteed employment schemes (Berg 1973; Ezekiel 1986; Drèze 1990a). The remarkable thing is that such a comprehensive strategy could be undertaken on such a large scale so often and with such telling results in such a poor country.

19. Concerning Ethiopia as a case in point see, in particular, Jansson, Harris, and Penrose 1987; see also Gill 1986; Giorgis 1989; and Chapter 5 in this book.

20. This railroad was actually built on the recommendation of the Famine Commission of 1880 (McAlpin 1983).

21. Economic assistance to Africa by USAID is about $900 million annually. The most famine-prone countries are not prime beneficiaries, with the exception of Sudan for much of the 1980s. Nor is Sudan currently.

22. India and China are opposites in this regard, with China having achieved remarkable success in improving public health and nutrition even while having suffered the worst famine—thirty million excess deaths—of the twentieth century (Ashton, Hill, Piazza, and Zeitz 1984). For a probing analysis of this contrast between the two countries see Drèze and Sen 1989.

23. Again, Botswana is a striking exception. Drèze (1988, 102n) notes that the report that laid the foundation for Botswana's very effective drought relief/famine prevention system "literally reads like an echo of the Famine Commission Report written in India almost exactly one century earlier." (Botswana's performance is assessed in Holm and Morgan 1985; Hay 1988; Moremi 1988; and Morgan 1988.) On the other hand, the relevance of India's experience for much of Africa is a matter of controversy. See McAlpin 1987; Clay 1988; Harriss 1988; and Drèze 1988.

24. A major exception was 1943–44, when the Bengal government refrained from declaring famine because it did not have the wherewithal to intervene, the declaration of famine being an official act with powerful implications.

25. Cutler 1985, 1987, and 1988 is equally dubious about high-tech detection. On the other hand, Wilhite and Easterling with Wood 1987 provide examples of remote sensing, meteorological monitoring, and crop forecasting that augur well. Cutler's misgivings and my own are political, not methodological. In addition, Cutler's are based on cost-effectiveness and a perceived mismatch between the technologies and the environments in which they are being applied.

26. The discussion that follows draws heavily on Corbett 1988; Walker 1989; de Waal 1989; and Currey 1992.

27. The abandonment of land is a final act of desperation, as is the sale of land in most instances because land sold is virtually impossible to recover when one is made destitute in other ways as well. An alternative to distress sale of productive assets is to seek credit or food from merchants and moneylenders, but doing so also exacts a price in the form of the long-term burden of indebtedness and powerlessness that accompanies credit under the circumstances.

28. Corbett's categorization of the final steps in the famine process is somewhat different from that presented here, but the meaning is the same.

References

Agency for International Development. 1986. "FEWS." AFR/TR, Washington, D.C. (3 March). Mimeo.

Anderson, Mary B. 1985. "A Reconceptualization of the Linkages Between Disasters and Development." *Disasters* 9, Harvard Supplement: 45–51.

Ashton, Basil, Kenneth Hill, Alan Piazza, and Robin Zeitz. 1984. "Famine in China, 1958–61." *Population and Development Review* 10 (December): 613–645.

Bates, Robert H. 1981. *Markets and States in Tropical Africa: The Political Basis of Agricultural Policies.* Berkeley: University of California Press.

Berg, Alan. 1973. *The Nutrition Factor: Its Role in National Development*, Appendix A: 211–221. Washington, D.C.: Brookings Institution.

Bonner, Raymond. 1982. "Famine." *New Yorker*, 13 March, 85–101.

Cahill, Kevin M., ed. 1982. *Famine.* Maryknoll, N.Y.: Orbis Books.

Carlson, Dennis G. 1982. "Famine in History: With a Comparison of Two Modern Ethiopian Disasters." In Cahill, 5–16.

Cekan, Jindra. 1990. "The Use of Traditional Coping Strategies During Famine in Sub-Saharan Africa." *Drought Network News* 2 (October): 5–6.

Clay, Edward. 1988. "Assessment of Food-Entitlement Interventions in South Asia." In Curtis, Hubbard, and Shepherd, 141–156.

Corbett, Jane. 1988. "Famine and Household Coping Strategies." *World Development* 16, 9: 1099–1112.

Currey, Bruce. 1981. "14 Fallacies About Famine." *Ceres* (March–April): 20–25.

Curry, Bruce. 1992. "Is Famine a Discrete Event?" *Disasters* 16 (June): 138–144.

Curtis, Donald, Michael Hubbard, and Andrew Shepherd, eds. 1988. *Preventing Famine: Policies and Prospects for Africa.* London and New York: Routledge.

Cutler, Peter. 1984. "Famine Forecasting: Prices and Peasant Behaviour in Northern Ethiopia." *Disasters* 8, 1: 48–56.

Cutler, Peter. 1985. "Detecting Food Emergencies: Lessons from the 1979 Bangladesh Crisis." *Food Policy* 10 (August): 207–224.

Cutler, Peter. 1986. "Famine Warning, Famine Prevention and Nutrition." *Nutrition Bulletin* 46 (January): 23–28.

Cutler, Peter. 1987. "Early Warning of Famine: A Red Herring?" *Proceedings of the Nutrition Society* 46: 263–266.

Cutler, Peter. 1988. "Preparation for Early Response to Disasters." Paper presented at the WHO/ACC/SCN Conference on Nutrition in Times of Disasters, World Health Organization, Geneva, 27–20 September.

Devereux, Stephen, and Roger Hay. 1986. *Origins of Famine: A Review of the Literature.* 2 vols. Oxford: Oxford University. Food Studies Group. Scheduled for publication by Harvester Wheatsheaf as *Theories of Famine.*

Devereux, Stephen. 1988. "Entitlements, Availability and Famine: A Revisionist View of Wollo, 1972–74." *Food Policy* 13 (August): 270–282.

de Waal, Alexander. 1988. "Famine Early Warning Systems and the Use of Socio-Economic Data." *Disasters* 12, 1: 81–91.

de Waal, Alexander. 1989. *Famine That Kills: Darfur, Sudan, 1984–1985.* Oxford: Clarendon Press.

Downing, Thomas E. 1990. "Monitoring and Responding to Famine: Lessons from the 1984–85 Food Crisis in Kenya." *Disasters* 14, 3: 204–229.

Downing, Thomas E. 1991. *Assessing Socioeconomic Vulnerability to Famine: Frameworks, Concepts, and Applications.* FEWS Working Paper 2.1, Final Report to the U.S. Agency for International Development, Famine Early Warning System Project, 30 January.

Downs, R. E., Donna O. Kerner, and Stephen P. Reyna, eds. 1991. *The Political Economy of African Famine.* Philadelphia: Gordon and Breach.

Drèze, Jean. 1988. *Famine Prevention in India.* Monograph No. 3, The Development Economics Research Programme, London School of Economics.

Drèze, Jean. 1990. "Famine Prevention in Africa: Some Experiences and Lessons." In Drèze and Sen 1990b, 123–172.

Drèze, Jean, and Amartya Sen. 1989. *Hunger and Public Action.* Oxford: Clarendon Press.

Drèze, Jean, and Amartya Sen. 1990a, eds. *The Political Economy of Hunger.* Vol. 1, *Entitlement and Well-Being.* Oxford: Clarendon Press.

Drèze, Jean, and Amartya Sen. 1990b, eds. *The Political Economy of Hunger.* Vol. 2, *Famine Prevention.* Oxford: Clarendon Press.

Drèze, Jean, and Haris Gazdar, eds. 1991. *Hunger and Poverty in Iraq, 1991.* Monograph No. 32, The Development Economics Research Programme, London School of Economics.

Edelman, Mark L. 1986. "Statement of the Honorable Mark L. Edelman, Assistant Administrator for Africa, Agency for International Development, Before the House Foreign Affairs Committee, Subcommittee on Africa, September 23, 1986." Mimeo.

Ezekiel, Hannan. 1986. "A Rural Employment Guarantee Scheme as an Early Warning System." International Food Policy Research Institute, Washington, D.C.

Field, John Osgood. 1987. "Multisectoral Nutrition Planning: A Post-Mortem." *Food Policy* 12 (February): 15–28.

Field, John Osgood, and Robert M. Russell. 1992. "Nutrition Mission to Iraq for UNICEF." *Nutrition Reviews* 50 (February): 41–46.

Franke, Richard W., and Barbara H. Chasin. 1980. *Seeds of Famine: Ecological Destruction and the Development Dilemma in the West African Sahel.* Montclair, N.J.: Allenheld, Osmun.

Gill, Peter. 1986. *A Year in the Death of Africa: Politics, Bureaucracy and the Famine.* London: Paladin.

Giorgis, Dawit Wolde. 1989. *Red Tears: War, Famine and Revolution in Ethiopia.* Trenton: Red Sea Press.

Glantz, Michael H., ed. 1987. *Drought and Hunger in Africa: Denying Famine a Future.* Cambridge: Cambridge University Press.

Greenough, Paul R. 1982. *Prosperity and Misery in Modern Bengal: The Famine of 1943–1944*. Oxford and New York: Oxford University Press.

Harriss, Barbara. 1988. "Limitations of the 'Lessons from India.'" In Curtis, Hubbard, and Shepherd, 157–170.

Hay, Roger W. 1988. "Famine Incomes and Employment: Has Botswana Anything to Teach Africa?" *World Development* 16, 9: 1113–1125.

Holm, John D., and Richard G. Morgan. 1985. "Coping with Drought in Botswana: An African Success." *Journal of Modern African Studies* 23, 3: 463–482.

Independent Commission on International Humanitarian Issues. 1985. *Famine: A Man-Made Disaster?* London: Pan Books.

International Study Team. 1991. "Executive Summary: Health and Welfare in Iraq After the Gulf Crisis: An In-Depth Assessment." Harvard Law School (October). Mimeo.

Jansson, Kurt, Michael Harris, and Angela Penrose. 1987. *The Ethiopian Famine*. London: Zed Books.

Lipton, Michael. 1976. *Why Poor People Stay Poor: Urban Bias and World Development*. Cambridge: Harvard University Press.

Lofchie, Michael F. 1975. "Political and Economic Origins of African Hunger." *Journal of Modern African Studies* 13 (December): 551–567.

May, Clifford D. 1987. "The Roll of the Media in Identifying and Publicizing Drought." In Wilhite and Easterling, 515–518.

McAlpin, Michelle Burge. 1983. *Subject to Famine: Food Crises and Economic Change in Western India, 1860–1920*. Princeton: Princeton University Press.

McAlpin, Michelle Burge. 1987. "Famine Relief Policy in India: Six Lessons for Africa." In Glantz, 391–413.

Moremi, Tswelopele C. 1988. "Transition from Emergency to Development Assistance: Botswana Experience." Paper presented at the WHO/ACC/SCN Conference on Nutrition in Times of Disasters, World Health Organization, Geneva, 27–30 September.

Morgan, Richard. 1988. "Drought-Relief Programmes in Botswana." In Curtis, Hubbard, and Shepherd, 112–120.

Palmieri, Victor H. 1982. "Famine, Media, and Geopolitics: The Khmer Rouge Effort, 1980." In Cahill, 19–27.

Ram, N. 1990. "An Independent Press and Anti-Hunger Strategies: The Indian Experience." In Drèze and Sen 1990a, 146–190.

Ravallion, Martin. 1987. *Markets and Famines*. Oxford: Clarendon Press.

Sen, Amartya. 1981. *Poverty and Famines: An Essay on Entitlement and Deprivation*. Oxford: Clarendon Press.

Shawcross, William. 1984. *The Quality of Mercy: Cambodia, Holocaust and Modern Conscience*. New York: Simon and Schuster.

Shepherd, Jack. 1975. *The Politics of Starvation*. New York and Washington, D.C.: Carnegie Endowment for International Peace.

Shoham, Jeremy. 1987. "Does Nutritional Surveillance Have a Role to Play in Early Warning of Food Crisis and in the Management of Relief Operations?" *Disasters* 11, 4: 282–285.

Timberlake, Lloyd. 1985. *Africa in Crisis: The Causes, the Cures of Environmental Bankruptcy*. London: Earthscan.

Vaughan, Megan. 1987. *The Story of an African Famine: Gender and Famine in Twentieth-Century Malawi*. Cambridge: Cambridge University Press.

Walker, Peter. 1989. *Famine Early Warning Systems: Victims and Destitution*. London: Earthscan.

Watts, Michael. 1983. *Silent Violence: Food, Famine and Peasantry in Northern Nigeria*. Berkeley: University of California Press.

Wilhite, Donald A., and William E. Easterling, with Deborah A. Wood, eds. 1987. *Planning for Drought: Toward a Reduction of Societal Vulnerability*. Boulder: Westview Press.

Index

Tanganyika African National Union
(TANU), 175
Tassacht Association of Mali, 181
Technocratic VDOs, 192–93, 200,
202n.4
Tigray, 76, 77, 93, 94–95, 96, 110, 158,
160
Tigrean Peoples Liberation Front
(TPLF), 95, 108, 109, 113, 115,
119nn.10, 11, 158, 159
Togo, Naam organizations, 180
"Transmission-belt" VDOs, 184–87,
200–201
Truman, Harry S, 90–91
Twareg herders, 63, 65

*Union de Féderations de Groupement
Naam* (UFGN), 179
SIX-S/UFGN, 188–93
United Nations Children's Fund
(UNICEF), 20, 80, 153, 162,
163–65
United Nations Development
Programme (UNDP), 79
United Nations Disaster Relief
Organization (UNDRO), 20, 101
United Nations Educational,
Scientific and Cultural
Organization (UNESCO), 79
United Nations High Commissioner
for Refugees, 20
United Nations Office for
Emergency Operations in
Ethiopia (UNEOE), 83–84
U.S. Agency for International
Development (USAID), 20, 48,
49, 51, 52, 82, 96, 97–98, 111, 165,
195, 221
Bureau for Food for Peace and
Voluntary Assistance, 104–5
Famine Early Warning System
(FEWS) project of the, 259
U.S. Department of Agriculture, 104,
116
U.S. Department of Commerce, 105
U.S. Department of the Treasury,
104, 105
U.S. General Accounting Office
(GAO), 82
U.S. Office of Management and
Budget (OMB), 104, 105

Voluntary development organizations (VDOs), African, 172–204

Walker, Brian, 153
War, food shortages and, 136
Wheat production, 40
Wilson, Woodrow, 90
Wodaabe herders, 62, 64, 65
Wollo, 76, 77
Wolpe, Howard, 99
Women
AETA fuel-efficient stove project,
184–85, 198
vulnerabilities to disasters, 134–35
women's organizations, 198–99
World Bank, 195, 230
World Food Programme (WFP), 99,
221
World Vision, 111

Yako Region Committee, 181